# CULTURE REPORT
# EUNIC YEARBOOK
# 2012/2013

# CULTURE REPORT
# EUNIC YEARBOOK 2012/2013

Although a painting can never stop a bullet, a painting can stop a bullet from being fired. Culture is a central component of conflicts between different groups and ethnicities. So what could be more appropriate than using culture as a tool for conflict resolution? After centuries of war, Europe has particular experience in how to create peaceful and cooperative ways of co-existing. What kinds of external cultural policies does Europe need to embrace that will allow art, education and intercultural dialogue to open doors and build trust between communities – and help prevent conflicts around the globe?

# Lifting the veil

*By Sebastian Körber*

Culture has a vital role to play in conflict regions. It can build bridges but it can also increase divisions. What are the opportunities and challenges, the risks and limitations of cultural engagement in regions beset by crisis and conflict? This question has of course been a central focus of international relations for more than 20 years, but there is still no clear answer. Former UN Secretary-General Boutros Boutros-Ghali put this item on the agenda of the United Nations as far back as 1992. In 1993 Samuel P. Huntington's thesis on the Clash of Civilisations unleashed a long-lasting debate on the geopolitical significance of culture, and after the terror attacks of 11 September 2001 it soon became clear to everyone that considering the role of culture in international relations is not just an intellectual exercise. In parallel to this, the limited success achieved by military interventions in Somalia, Afghanistan and Iraq pose the question of whether other, softer, approaches would be more effective. Even international development assistance, something that – as Damien Helly discusses in this report – finds itself in a state of existential crisis, is on a quest for find alternative ways of dealing with fragile states. So it is logical that the network of European Union National Institutes for Culture (EUNIC) should ask what role cultural activity can play in conflict resolution.

First the good news: the number of extremely violent conflicts has dropped by 40 percent since 1992, as the journalist Michael Gleich notes in his contribution. He believes the fact that many people find this surprising is down to the media's distortion of reality. It is not violence that has increased but the reporting of violence. The media is not interested in successful approaches to crisis prevention and the absence of conflict. And do academics and researchers also suffer from this blind spot? Gleich believes there can surely be no more urgent topic for research. But the quiet work being done by culture is drowned out in journals and at conferences by – as Chinese poet Yang Lian puts it – the "tumult of conflict".

But when it is a question of proving that cultural activity is an effective tool in conflict resolution, the representatives of cultural relations institutes also often find themselves resorting to vague statements. So Gottfried Wagner, former Director of the European Cultural Foundation in Amsterdam, warns against the use of glib cultural rhetoric when it comes to conflicts. The writer Slavenka Drakulić says, "When talking about the role of culture in the reconciliation process, we should not ignore its capacity to produce ideology and propaganda", and reminds us of the writers, journalists and philologists who became cogs in the nationalist propaganda machine during the war in the Balkans. Political scientist Jochen Hippler concludes that if a conflict is interpreted as a clash of cultural values, then a conflict about interests becomes a conflict about identity, something that is much more difficult to resolve. This culturalisation of conflicts ensures that practical interests such as guaranteeing supplies of raw materials and energy disappear behind a cultural smokescreen. Hippler believes that for this reason the job of cultural dialogue should not be to resolve conflicts but to open up new perspectives on the causes of conflict.

"Humans always want to make sense of things and need things to make sense. Ongoing violence also requires a narrative framework", says Jerusalem-based conflict expert Gudrun Kramer, describing the "signification spiral" of values, symbols, songs, monuments and street names. So it is a question of stopping the growth of emotion-laden myth-building and entrenched ideologies, which simply help to escalate conflict. Curator Moukhtar Kozache speaks of a "process of unlearning" and urges us to overcome the "non-creative and catastrophic notion of a 'clash of civilisations'" and instead to accept the interwoven history and mutability of civilisations.

Robin Davies, who recently joined the British Council from NATO headquarters, admits that he has long underestimated the transforming power of culture and therefore stresses all the more that we should no longer see culture as being separate from mainstream policies on international relations.

And EUNIC? Raj Isar, who currently holds teaching posts at universities in Sydney and Paris, proffers a controversial opinion. Although he values the potential of art as a vector and instrument of conflict resolution, he recommends that the network should of course offer moral support but otherwise leave the complex task of conflict resolution to the experts. He points to "concord organisations" that bring together people with fundamentally opposing views, as is the case in divided societies, in order to initiate dialogue or offer training in conflict management.

But this report also has its share of optimistic voices. Austrian diplomat Martin Eichtinger speaks of a "noble task". The cultural institutes should make use of courageous and thought-provoking programmes to prepare the ground for breaking down stereotypes and prejudices. Little strokes fell big oaks. Echoing Winston Churchill, he praises the culture of listening: "In a conflict, it requires courage not just to stand up and speak, but also to sit down and listen." The current EUNIC President, Delphine Borione, points out that the European cultural institutes have particular credibility with regard to the contribution of culture to economic, social and human development because they represent countries that have experience of conflict stretching back over many hundreds of years.

This is the fifth edition of the Culture Report on the progress and shortcomings of Europe's cultural relations, and it is the second edition that also serves as the EUNIC Yearbook. I would like to thank all the contributors, translators and editors, along with the members of the EUNIC network, for their valuable assistance. My special thanks go to the Robert Bosch Foundation for funding the Culture Report from the very beginning. I am also delighted that it can once again appear in several languages thanks to the support of the British Council, the Gulbenkian Foundation and the French Foreign Ministry.

Sebastian Körber, Deputy General Secretary and Head of the Media Department at the Institute for Foreign Cultural Relations

# The Potential of Culture

**There is no doubt that culture can help to resolve conflicts (and can also be abused in order to fuel them). But cultural activity cannot be a substitute for political (and economic) initiatives for conflict resolution. How can culture help with conflict management? How can we make the best possible use of the positive role of culture? And what cultural policy initiatives does Europe need to set in motion in order to help regions beset by conflict?**

## Beyond the cultural smokescreen

For as long as a conflict is predominantly about differences in interests, it is often easier to find pragmatic compromises. However, if the same conflict is also interpreted as a conflict between different cultural values, then the dispute over different interests becomes a dispute over identity. So what could be more obvious thanto into involve culture in conflict resolution? *By Jochen Hippler*

Since the 1990s, and especially since the terror attacks of 11 September 2001, the relationship between culture and cultural factors and potential or actual violent conflicts has attracted an increasing amount of attention from politicians and academics alike. This discussion actually goes back much further, though it has not always been carried out with the same degree of fervour. When Samuel Huntington published his widely acclaimed article in 1993 on the "Clash of Civilisations" (followed up by a book of the same name) it prompted intensive global discussion and was a key factor in the decision by the United Nations, at the suggestion of Iranian President Mohammad Khatami, to declare 2001 to be the "Year of Dialogue Among Civilisations". Ironically, it was in this very year that the Al-Qaeda attacks of 11 September took place.

Relations between Muslims and the West were placed under considerable strain as a result of this criminal act and the subsequent 'War on Terrorism' (including Guantanamo and Abu Ghraib), as well as the wars in Afghanistan and Iraq. Many governments and numerous private agencies also tried to improve Western-Islamic dialogue in an attempt to mitigate the current conflicts and avoid future ones. However, these efforts tended to tail off after a few years as the dramatic pictures from 11 September started to fade from people's memories.

The public soon started to take an interest in another aspect of the relationship between culture and conflict. The problem of fragile and failing states and the limited success of attempts to bring stability to Afghanistan (and, for some years, Iraq), despite the deployment of huge numbers of personnel and resources, raised the question as to whether attempts at conflict resolution based on a security policy approach (especially military deployment) were not overrated, and whether other, 'softer' instruments might not be possible and potentially more successful. This question is all the more relevant given the fact that the dynamics of many conflict situations are bound up with ethnic or religious – and therefore cultural – issues and cannot be readily influenced by military means. This suggests that better use could be made of culturally-oriented approaches in such cases, which in turn would raise the profile of European Foreign Cultural and Education Policy (FCEP), which was and still could be an important vehicle for intercultural dialogue.

Internal or inter-societal conflicts are mostly the result of a clash of competing interests. When individuals or groups are pursuing similar interests, conflicts are much less likely. If conflicts do arise, perhaps due to a misunderstanding or because of psychological factors, then they tend to be short-lived and solutions are relatively easy to find, usually through some form of compromise. Conflicts tend to be of a more serious nature and so harder to resolve in cases where the interests of the parties involved are at odds with each other. Conflicts based on a zero-sum outcome (what one side gains, the other loses) are usually much more problematical, and, if they revolve around vitally important commodities or issues, they can be particularly intractable, bitter and difficult to resolve.

However, reference to different, contradictory or exclusive 'interests' can lead to the over-hasty conclusion that the resulting conflicts are somehow 'objective' in nature. This may well be true in certain extreme cases, if for example one side needs a non-divisible resource for its own survival and the other side needs it for the same reason, but as a general rule 'interests' are not 'objective' per se, but tend to be socially mediated.

My interests cannot be measured by a calculator or ruler, but are dependent on my needs, intentions, characteristics and other factors, which is to say they are defined by who I am and what I consider to be important or unimportant in life. Whether and to what extent I consider alcohol, art, conviviality, tranquillity, money, prestige, sports cars or other things to be central or of lesser importance to my life is dependent on what sort of person I am and how I want to live my life.

The same applies to smaller or larger groups or even whole countries. Gaining Lebensraum in the East was a key national interest for Germany in the 1930s and early 1940s, but in the 1960s it was no longer an issue, and this remains the case today.

## *Competition between particular political cultures*

To put it another way, the 'interests' that play a key role in the origins and outcomes of conflicts are first and foremost determined by social, subjective and 'cultural' factors, but they are also changeable. We could say that interests are the societal and cultural articulation of common, socially-negotiated goals, intentions and needs that arise out of intra-societal disputes and debates. They are therefore a product of the 'political culture' of a group or society and develop out of the competition between the specific political cultures of individual sub-groups.

There is no doubt that 'objective' aspects can be included in this (export needs, pastureland, relieving population pressure, etc.). Ultimately, however, the importance of 'interests' lies in the fact that they are an articulation of the perception of the objective requirements for reproduction, rather than the requirements themselves. These requirements are rarely direct and irrefutable, but are mostly dependent on a particular path chosen (if an economy becomes more reliant on its internal market, its dependence on exports goes down; a switch from intensive animal husbandry to cultivation reduces the need for pastureland) and are culturally defined. As a result, the political culture of a society or group becomes a key factor in the origins of a conflict, and therefore also in its potential resolution.

There is a second aspect to the culturally-influenced articulation of the 'objective' requirements for reproduction: it is often the case that when a conflict starts it is not only one's own interests that are articulated but also those that are bound up with one's own identity and one's perception of others or of the opposing party. It is no longer only what I want, but also who I am (or who the opposing party is or allegedly is) that becomes an integral part of the conflict. In this way, prejudices and distorted pictures of a group of others can also play a significant role.

To put it another way, individuals and groups often see challengers for power or resources not just as competition, but also as culturally or ethnically 'different', especially in heterogeneous societies. And this fact of being different is often used as a justification for conflict, even if it is actually about tangible interests such as land, jobs or influence. In this way, conflicts can become 'culturalised', which makes them much more difficult to resolve.

For as long as a conflict is predominantly about differences in interests, it is often easier to find pragmatic compromises, such as introducing quotas in the civil service or the sharing of land and resources. However, if the same conflict is also interpreted as a conflict between different cultural values, then the dispute over different interests becomes a dispute over identity. And when this is the case, finding compromises becomes much more difficult. Groups may be able to resolve their different interests through compromise, but compromises are rare when it is a matter of individual identity. Who I am is not up for negotiation; at best we can talk about what I want. And anybody who is prepared to limit their own spheres of interest in order to mitigate a conflict is unlikely to put their own identity on the line.

A third aspect of cultural influences on conflict dynamics exists in the relationship between external demarcation and internal mobilisation. Political culture, especially political identities, can become resources for political actors, but can also take on a life of their own that

"The political culture of a society or group becomes a key factor in the origins of a conflict, and therefore also in its potential resolution".

under certain circumstances can get out of control. Political identities, including ethnicities in the broadest sense (taking into account national, religious or tribal aspects) are generally not as clearly defined, or as easy to define, as many actors claim and many observers assume.

The very fact that they are not clearly defined makes it possible to use these political identities as a method of demarcation and as a way of defining who is in the in-group and who is in the out-group. They can be used in an integrative way (all Muslims are the same and form one large community, even if they are from different nations and speak different languages), but also in a divisive way (Shiites are not real Muslims but heretics). However, this kind of demarcation is not reflected in reality in most societies, which are normally characterised by a whole series of overlapping identities. It is possible to be Iraqi, Muslim, Sunni, Kurd and secular as well as an intellectual, a man, a member of a particular party, a musician and a father, to name just a few possibilities. Creating a personal identity generally consists of bringing all these individual characteristics and part-identities together, establishing priorities, resolving or reconciling and, if possible, integrating potential contradictions. This is a creative and 'cultural' task carried out by individuals and groups with varying degrees of success.

When political and social conflicts flare up or escalate, especially if they are violent in nature, certain aspects of identity can come under pressure, especially those with potential or real political implications. If, for example, members of a religious, national or ethnic group are systematically persecuted, then membership (or non-membership) of this group and hence the corresponding part of their identity becomes more important. In extreme cases, membership or non-membership of a particular group can become a matter of life and death (for example, Hutu/Tutsi, Jewish/ 'Aryan').

### *Ethnic identity becomes a matter of personal safety*

Redefining or re-evaluating group membership can fundamentally change the political culture of a country and is often a key component of the dynamics of conflicts. The importance of such factors in the escalation of political violence is clear for all to see in the former Yugoslavia, Iraq and Syria. When a certain level of violence is exceeded in such a context, demarcation tends to both accelerate and deepen, and ethnic identity can quickly turn into a matter of personal safety. The threat of danger comes either objectively or subjectively from another ethnic group, and protection can only be guaranteed through militias or other entities from one's 'own group'.

The justified or unjustified feeling of being threatened by an 'alien' group and the possibility of being protected by organisations within one's 'own' group can be the trigger for mobilising political support and inspiring activism and recruitment by those carrying out ethnic violence. This can lead to the division of society into large hostile groups that constantly threaten each other, along with a growing pressure towards conformity and discipline within these groups. The political elites can use this division and confrontation externally in order to legitimise and strengthen their power internally and to generate and manipulate activism in society. I should add at this point that these aspects of 'political culture' that we have talked about so far all exist at an individual and collective level, and so are based on a broad understanding of the term culture. However, these issues are also closely bound up with what we understand by culture in the narrower sense. Musicians, archaeologists, linguists and other creative artists can play an important role in sharpening or even creating ethno-national, ethno-religious or other political identities – perhaps through the construction or standardisation of a national language, the retrospective creation of a 'national history' or the postulation of a national literature, music or culture in general.

The more that art and culture is used to create identity, the more people have a reason or opportunity to identify with a large social group at an emotional level, something that did not exist in this form in the past, or at most to a limited extent. Depending on the context, need or situation, historical science can therefore carve out real historical commonalities, systemise them ideologically and place them in a new context, or project the national concept of the present back to the past in order to revive old myths or create new ones. A good example is provided by the view of a German nation evolving seamlessly from and continuing the history of the Germanic peoples, and which reveres the "Hermann" of the Battle of the Teutoburg Forest as a quasi-German hero. Poetry, history, painting, music and architecture ('Hermann's Memorial') all played an important part in creating out of all the many German identities a single unified identity that could be directed against the 'Latins' (Romans and French).

The second half of the 19th century (and often the first decades of the following century) was an era of culturally-supported, nationalist identity-building, particularly in Central, Eastern and Southern Europe. A similar process was undertaken and continues to be undertaken amongst ethnic groups, religious movements and larger tribal entities, but this is clearly just one political-historical option among many, as other 'nations' or ethnic groups have gone down a completely different path in the course of their history. Art and culture, in the narrower sense of the terms, can also play an increasingly important role in the strengthening or weakening of old and new political identities, as well as influencing the dynamics of conflicts. This means that both governmental and non-governmental cultural policies can be relevant to conflict situations.

So far we have talked either explicitly or implicitly of group conflicts within a society, but culturally-charged conflicts can arise between nations too – we only have to think of the earlier traditional German-French enmity that was supposedly rooted in fundamental differences of mentality, cultural systems and values.

Culturally-influenced conflicts can also arise at a level that goes beyond or is tangential to individual nation states. This can be the case on a regional scale, where, for example, specific cultural, ethnic or other identity groups live in several neighbouring countries (for example, Kurds in Turkey, Iran, Iraq and Syria) where conflicts are directly or indirectly linked and influence each other.

The conflict for potential is somewhat different when such groups live in other, possibly distant diaspora communities (such as Turkish and Kurdish migrants in Germany or North Africans in France). When diaspora communities live under the influence of foreign cultural and legal systems and are only involved in limited interactions with the original societies, then additional factors come into play within the dynamics of conflict that arise from their degree of integration or non-integration into their new homeland. However, we are not in a position to investigate all these issues here.

One special case in the relationship between culture and conflict can be seen at a very general level: that of the aforementioned Western-Islam relations. It is a special case, firstly because the term 'Western' cannot be positively defined and the group of people covered by the term is very unclear.

In addition, two groups are set against each other that are in fact very difficult to compare. 'Muslims' can clearly be defined in religious and cultural terms, but they are not being compared to Christians (or any other religious community, or even atheists), but to a large group that cannot be defined in religious (or anti-religious) terms, but only on the basis of some vague cultural aspects. Christianity is often explicitly or implicitly attributed to the West, but this would also mean that Copts, Maronites and other Christians in the Middle East as well as the many Christians in Asia, Africa and Latin America would by definition be part of the West due to their religious affiliation, something which makes little sense. The opposite is also true – being part of the West can also not be defined by agnostic, secular, anti-religious or atheist attitudes, otherwise many US citizens and Europeans would be excluded.

What is also not clear in this concept is whether the millions of Muslims living in Europe or North America belong to the 'Muslim' or 'Western' side of the equation.

> "Art and culture, in the narrower sense of the terms, can also play an increasingly important role in the strengthening or weakening of old or new political identities, as well as influencing the dynamics of conflicts."

### *Rejection of the West*

Although the groups referred to in the Western-Islam antithesis may be difficult to define, there is no doubt that they harbour a real potential for conflict. Just as Western policies and military interventions are not really directed against Islam itself (although the people of the region are often only too happy to assume this), but rather are intended to look after specific interests, so Muslim societies are not really permeated by a blanket rejection of the West and Western culture. Antipathy and opposition is often directed towards the United States and the US government and its policies, which are often perceived as imperialist and arrogant. Indeed, this is a view that is also shared by many (Western) Europeans, but in cultural terms it is articulated in a different way. Anti-Americanism in Europe is rarely clothed in religious formulas.

There appear to be a combination of several key factors that underlie the conflict between the West and Islam:

- The clear imbalance of power between North American/Western European countries and those of the Near and Middle East
- The convergence of economic, political and cultural crises in many countries in the Near and Middle East
- The contradiction between an admiration for Western achievements (technological, economic, political and cultural) and a desire for equality and the protection of their own independence and identity
- The experience that many dictators and repressive regimes in the region are or have been supported by Western governments (USA, France and others) and that they serve the interests of these supporters more than they do the interests of their own people
- Western governments' direct or indirect support of Israel's occupation of the Palestinian territories
- The foreign and military policies of Western countries in the Near and Middle East (and, again, especially the USA), which are perceived as being imperialist and arrogant, as symbolised for a time by the occupation of Iraq.

The Western-Muslim conflict is, therefore, essentially political, even if it is also bound up with development crises and deficiencies within the societies of the Near and Middle East (corruption, dictatorships, stagnation, etc.) and also includes cultural components (a desire for cultural independence and identity that is often articulated in religious and not just nationalistic terms).

### *Secular and political origins*

Ultimately, the origins of the conflict are essentially secular and political and a reflection of differences of interest. The relationship between the West and Islam (more accurately the relationship between the most important Western countries and the Near and Middle East) revolves around issues relating to energy supplies, stability and security, the security of Israel, the prevention of mass migration to Europe and the optimisation of Western power in the region. Many of the region's ruling elites have been keen to work closely with Western politicians, despite the fact that large sections of their people often rejected these policies, proving once again that the dividing line does not simply run between the West and Islam (or the Muslims).

As with many interest-based conflicts, the conflict between the West and Islam has also been heavily culturalised and thus turned into ideology, making it out to be a "clash of civilisations". As a result, 'Islamic' and 'Western' societies suddenly find themselves locked in an apparent battle that is no longer about specific interests, but about 'values' and political cultural identity. This makes it much more difficult to find a solution to the conflict and leads to a hardening of political and ideological stances, which in turn are presented as a sign of cultural self-assertion.

The idea of a "clash of civilisations" becomes more plausible when it is confirmed by dramatic acts of violence (such as the September 11 and other terrorist attacks on Western countries, the wars in Afghanistan and Iraq and the occupation of Palestine). Interest and political power-based conflicts give the impression of being about values and identities, with the result that these kinds of cultural dimensions become even more important in reality. For example, the Islamic religion is used, under certain circumstances, as a kind of cultural and linguistic code to articulate anti-Western opposition.

This is where the cultural dialogue referred to above can and should be employed. As long as it is not just empty rhetoric, it can be used to counter the culturalisation and manipulation for ideological purposes of the underlying disputes and bring the focus back to the real interests and political structures involved. Intercultural dialogue cannot resolve the conflict per se, because the origins of the conflict do not lie in cultural differences or practices. But it can play an important subsidiary role, as long as the political conflict is also resolved politically at the same time.

If this does not happen, there is a risk that it will just become a cultural smokescreen, designed to hide the 'real' politics, with people talking about religion, cultural values and commonalities, while pursuing an uncompromising policy of interests. However, if intercultural dialogue takes place in parallel to the political solution of conflicts and is accompanied by development policy measures and economic cooperation, then it can have some real value and make an important contribution. For it to succeed, it is vital that it is not seen as a substitute for policy, but as just one element of an overall conflict resolution package.

Against this background of a potential relationship between conflicts and culture, the question remains as to whether there is a role that Europe's foreign cultural policy can and should play, and what form this role should take. This presents a major challenge, as the European Union is a civilian power that is the neighbour of an unstable crisis region. But this is an area where it could and should be more active, not in competition with national

"Intercultural dialogue cannot resolve the conflict per se, because the origins of the conflict do not lie in cultural differences or practices. But it can play an important subsidiary role, as long as the political conflict is also resolved politically at the same time."

foreign cultural policies but in a coordinating role, and the still-young European External Action Service should be set up in such a way that it is up to the task.

It should not simply be a question of giving foreign cultural policy an important role within European external policy, but rather that it should be tailored more towards conflict prevention and resolution in a wider cultural sense. There have been some tentative steps in this direction and these initiatives should be further encouraged and strongly reinforced.

But we should remind ourselves that these efforts are often undertaken in difficult environments, during crises and in conflict zones. These difficult circumstances often lead to limited chances of success. Potential or acute violent conflicts can have a major impact on foreign cultural activities and to a large extent determine their possibilities and limitations. Once a violent conflict has escalated, external cultural policy can become unworkable because the danger to personnel becomes too acute. By then it is too late for it to have some form of preventive effect in the short or medium term. The prevailing political situation often also presents a serious obstacle. In this case, it is a serious mistake to pay insufficient attention to the context of the conflict or to have unrealistically high expectations. It is therefore critical that foreign cultural policy takes all these aspects into consideration. However, it would be shortsighted to see the relationship between foreign cultural policy and conflicts only in negative terms. In many cases it can be designed in such a way that it can make a valuable contribution to conflict prevention or resolution. However, for this to work, the approach needs to be specifically tailored to the needs of the situation, the conflict should not have become too advanced and it should not be burdened by excessively high expectations.

European and national external cultural policies might then have a chance of success and gain in importance. Ethno-cultural identities are not readily accessible to classical diplomacy, but a well thought-out cultural policy can at least try to help reflect the character of separate identities, promote a pluralistic pattern of perception and counter the culturalisation of conflicts.

## *Appealing to feelings*

We should of course not overestimate the importance of cultural work, but in combination with other tools of conflict management it can make a valuable contribution. When representatives of different identity groups come together to work on film, theatre, dialogue processes and joint artistic activities, this at least provides the possibility of not only appealing to people's sense of self-interest but also to their feelings and identities and encouraging them to reflect on their relationship. Films made against the background of the Palestine/Israel and India/Pakistan conflicts are good examples of this. The film "The Heart of Jenin" tells the story of a Palestinian who donates the organs of his dead son to Israeli children. The short film "Wagah" takes a humorous look at the border crossing between India and Pakistan. European and German foreign cultural policy has played a positive role in promoting these two projects.

In Germany in 2001, as part of the political reaction to the 9/11 terror attacks, foreign cultural and education policies were given a stronger and more concrete role in conflict prevention and management. Large sums of anti-terror funding were fed into external cultural policy and into initiatives such as dialogue programmes organised by intermediary organisations. This trend towards involving cultural policy more closely in peace and security policy initiatives was demonstrated in 2004 when the German federal government published its "Civilian Conflict Prevention, Conflict Resolution and Post-Conflict Peacebuilding Action Plan". This Action Plan clearly states that crisis prevention has an important cultural dimension and that intercultural understanding and respect for other cultures are major prerequisites for crisis prevention. With this, Germany's foreign cultural and education policy opened up an important field of activity that included dialogue and exchange, but also "culturally-sensitive methods of communicating the values and instruments of crisis prevention as well as support for education systems that promote non-violent approaches to dealing with conflicts and allow different points of view, especially with regard to contemporary history curricula".

"It should not simply be a question of giving foreign cultural policy an important role within European external policy, but rather that it should be tailored more towards conflict prevention and resolution in a wider cultural sense."

The paper refers to the German Foreign Office's Dialogue with Islam, its participation in the Year of Cultural Dialogue, the activities of the Goethe-Institut and of the Institute for Foreign Cultural Relations. It also states: "Capacity-building measures for local institutions are an integral part of the Federal Government's cultural relations and education policy. The German Academic Exchange Service (DAAD), the Alexander von Humboldt Foundation and the German Rectors' Conference are engaged in peacekeeping and crisis prevention activities in the context of international endeavours to promote stability" in areas such as South Eastern Europe and Afghanistan.

But since then, a certain amount of disillusionment seems to have crept in. It is not always clear whether fundamental statements of principle are really being taken seriously and implemented in full.

In its new concept, announced in September 2011, entitled "Foreign Cultural and Education Policy in the Age of Globalisation", the German Foreign Office made it clear that it was focusing on foreign cultural policy and raising the bar in this respect. It stated that securing peace was one of the three main aims of this initiative and that it would "contribute to the resolution of regional and local conflicts, particularly in places where they arise out of differences in cultural, religious or ideological views". The paper goes on to say: "Cultural dialogue and educa-

tional opportunities can provide a basis for political and societal stabilisation. Our aim is act earlier to use cultural and educational programmes to avert acute crises in countries and territories that are prone to conflict."

These are all worthwhile and meaningful policy objectives, but the striking thing is that they have been turned into a central focus of foreign cultural policy, or at least this is the intention. It is somewhat less clear whether this intention will become reality. This is particularly true of the Dialogue with Islam, a programme that is no longer being run by a special representative appointed by the Foreign Minister but instead has been integrated into the normal responsibilities of the Foreign Office. Indeed, over the last few years it seems that the emphasis on conflict management in Germany's foreign cultural policy and its efforts to initiate dialogue have dwindled rather than increased. This is most regrettable, and is a reason why European initiatives in this respect are particularly desirable and beneficial.

Overall, the possibilities – but also the limitations – of foreign cultural policy as an instrument of crisis prevention and management are very clear. It is evident that they alone will have little chance of resolving entrenched conflicts within or between nations and societies, such as in the Middle East, Afghanistan, or between India and Pakistan. Political approaches to resolving these conflicts are also necessary, and above all the exercise of political pressure and influence by means of coordinated European and national endeavours. If this kind of political approach is followed, then foreign cultural policy can make a useful, even significant, supplementary contribution. If such political solutions are lacking or not seriously pursued, then foreign cultural policy cannot provide a replacement. Foreign cultural policy as a European instrument of crisis prevention and management is particularly effective in two areas. The first of these is in intensifying and redirecting dialogue with the Islam world to counter the still prevalent idea of a "clash of civilisations". In this respect, the Arab Spring has opened up new opportunities but also thrown up new exigencies. Secondly, Europe should do more to promote more pluralistic behaviours in heterogeneous societies and work to counter the culturalisation of conflicts. In these two areas, it is to be hoped that Germany and Europe can find new impetus to turn their good intentions into reality.

**Jochen Hippler** is a Political Scientist and Peace Researcher at the Institute for Development and Peace (INEF) at the University of Duisburg-Essen. One of his main areas of research is the relationship between political force, governance, political identities and military intervention by Western nations. His work focuses on the Middle East region, along with Afghanistan and Pakistan.

# More culture in global politics

Europe needs to invest more in cultural relations worldwide to capitalise on its experience of peaceful coexistence, artistic sources of inspiration for governance initiatives, cultural and multilingual dialogue and the practice of confidence-building in the EU. Europe also has experience with intellectual freedom that could be of benefit elsewhere. These are all recipes for tackling conflicts and, above all, for preventing them. *By Damien Helly*

The debate on the cultural components of the EU's external action is expanding. While less than a decade ago, the relevance of cultural relations in EU's diplomacy was still being questioned, today it is almost taken for granted. Diplomats now see that Europe, beyond nation branding, needs to develop a proper cultural diplomacy as a block in an increasingly multipolar, if not interpolar, world. The military found itself dramatically exposed in Afghanistan, Pakistan, Lebanon and Africa and had to learn the value of culturally-sensitive approaches to crisis management. The development aid community is currently experiencing an existential crisis and looking for alternative approaches to international cooperation. National cultural diplomacies are at risk of being diluted in a globalised world where transnational communities have now learned how to develop their own multicultural initiatives.

Networks that have understood that their ideals of equality, common humanity and imagination could potentially lead to multi-dimensional and multi-lingual dialogues and conversations have finally recognised that, in this environment, cultural relations are suited to playing a central role. From NGOs and lobbying networks to supranational institutions, from cultural institutes to the European Parliament, experts in international affairs are recognising that culture really matters and are asking for more culture in global politics.

At last, some decision makers, politicians and donors are now convinced that, in the interests of all Europeans, cultural relations require sound, smart and ambitious policies in every corner of the globe. Policy-making is a dangerous pastime and a double-edged sword – too much strategy, too many concepts and too much bureaucracy simply get in the way of action. Artists, curators, cultural activists, citizens, journalists and computer geeks have not been waiting around for the USA and the

EU to do what others are now preaching: doing culture tous azimut, tutti frutti and at all levels of globalisation. They know what they need to do to develop their projects and realise their ideas, and it's time that we listened to them.

Conflict prevention is just one of many tools used by the EU in its external action. Prevention is one example of an area where a great deal can be done. It constitutes a wide range of actions in a familiar cycle, moving from crisis prevention, crisis management, post-conflict reconstruction and peacebuilding to peaceful coexistence. I would now like to give a definition of cultural relations as a preventive tool.

As a preventive tool, cultural relations are about creating, sharing and performing metaphors for conflicts. It implies a degree of questioning; the identification of the tensions and violence that are to be prevented; an effort of reformulation, translation and transposition, in order to achieve a result that is a kind of cultural production characterised by its aesthetical strength and complex meaning. It does not necessarily have to be linked to the arts to be aesthetically strong: learning a language or new skills also has its own beauty. (For another definition, see Helmut Anheier and Yudhishtir Raj Isar, "Conflicts and Tensions", The Cultures and Globalization Series, page 281.)

### *Early warning and early action*

Cultural early warning is about putting conflict and violence on the stage before it erupts into reality. This can take many different forms. The concept of cultural rapid reaction intervention groups, suggested by Ferdinand Richard on the basis of his experience of working in Marseille with young hip-hop professionals, could inspire the creation of European cultural early warning and early response teams, on the model of existing CRTs (Crisis Response Teams). Deploying cultural professionals in conflict-prone areas to assess cultural prevention needs could be one way forward. This could initially be done via pilot projects in urban areas that studies have shown may be melting pots for social, political, environment and security-related tensions in the future.

The work of detecting risks of violence and crisis is known as early warning. Which members of society are better placed to have a sense of when things are going wrong than artists and cultural workers? Who creates the link between cultural production and social emergencies? And who better to deal with the surrounding issues than those who are sensitive to multi-layered identities, to misperceptions, miscommunications and multicultural tensions? One recent example of the prevention of cultural conflict within Europe is the *Art as LGBTQ (Lesbian, Gay, Bisexual and Trans) Activism: from Britain to Belarus* initiative which ran as part of the Transeuropa Festival 2011. It surveyed performance campaigns for lesbian and gay visibility across Europe and showed the burning issues of anti-gay violence in Belgrade, Zagreb and Minsk.

When things go well, the media don't bother to report it. Nor do they acknowledge that some people are working to make things go well. Cultural relations and social relations are a garden that has to be cultivated, cared for and watered. Cultural relations provide the means to help us live together, despite all the economic hardships. Take them away, and relations soon start to fall apart. The destruction of symbols engenders hatred. The part played by a TV series depicting the peaceful co-existence of communities that was developed by the NGO *Search for Common Ground* in Macedonia and Sierra Leone is a good example of the preventive work that can be done using traditional media. There are many other examples around the globe, such as in Sri Lanka, where theatre has been used to address inter-community violence, (for more on this see Helmut Anheier and Yudhishtir Raj Isar, "Conflicts and Tensions", pages 296-305. This same book also includes a chapter on radio stations in Colombia and Afro-Reggae in Brazil).

Culture is the hope that, like flowers and trees, grows from seeds planted in the ruins. Rainfall and oxygen are all that is needed to make human ecosystems fresh and fertile once again. Likewise, culture can restore hope to destroyed psyches and communities and help them move beyond nightmares, grievances and revenge. It is not justice, but it voices it and spells out new possibilities for the future.

"The work of detecting risks of violence and crisis is known as early warning. Which members of society are better placed to feel when things are going wrong than artists and cultural workers?"

## *A worthwhile investment*

Cultural activism in post-conflict settings is a worthwhile investment: it can go from clowning performances by soldiers in the wake of a battle (as in the case of Brazilian troops in the shanty town of Cité Soleil in Haiti in 2007) to the revival of cultural infrastructures after a conflict and the relaunch of cultural initiatives that were brought to a halt by conflict. Other initiatives related to transitional justice and mediation may also entail strong cultural components, such as the Gacaca system in Rwanda, (for more on this see Helmut Anheier and Yudhishtir Raj Isar, "Conflicts and Tensions", pages 306-312).

When people have stopped believing in the outdated ambitions of their elders and the past, then it is time for new generations and for those artists who have remained young at heart to reinvent their heritage beyond their all-too-familiar horizons. When Europe is suffering political decline, when those who represent our democracies cease to fight for them, then it is time for cultural relations to take to the streets, change its face, compose new songs and write new plays.

How is it possible to ensure peaceful co-existence without becoming an empire or returning to the nationalism of the 1930s? The European renaissance is a scenario that has begun to be written in blogs, music scores and European films both long and short. It is the fresh and aromatic surf on the new waves that lap the hospitable shores of Asia, Africa and America, driven onward by the movements of a new Europe riding her mythological bull. Films by Fatih Akin such as "Gegen Die Wand" are metaphors of contemporary Germany and Turkey, where language, migration and contemporary mental nomadism represent the complexity of European culture, and how individuals are experimenting with it. It links people with our societies and with the collective concerns we have about peace. However, the establishment of spaces for cultural relations should not be a goal in itself unless it is backed up by a strong collective consensus on method and values. Europeans still need to reach this consensus by holding thorough debates on controversial topics.

### *Preventive power or an instrument of hegemony?*

The first of these is the relationship between cultural relations and the use of force: is the military justified in carrying out cultural work or even being associated with preventive cultural initiatives? Isn't "the military" and "cultural prevention" a contradiction in terms? Or should we try to think of ways in which the role of the military is acceptable in the field of cultural relations?

The second issue that Europeans need to debate is the link between cultural relations and international political domination. In other words, under which conditions is European soft power a force for prevention rather than a tool for hegemony, neo-colonialism or neo-imperialism? Can hegemons claim that their cultural diplomacy is based on the principle of a partnership of equals?

The third challenge for Europe's external cultural preventive action is to combine cultural relations and social class disparities. This dilemma is not a new one for cultural policies, but it still applies in the case of cultural diplomacy: are cultural relations the preserve of the elite? How should cultural relations deal with social inequalities and class warfare?

Finally, it is important to discuss the question of compliance with a set of values relating to the protection of human rights, and these values must be established before the launch of any new initiatives. Cultural relations cannot afford to be accused of breaches of human rights and compromises are not acceptable. But to what extent is this really possible in every context, when the boundaries between effectiveness, interests and values become blurred and when culture is used as a temporary and by-default mediation tool to promote (legitimate) change?

To cut a long story short: Europe needs to invest more in cultural relations world-

"Culture can restore hope to destroyed psyches and communities and help them move beyond nightmares, grievances and revenge."

wide in order to capitalise on its existing experience of peaceful coexistence, of artistic sources of inspiration for governance initiatives, of cultural and multilingual dialogue and the practice of confidence-building, of intellectual freedom as a multiplier of utopian projects. This is a recipe for tackling conflicts and, above all, preventing them. The European Parliament's 2011 report on the cultural components of the EU's external action has harnessed most of what needs to be done in terms of policy: it needs the kind of intelligent, assiduous and thorough attention to detail that our institutions are well placed to execute. It is time to act and to implement these recommendations, working closely with the cultural relations institutions and organisations around the world that are already representing Europe but still desperately lack support from those who have – democratic – power and money.

Europe should no longer be a goal per se, provided, as Javier Solana once said, that the "spirit" of the treaties is implemented whole-heartedly. In a way, our goal has already been reached with the latest treaties and the creation of the Union. It is now time for Europe to be more creative in the way it expresses itself. The temple has been built, now it just needs some performances and ceremonies It needs its own metaphor. It needs its own mythology, its own sacrifices, its own symbols.

Spreading these freely-accessible European temples of culture across the globe and in the process creating and supporting spaces for cultural relations (such as museums, theatres, houses of creativity where cultural relations can develop) will provide the basis for the establishment of spaces for the prevention of cultural conflict.

**Damien Helly** has worked for the EU think tank, the EUISS (European Union Institute for Strategic Studies) since 2008. His main areas of focus are Sub-Saharan Africa, European-African relations and the Common Security and Defence Policy (CSDP). He has carried out research into conflict prevention and conflict management. Before joining the EUISS, he was head of the Port-au-Prince, Haiti, office of the NGO, International Crisis Group. From 2005-2006 Helly was head of an EU branch of the British NGO Saferworld in Brussels.

# Signification spirals and moral imagination

Culture can be the missing link between the adversaries of structure and the power to act. It is one dimension of social reality that enables us to understand the 'why' and 'how' of human conduct. It is a weighty element of social practices, which are in fact always coloured by culture. It is important that this potential is used in conflict management. *By Gudrun Kramer, Thomas Ernstbrunner and Wilfried Graf*

"The Moral Imagination" is a major work on conflict transformation. Its author, the American conflict researcher John Paul Lederach, is at pains to demonstrate a deplorable gap in current efforts to transform violent conflicts into drivers of peaceful social change. Our mind, our cognition, our rational perception are blank and blurred when thinking about ways of tackling deadly local and international conflicts. Lederach calls on us to fill the gap with human imagination and our ability to create. He calls for serendipity – allowing moments of epiphany and chance discoveries to occur. He calls for morality as an impetus and innovation as a tool. In a word, he calls for creativity.

Lederach wants to change the ways in which people and societies respond to challenges by making use of facets of human nature that are normally not considered as integral, necessary or even desirable components of initiatives for conflict transformation. In this way, he involves the artistic, cultural and creative dimension of human beings in the process. But he also asks how best we should do this. How can we translate this inspiring call for more imagination into practical conflict transformation? What does engaging in culture mean in this context?

In this complex and chaotic world, myriad events, actions, phenomena, causalities and underlying interdependences interact in a chaotic quagmire. It is amazing that people can even begin to get their bearings in this muddle, that they manage to act without being constantly overwhelmed and paralysed. Amongst other things, culture provides such bearings. It gives people tools that enable them to do things but that also limit them and in this way reduce the randomness and complexity of existence. These tools are assumptions, norms, values and customs. For the sake of interaction, we proceed from this basic foundation of common values and norms and frame expectations. Having said that, culture is a guiding framework that is normatively charged and deeply integrated. In this way, we tacitly know, or rather feel, what is good, beautiful or the right thing to do. This includes that we also tacitly know, or feel, what is the bad, ugly or wrong thing to do. It is a normative framework that is deeply internalised and gives us a shared system of rules.

When considered in this way, culture denotes a specific way of living that is inextricably intertwined with a (moral) evaluation. To a certain extent, it shows a way of living that is worth striving for and that is valid for every member of society. There is no space for the plural – cultures – but instead it is predominantly used in its singular form and appears to be a doxa. However, its normative basis and symbolic force or power is mostly denied. It taps into our internalised shared understanding of what the world should and should not look like in order to 'naturally' impose norms and values on all members of society. In this way it creates boundaries, distinctions and in the end a 'We' that is in the possession of the 'right' way (of life). Conceived in this way, culture is an ultimate argument, unchangeable, monolithic in its impact, and strongly excluding, degrading and derogative.

"In this complex and chaotic world, myriad events, actions, phenomena, causalities and underlying interdependences interact in a chaotic quagmire."

## *A culture of misunderstanding*

Since Samuel Huntington's theses on the "clash of civilisations", we can detect an increasing orientation towards cultural aspects. It is a prominent example of social sciences embarking on the unchangeable nature of culture that ultimately is destined to steer individuals within its orbit – dazzling and deceiving – towards a battle of good against evil. In Germany, Thilo Sarrazin stirred up a similar debate, arguing that Germany has an integration problem due to cultural differences. According to Sarrazin, Turkish and Arab immigrants are unwilling to integrate for cultural reasons. His stance on integration revealed a culture of misunderstanding and promoted a deep, underlying view that immigrants are unteachable and incapable of change. In this way, Sarrazin reduced social, political and economic problems and shortcomings to cultural differences.

Not least because of this constant tendency to simplify, reduce and ultimately 'culturalise', social scientists and conflict researchers have tended to deny this level of social reality or have simply refused to engage in it. It cannot be emphasised strongly enough that we totally reject this idea of culture. Culture is just one dimension of social reality that is still extremely worthwhile in its own right. When reflecting on culture, one needs to set it in relation to the social structures manifested by both society and individuals.

In fact, these poles can be seen as the points of a triangle. The first point is structures, institutionalised relations within and between societies that enable actors to operate, but that influence the behaviour of those actors. This is the realm of the 'outside' world.

The second point of the triangle is culture as the shared world of societies and collectivities. These are the shared patterns of assumptions, attitudes and meanings, including the collective psychology of groups; this is the shared 'inner' world.

The third point is human (inter)action, dealing primarily with the actors as individuals and groups who act out conflicts in the social world and are endowed with a certain amount of power to act, and with their behaviour. Here, the inner and the outer worlds meet, shaping and influencing the behaviour of the actors as individuals and groups.

At this stage, we can already see the implications for conflict transformation. It is important to understand that culture is just one dimension of social reality. In this sense, the surrounding culture informs, frames and structures individual behaviour. But this perspective does not do justice to individuals and social structures. People are not just 'cultural dopes'. They have the potential to be creative, independent of socio-cultural influences. Social interaction can therefore also be creative and transformative. Social structures are laden with culture, giving us an impression of how modes of domination are signified and symbolised. However, this falls short, of a more structural account of how power or domination is typically established (in terms of possession or exclusion). It is therefore pivotal to take into account the social dimension and social structures, especially when engaging in conflict transformation. To put it bluntly, it is counterproductive to gear initiatives towards cultural change without considering or addressing structural power asymmetries. Such a transformation would result in the 'pacification' of groups without social justice.

### *Culture as the 'missing link'*

In this relational context, culture has much to offer, with insightful potential that should not be thrown out with the 'culturalism' bath water. Our understanding of culture defines it as the totality of internalised norms and values, of the knowledge and practices required for meaningful membership of groups and intersubjective actions. Thus, culture can be the 'missing link', the mediator between the adversaries of structure and the power to act. It is one dimension of social reality that enables us to understand the 'why' and 'how' of human conduct. Culture, in this concept of it, is a weighty element of social practices, which are in fact always coloured by culture. Internalised shared meanings and practices impinge on our behaviour – they inspire and encourage certain forms of behaviour as much as they dishearten or discourage others. The tacit, bodily knowledge of this normative structure binds us together in groups and communities. They mark boundaries – geographically as well as emotionally. In this way, culture creates a 'We', a cultural, social identity that connects us to our community and its history. Culture enables the 'lived' internalisation of and identification with emotionally-laden events in history, adopting it through shared symbols, rituals or other cultural tokens.

"It is counterproductive to gear initiatives towards cultural change without considering or addressing structural power asymmetries."

We rarely, indeed hardly ever, question the governing and guiding aspects of our culture; not to mention assessing their destructive, malignant or even violent elements. Because these principles are so deeply-rooted within us, often unconsciously, these sensuous cultural guidelines can at times be tapped into or instrumentalised. They provide the raw materials for the dynamics of conflict escalation, polarisation and ultimately the dehumanisation of others, which in turn are exacerbated by populist and fundamentalist policies.

Particularly in times of crisis, when a group is faced with a complex situation yet needs to maintain consensus in order to (re)act effectively, culture is steered towards creating emotional social cohesion, which no longer allows pluralistic views. Anyone who is not with the group is automatically perceived as being against it. Culture is misused to create enemy images and to portray others as non-human. Dehumanisation is, in fact, a socio-cultural frame of perception that on the one hand creates images of people who we mourn, and on the other hand, images of people who cannot be mourned as their very existence as a human being is denied in the first place.

### *Legitimising violence*

When individuals or parties are dragged by personal and situational dynamics into a vicious cycle of violent conflict, they can advance to a point where the other is no longer perceived as human. Violence is legitimised in this context and directly centred on the human condition, shattering social ties and divesting individuals or groups of their humanness. Yet, de-humanisation is just one of several extreme forms of moral exclusion. 'Psychological distance' (perceiving others as objects, as non-existent), 'condescension' (patronising others as inferior or irrational), and so on all hamper genuine human relations.

It is already almost a truism that large-scale violence affects collectives as much as individuals. But despite all the similarities, we have to imagine the different effects. We cannot put individual trauma on the same level as collective trauma. Individual trauma responds to therapy. We cannot simply put groups, communities or societies on the couch and treat them with a 'talking cure', as it does not work at a collective level. Communities try to cope with collective traumas in a different way. Culture is in fact one of the coping mechanisms used by groups for dealing with traumatic events.

In desperate times, people struggle to make sense of their situation. Humans always want to make sense of things and need things to make sense. Lack of meaning is the arch-enemy of human existence. It is an existential fear that generates a stampede towards a formula for meaning that provides us with values and a blueprint for life. Values tell us not only why we live but also how to live.

Ongoing violence also requires a narrative framework and meaning. Individuals and societies need to find sense in the violence that answers the question why and tells them how to deal with the ongoing violence and its effects. As it progresses, groups and communities develop certain beliefs that enable them to cope with it and give meaning to their senseless suffering.

So the narrative of where we come from, where we are now and where we are going is damaged by the experience of large-scale violence and collective trauma. This damaged narrative is passed on from one generation to the next through norms, values, symbols, myths, songs, poems, monuments, street names, etc. The narrative of the victim is coloured by the longing for revenge and the narrative of the perpetrator is coloured by the desire for victory and glory. The narratives are kept alive by the media or other representatives of the collective who take the narrative and modify it through a 'signification spiral'. In this way, the coping mechanism for past collective trauma becomes the basis for legitimising violence in the present.

Culture can not only pose a considerable obstacle to efforts at conflict transformation, but it also can be a vital

"We cannot simply put groups, communities or societies on the couch and treat them with a 'talking cure'."

resource. As such, societal beliefs, narratives and values are a helpful signpost in navigating the respective cultural fields.

Norms and values need to be fostered to enable an environment or culture of responsiveness. If this goal is to be achieved, then 'pathological' cultural adaptations need to be addressed and transformed. Change and transformation is not intended to be exclusively externally triggered or co-opted. Local culture can present as many obstacles as solutions. Therefore it is important to work together to foster and fortify peacebuilding cultural resources that are capable of overcoming persistent obstacles such as de-humanisation.

One way that conflict transformation can engage in the cultural field is to facilitate the reframing and renegotiation of those perceptual frames. Here, rehumanisation is the reversal of the destructive dynamics of conflict and violence towards fostering the right values and attitudes towards others. The key to conflict transformation is therefore fostering a culture of rehumanisation and responsiveness. Alongside this relational idea of reframing and dismantling enemy images, rehumanisation also includes our role as victims or perpetrators.

In violent conflicts, we can lose our inner link to our humanity. Above all, sexual violence such as that practised in patriarchal societies cuts deep into the social fabric, leaving behind stigmatised victims. These victims and victims in general often find themselves ostracised, marginalised and excluded, made even worse by their loss of honour, fertility and fears of 'contamination'. In protracted conflicts, perpetrators also lose some part of their humanity in the haze of atrocities and so feel the psychological need to restore their self-image as a moral person. Feelings of guilt due to the breach of shared values and norms place perpetrators outside the cultural community and they may also find themselves excluded, marginalised or suppressed.

Having said this, it is vital to integrate the backdrop to the ultimately different experiences of victims and perpetrators in violent conflicts. Whatever perpetrators may have gone through, it is the result of destructive actions and strategies against their victims, and as such we must reject premature efforts to integrate perpetrators. These normally arise when social structures remain untransformed and there is still an imbalance of power. For that matter, the importance of a culture of responsiveness has gained ground over the last decades as the focus has turned more to the bolstering or weakening effects of the political and socio-cultural environment on traumatised victims. It is now clear that social and collective support helps the individual in coping with potentially traumatic events.

Academics and experts in transitional justice have highlighted the positive impact of acknowledgement, reparations, truth commissions and war tribunals in this context. Fostering a culture of responsiveness is therefore a vital part of conflict transformation. As such, it includes rethinking concepts of the enemy as part of paving the way for a culture of responsiveness (by acknowledging the suffering inflicted on victims) and reintegrating victims and perpetrators into the moral community by coming to terms with the past.

## *Acknowledging suffering*

Cultural activities and events can provide the reflective social space that is needed for transforming norms and values. An example is the establishment of the Cultural Resource Center in the Palestinian refugee camp Talbiyeh in Jordan, supported by the Gesellschaft für Internationale Zusammenarbeit (GIZ) on behalf of the German Federal Ministry for Economic Cooperation and Development (BMZ).

The Cultural Resource Center conducts art workshops on topics such as photography, film, animation and social media, and organises public lectures and video screenings. These art workshops give young people an opportunity to express their creativity, while also finding a constructive way of questioning norms and values that have become set in stone within the diaspora but no longer fit in with present-day society. Through public installations, the people of the camp are invited to join a public debate about contemporary identity.

Young people dealt with the issue of collective trauma by interviewing and filming survivors of the Nakba (the displacement of Palestinians that followed the Israeli Declaration of Independence 1948) in the camp. In future, these historical archives might become a source for healing the 'damaged' Palestinian narrative. At the same time, engaging with contemporary Palestinian culture and art is reviving the camp's cultural life, which had degenerated into nothing more than folklore.

In this way, the Cultural Resource Center supports the transformation of norms, values and social practices (culture). However, it also addresses the transformation of institutionalised relationships (social structure). The Center is run by women and for the first time girls and boys are learning together.

The establishment of the Cultural Resource Center in Talbiyeh shows that development cooperation does not have to be restricted to fulfilling basic material needs. It can also fulfil immaterial needs such as identity. Socio-cultural empowerment fosters creativity and thus supports the critical factor in conflict transformation – what John Paul Lederach calls “the moral imagination”.

**Gudrun Kramer** is head of the Regional Social and Cultural Fund for Palestinian Refugees and Gaza Population run by the Gesellschaft für Internationale Zusammenarbeit (GIZ) in Jerusalem. The aim is to help improve the way the population of Gaza and Palestinian refugees in the region are able to deal with the ongoing conflict and to develop new long-term prospects for themselves and the community. **Thomas Ernstbrunner** is a freelance research assistant at the Herbert C. Kelman Institute for Interactive Conflict Transformation and Peacebuilding (IICP) in Vienna. **Wilfried Graf** is active as a researcher, adviser and trainer in conflict regions and post-conflict societies (Sri Lanka, Central Asia, and currently predominantly in Israel/Palestine). He is co-founder of the Herbert C. Kelman Institute for Interactive Conflict Transformation and Peacebuilding (IICP) in Vienna.

# Message in a bottle The Mediterranean is a cultural melting pot that people have always wanted to claim, possess and control. Are the basic premises of diplomacy still relevant today? Or should the more popular soft power strategies be exchanged for more nuanced, horizontal and sincere strategies?

*By Moukhtar Kocache*

Over the last fifteen years, exchange, interaction and support within the culture sector has been at the heart of a significant number of programmes, resources and meetings between Europe and its Southern Mediterranean neighbours. This has given rise to both a significant amount of debate and some criticism, but it has also provided thousands of citizens on both sides of the sea the opportunity to learn something new. The fact remains however, that cultural development, dialogue and partnership policies and programmes are generally unwieldy and tend to go in one direction only, from North to South. The fragile nature of political, civic and public spheres in the Southern Mediterranean states is no doubt partly to blame for this situation. There seems to be consensus, in the South at least, that in spite of the large number of initiatives that have been undertaken, few schemes have been able to create the kind of familiarity and closeness that can arise in certain disciplines and communities out of a genuine sense of curiosity or intellectual exchange. The majority of initiatives are dominated by the large number of formal, institutional and public programmes and projects that naturally tend to convey and reinforce European political thinking and ideology.

Since 2000, culture seems to have resurfaced as an essential component of successful diplomatic relations between Europe and its Mediterranean neighbours to the south. Over the last few years, the European Commission has repeatedly reminded us of the key role that culture has to play in building international and external relations. Several states have also adopted an official or even unofficial policy of integrating culture into their diplomatic efforts. Many national cultural institutions have expanded their activities and sought to create meaningful programmes and services at their centres of operation in the South.

What is perhaps not clear is what they are actually hoping to achieve and whether they have been successful. Just how successful is traditional and modernist diplomacy in this day and age? Are its premises and assumptions still viable for our contemporary world and the one we seek to build in the future? It seems that outdated strategies of 'soft power' and binary, oppositional dialectics need to be replaced with more nuanced, horizontal and sincere strategies that move away from notions of conflict management towards genuine needs and values based on mutuality, sharing and commonality.

At this point, it is worth mentioning the "More Europe" initiative, a new cultural civic initiative that seeks to highlight and reinforce the role of culture in the EU's external relations. It calls on Member States, civil society and EU institutions to work together in order to pursue a common vision, pool resources, and coordinate activities. "More Europe" is, however, only supposed to be a temporary platform, whereas this type of work needs sustained and long-term effort and commitment.

## *Psychogeography of the Mediterranean*

Over time, the psychogeography of the Mediterranean has tended to fluctuate between division and commonality. Some have seen it as a bridge between peoples, others as a gulf. Throughout history it has always been a place that awakened a sense of longing or fascination, a place that either had to be feared or defended against.

Nevertheless, the Mediterranean has always been and continues to be a transitional space, a place of cultural fusion, a space to claim, own and manage. There is no doubt that controlling it has been at the heart of various civilisations. It is perhaps no coincidence that arguably one of Europe's first nationalist empires not only claimed it, but gave it the name "mare nostrum", our sea. It is no surprise that the concept of the Mediterranean was created in Europe with the advent of colonialism and the solidification of yet another concept, that of the nation state.

The Northern discourse that has shaped its political, geographic and historical classification seems to have constrained the cultures and peoples of the Mediterranean and prevented overlapping and complimentary historiographies, identities, narratives and opportunities from emerging ever since. The rich and enriching organic linguistic, literary, musical, culinary and intellectual development and joy of creation of the past seem to have lost their way, both in form and function, with the solidification of nationalist, modernist and totalitarian modes of governance and hegemonic ideologies. The people that inhabit the coast of the Mediterranean today deserve better opportunities for creativity when it comes to highlighting their common heritage, pursuing forms of cultural fusion and creating new Mediterranean platforms and modes of belonging that will allow them to better project themselves in the world.

Historical, philosophical and theoretical studies of the peoples and cultures of the Mediterranean should, in my opinion, accompany our exploration, analysis and development of systems and structures of exchange, partnership and dialogue that seek to foster the wellbeing of communities in Europe and the Southern Mediterranean. The cultural realm, with artists, intellectuals, cultural critics, theoreticians and philosophers at its helm, seems to me to be the ideal vehicle to take us on a voyage of rediscovery into our common past. We need to start a process of deconstruction, re-imagination and transformation of the ideological, institutional, governance and political frameworks that determine the relationships between Europe and the Mediterranean. This will be a delicate, complicated and not particularly reassuring journey, because a process of generous and serious reaching out towards the 'other' will also require the need to revisit and rewrite one's own narratives, which in most instances have been created in direct opposition to that very same 'other'.

The history of exchanges between Europe and the Southern Mediterranean is rich but also chaotic. There are a whole range of formal initiatives that we can scrutinise and learn from. These include the Euro-Mediterranean Partnership and its Euro-Mediterranean Strategy on Culture, the Euromed Heritage and Euromed Audiovisual programmes, the Anna Lindh Foundation for the Dialogue between Cultures in the Mediterranean, the European Neighbourhood Policy, the efforts of the Union for the Mediterranean and the Council of Europe as well as a cluster of civic and non-governmental programmes and initiatives. The intelligent work of the European Culture Foundation is particularly worth noting in this connection. Given such a wide range of sometimes contradictory programmes, there has been very little in the way of coordination between civic, private and public initiatives and a great deal of confusion on the ground in the cultural sector that these programmes are meant to serve. Despite the fact that a great deal has happened and that there is a much more lively exchange between North and South these days, there is still much to be done. Too often, Southern 'partners' feel frustrated and left out of the creative and analytical process.

There are many ways to help diffuse and improve this situation. There is often an assumption that Southern partners and societies need to embark on a 'learning process'. In many respects this is either doubtful or even completely untrue. I believe it is just as important, however, for European structures and societies to also

"The people that inhabit the coast of the Mediterranean today deserve better opportunities for creativity when it comes to highlighting their common heritage, pursuing forms of cultural fusion and creating new Mediterranean platforms and modes of belonging that will allow them to better project themselves in the world."

evaluate whether embarking on a process of 'unlearning' might not also help them to put divergences into perspective, to re-evaluate their modus operandi and bring radical creativity into their processes. Without that willingness, Northern partners can be left with a reductive, limited and perhaps even dishonest notion of their actual and potential partners, who tend to have to start culture and policy work from the ground up because they lack the necessary framework or background. With much behind us in terms of accomplishments and lessons, the coming period calls for in-depth reflection, synthesis, learning, humility, honesty and radical creativity in terms of self examination and the envisioning of a better common future for all.

In October 2011, the Young Arab Theatre Fund (www.yatfund.org) organised its fourth meeting of cultural spaces in the Arab region. This latest meeting was organised in partnership with Marseilles as 2013 European Capital of Culture. One of the goals of the meeting was to engage the fifty or so representatives of independent cultural organisations from the Arab world in an informal process of reflection on the cultural relations between Europe and the Arab world and to gather their impressions. What follows is a personal summing up – not an official declaration – of the salient issues and ideas discussed by the group. These examples can serve as benchmarks, points of discourse and insights into the nature of this complex relationship from a Southern perspective and allow the message in the bottle to finally land on the Northern shore of the Mediterranean.

## *Celebrating interwoven histories*

The current frameworks that have helped shape and govern relationships between Europe and its Southern Mediterranean neighbours are modernist in nature and fail to grasp the desires and needs of the people and cultures of the individual regions. Rather than having a "geometrically induced logic" of boundaries, barriers and differences, what is urgently needed is a framework that acknowledges and celebrates overlapping practices and interwoven histories. This would favour less rigidity, more visceral and practical comprehension and a respect for the multiplicities and complexities of the relationships and dynamics.

I believe that all efforts since the 19th century to separate and regiment the cultures and peoples of Europe and the Southern Mediterranean ideologically, intellectually and legislatively have played an implicit role in bringing us obliquely into the current depressing, non-creative and catastrophic notion of a "clash of civilisations". What the North and South or the Orient and Occident urgently need is an acknowledgement, promotion and celebration of the mutability, layering and fusion of the cultures of the extended Mediterranean. This would allow for hidden narratives, suppressed identities and alternate historiographies to emerge. This would

SONJA
Jimmy
S.R
SONJA
Jimmy

complicate, but also support the process of breaking down differences between the peoples of this region.

The modernist paradigm that has characterised itself in the universal right and freedom to travel and migrate in our contemporary world translates into a gross lack of freedom and inequity in terms of access and opportunity. Strangely enough, market forces and economic policies cloaked with notions of freedom do not run into the same obstacles and limitations and are increasingly creating challenges for both Europe and the Southern Mediterranean that threaten fundamental rights and freedoms in the areas of health, education and food.

## *An acute sense of inclusion and exclusion*

The nationalism of the 19th and 20th centuries has taught us how crucial it is to identify the 'other' in order to create homogeneity within specific political, civic and cultural boundaries, or at least a semblance of it. In recent decades, the same principles have applied in newer forms of societal consolidation such as the European Union. Never before has there been such an acute sense of inclusion and exclusion in the relationship between Europe and the Southern Mediterranean. This is perhaps emblematised most strongly in the ability of Europeans to travel to Southern Mediterranean countries freely and without the need for prior approval, whereas Southern Mediterranean citizens not only need to go through a convoluted, humiliating and expensive process to receive permission to travel to Europe, but also have to go through the same process if they just want to transit through Europe on their way to another destination like Asia or America. The presence of the 'other' is not tolerated and differences are even reinforced between two gates of Europe's international airports.

At risk of sounding polemical, Europeans need to urgently work through a conscious and unconscious past in which colonialism and empire have helped crystallise notions of identity, culture, race and progress. The current European crisis, which is clearly not just economic in scope, provides Europeans with an opportunity to deconstruct appropriated and imagined histories and explore alternatives to Cartesian nationalism and rationalism. They can reshuffle notions of otherness where the self is not constructed, valued and defended in opposition to the other.

In many ways, the crisis in Europe today stems from a mismatch between politics, philosophy and culture. The European Union project, which calls for increased federalism, is currently threatening the notion of the nation state that has in great part been responsible for the construction of European identities. However, federalism would eventually mean decentralisation and local governance. Local governance endangers the nation state not only because it shifts decision-making processes away from a centralised system but also because it celebrates local identities, ethnicities, languages and practices. However, there will be no escaping regionalism as Europe heads towards a more federal structure. Too much hesitation in this in-between stage will be dangerous and disruptive.

I imagine that a truly federated Europe would encourage the re-emergence of local narratives and associations, allowing communities to develop more genuine exchanges and alliances with other communities.

Europe has been a bastion of radical, creative, discursive, political, philosophical and theoretical thinking and this coming period will require unconventional leadership and bravery to propose new ideas, structures and governances for communities and cultures to live and prosper together.

What might be required is not just a healthy critique of the ills of colonialism and a sense of guilt, remorse or shame on the part of Europeans towards a 19th century that was rife with expansionist, racist and reductive ideologies, systems and beliefs. What is primordial at this point and perhaps also timely, is to investigate and alter how historical, cultural and political structures of the past continue to frame and propagate inequity, injustice and institutional power while simultaneously brandishing civilising notions of democracy, universal human rights, liberty and freedom.

"Never before has there been such an acute sense of inclusion and exclusion in the relationship between Europe and the Southern Mediterranean."

This in no way seeks to discredit the rich heritage and principles propagated from and since the Enlightenment, culminating in Western modernity. Rather it is a call to excavate, to expose the ambiguities, incoherencies and relentless logic of this heritage as it impacts a European world view at a time when the Western template is being increasingly challenged. Can this materialise without a sense of fear, threat or conflict and a feeling that these new realities are being imposed? Owning this process and determining the modalities of its operation clearly seems to be the wisest way of engaging with these shifting landscapes and a new world that will require the inclusion of multiple, diverse and divergent values, perspectives and paradigms.

Using existing and failing parameters of knowledge and analytical frames could then limit the realms of thought and creative problem-solving. New geographies of association and representation as well as new historiographies are necessary in order to allow for new configurations and possible systems to emerge in the future. But how can all this be implemented in practical terms?

The almost complete absence of European philanthropy in this field is remarkable. Creative and sustained efforts must be made to encourage European foundations and the emerging philanthropic sector in the South to engage in and with this topic. There is an urgent need to diversify the actors involved and the supporters of European and Southern Mediterranean relations. This will not only help reduce the burden on and expectations of official European institutions and structures, but will help foster a diversity of projects that are more personal, including community- and affinity-based collaborations and support.

Very often, the assumption in Europe is that working with communities and organisations from the South will help to reach immigrant communities in Europe or help in addressing some of the social problems they are facing in Europe. This premise may at times make sense, however it must be understood that these are primarily European-based incentives and concerns that in most cases do not reflect the concerns of people on the Southern shores of the Mediterranean – even if this where most migrants have come from over the last 100 years. In many instances, European immigrants are working class, may have left their homes in the South many years ago or even several generations ago. They could perhaps be more traditional or even nostalgic in their tastes and morals and may not be drawn to or appreciate the contemporary culture being produced today in the South. Europe needs to have a better understanding of these differences and realities.

## *Lack of cohesion*

Northern partners should also understand that partnerships and projects that are initiated in the North may interfere with the needs, responsibilities and commitments that Southern partners have towards their own institutional development, aims and constituencies. As such, there is much work to be done by Northern partners to gain deeper knowledge of the organisations, individuals, infrastructure and the context in which the Southern partners function.

Northern partners need to take into account the lack of cohesion in the cultural landscape of the Southern nations where a significant rift exists between official and independent cultural structures. In a sense, there are disparate cultural policies at stake and being promulgated. This will remain the case until governments in the South become truly representative and democratic and ministries and official instruments of culture organise themselves in the service of their citizens. As such, Northern partners should be cognizant of this when envisaging programmes with multiple players in the South or within the same cultural landscape and nation.

Although limitations exist administratively, financially and politically, European institutions should strive to develop policies and programmes that are flexible and tailored to each context and not just

"Europe has been a bastion of radical, creative, discursive, political, philosophical and theoretical thinking and this coming period will require unconventional leadership and bravery to propose new ideas, structures and governances for communities and cultures to live and prosper together."

created in blanket fashion for the entire Southern region.

Clearly, the greater the differentiation and contextualisation, the more nuanced, deeper and more sustainable the results of the partnerships will be. Despite various mobility programmes between Europe and the Southern Mediterranean over the past decade, the mobility of cultural workers remains weak and the institutions that support them continue to struggle with basic funding and sustainability. There is absolutely no excuse for the lack of strong, sustained and well-funded mobility platforms. European funders and donors need to make this a priority. The strange fact is that mobility is relatively inexpensive to support! Mobility for independent culture professionals and groups also needs to be accompanied by the need to expand professional networking between North and South and to create frameworks of long-term knowledge-building and sharing and the creation of affinities between people.

Equally, culture professionals in the South need to urgently embark on a deeper learning and understanding of the various structures and contexts emanating from Europe. The Southern cultural sector needs to become more informed, educated and nuanced about the opportunities, funding, services and partnerships that are at their disposal from the North so they can be better prepared, proceed more selectively and have appropriate expectations of their partnerships with Europe. Everyone who is interested in Mediterranean cooperation needs to learn from the good models and initiatives launched by European cultural institutes in the South. A compendium of case studies is overdue. This work would help identify best practices but also offer insight into the type of programmes needed in the future.

### *A new institution in Europe*

I have a vision for a new, ongoing, focused Secretariat, a new institution in Europe that would help coordinate, inform, study and mobilise actors and policy-makers around cultural, educational and intellectual cooperation between Europe and the Southern Mediterranean. It is an urgent necessity to create an independent organisation that will monitor, assist, interpret, translate and speak up for clarity and quality in initiatives that already exist or that will be created to govern cultural relations between Europe and the Southern Mediterranean. This body would use public, international, private and civic initiatives to fill the vacuum between these spheres and help create a more holistic scope of intervention. Such an institution could produce more ongoing and intensive research and seek to simplify the presentation of the results so that they are accessible to a wider and more diverse set of players.

There is no doubt that at present there is a great range of ideas, programmes, policies, reflections and experiments that can all help us to better understand and develop future initiatives for promoting collaborations, partnerships and joint projects between Europe and the Southern Mediterranean region.

In order to define the process going forward, or at least to serve as an ultimate goal, we need to come together to tackle the issues, events and opportunities that impact the peoples of the North and South. Only then can we move from mere binary interactions towards a shared sense of common destiny. In a sense, we need to strive to go further than traditional notions of dialogue, understanding, cooperation and assistance. Building a process with shared interests, responsibilities and participation will be essential not only at the level of institutions but also and specifically amongst the communities and people who live in this region. As we seek a future with more exchange, creativity, respect, harmony and equity between various peoples, we currently seem to have in place outdated and perhaps also counterproductive instruments and institutions that are charged with the mission of helping to facilitate this goal. Vision and courage will be needed to re-imagine and redesign our existing structures, systems and world views, given that our future is inscribed in the political, cultural and social apparatus and foundations that govern our present.

**Moukhtar Kochache** is a curator and artistic manager. Until 2012, he was at the Ford Foundation in Cairo, where he worked on the development, sustainability, networking and infrastructure of art and artistic spaces. Prior to this, he was Programm Director for the Lower Manhattan Cultural Council (LMCC), where he devised and organised exhibitions, and he was also an advisor and university lecturer.

# "Self-confidence based on mutual respect"

How can cultural organisations on both sides of the Mediterranean work more closely together? What is required? For the North it would be better to promote the arts for the sake of cultural production rather than using it as a socio-political instrument. This was one of the ideas that emerged from the fourth conference on cultural spaces in the Arab region, organised by the Young Arab Theatre Fund.

The mutual connection between Europe and the Arab world exists across geographical, geopolitical, historical and postcolonial boundaries. This was the conclusion of the participants at the fourth meeting on cultural spaces in the Arab Region in October 2011, organised by the Young Arab Theatre fund.
They acknowledged that a post-colonial Europe is struggling to produce new relations with its former colonies and to turn existing relations into productive ones of mutual respect. It was recognised that this is also affected by political and economic imperatives that are not at all related to culture. The recent rise in right-wing populism and anti-Arab racism in Europe has emphasised the importance of cultural collaboration as a project for Europe. Europe's economic ability to act on these desires is a considerable source of arts funding for the Arab world. This may be changing due to the current economic climate. The Gulf States have the economic ability to support NGOs and art markets in both Europe and the Arab world, but the political reality of the Gulf region makes it an improbable partner for moral, ideological and ethical reasons.
The conference participants emphasised that Europe is a space for the intense, discursive, practice-based, and profitable circulation of art. Arab cultural actors and artist want to be more involved in this flow in order to open doors to a global career that would otherwise remain closed.
The promising but rocky road to a partnership of equals is hindered by the fact that Arab artists lag behind their European partners and do not have access to the same privileges of address, collaboration, authorship, remuneration and mobility. Relations between the Arab world and Europe are currently limited to a binary perception of two homogenous spaces. There is a lack of capacity on both sides that hinder the development of trusting cultural relations in interactions at all levels.

**EU initiatives are too event-led**

The predominant experience of Arab cultural organisations has been that EU-funded cultural initiatives are led too much by events, policies or objectives rather than by context and artistic expression. This has led to Arab artists and cultural actors feeling manipulated, particularly with regard to EU objectives on development, the promotion of democracy or even the prevention of emigration to Europe.
To cultural workers on the ground, these factors seem artificial and marginal. It would be beneficial for the North to encourage equity in terms of the status of artists and the arts for cultural production rather than as a socio-political instrument. There is also a feeling that the EU's evaluation and monitoring procedures reflect a myopic, positivistic impulse, requiring as they do unrealistically fast, quantifiable 'results'. It is important that European partners recognise that cultural expression is a long-term and often unquantifiable end in itself, rather than an immediate service provider.
Conditions of partnership are frequently imposed from above rather than as a result of dialogue. This can also apply to the cultural initiatives of European Member States. Groups in the South want partnerships to spring from mutual recognition and interest rather than from top-down visions.
Southern organisations with small capacity find the process of applying for EU funding unnecessarily arduous and 'almost' designed to filter them out. Southern partners identify a conscious bureaucratisation by European institutions geared towards making them work harder for equal and similar recognition. Lack of trust is felt across many levels. Additionally, Arab organisations applying for certain European funding resent having to state their non-affiliation with 'terrorism' in their applications, and perceive hypocrisy when the same European policies and funds either directly or indirectly support corrupt regimes and radical groups and institutions on the ground.
There is also criticism that Europe has tended to continue funding the 'usual suspects' of trusted Arab partners, but mistrusts emerging organisations, resulting in a lack of

risk-taking and investment and opportunities for innovation and the development of new leadership. Southern groups call for an attitude of trust, respect and risk-taking in partnering with existing and emerging ventures.
Inexperienced European actors (organisations, Member State cultural diplomats) lack the insight to know what is credible within specific Arab contexts. This can result in support for projects that are locally considered irrelevant and so do not contribute to artistic discourse. Worse, less determined Arab artists may begin to perceive an 'ideological market' and bend their practice falsely towards funding opportunities.

**Clear communication is needed**

The conference attendees expressed the hope that Arab and European actors should approach each other with clear communication and professional confidence based on mutual appreciation and common goals. Ideally, this appreciation would be fostered through the existence of long-term contact and face-to-face peer interest and recognition, rather than being triggered by sudden opportunities for funding. This would help ensure that cultural productions emerging from such partnerships are regarded by their audiences in all contexts as worthwhile, credible and relevant.
It is important for European cultural and civil society organisations to develop long-term research activities and relations with Southern organisations and artists that clearly share an affinity with their goals, rather than simply responding opportunistically and in the short-term to funding patterns. Partnerships should always retain a focus on cultural and artistic quality and excellence.
European cultural organisations struggle to take into account the impact of structural imbalances such as workload, risk, costs and visa procedures for Arab organisations and artists. Equal fundraising targets are often proposed in collaborations, representing a grossly disproportionate burden on their Arab partners. Another issue that has to be considered is the difference in currency value that makes travel to Europe disproportionately expensive for Arab partners. Collaborations can only truly be equal when they take into account the practical burdens of infrastructural imbalances affecting Arab organisations and artists. The conference also spoke up in favour of the allocation of funding to build the capacity of professional arts workers in the Arab world. This would allow a more realistic sense of institutional parity and respect, as well as diminishing the need for European experts (such as choreographers, projectionists, managers and designers) to be flown in at great expense. In order to specifically build the capacity of artists and managers, normal concepts of training and professional development should be expanded in terms of time and content and should not only function in a short-term manner.

**Advantages of a 'cultural visa'**

Particular administrative and financial support and tailored scheduling should be undertaken in light of the visa restrictions imposed upon visiting Arab artists. These should be considered as shared burdens and not private problems. The responsibility for setting timeframes, budgets, drafting contingency plans and administrative support for the visa applications of Arab artists should be borne equally. One possibility would be to create a 'cultural visa' instead of the Schengen system or to urgently come up with a parallel administrative system to process visas for artists and cultural workers.
European institutions should allow for more feedback and decision-making to take place on the ground in the South. For instance, cultural attachés should be given greater freedom to research civil society and new local organisations and put them on the cultural map. European staff on the ground could have greater autonomy in defining and building effective programmes and collaborations. This might help to introduce greater understanding, buy-in, transparency and responsiveness into the processes (qualities that many Southern actors feel are currently lacking), in order to move the relationship from 'funder' to 'partner'. Opportunities for learning from the Arab region have been under-explored. Arab cultural organisations have developed immense capacity to handle issues within the local context and could serve as a bridge for their partners. The conference participants stressed how members of the Arab diaspora in Europe and elsewhere have a unique experience that not only provides insight in terms of diverse cultural insight but can also

confound the logic of a cultural 'binary system' and thus expand our notion of local versus foreign identities. For this reason, they could be extremely relevant and exciting sources for building relations. European governments and embassies could seek out and employ qualified members of this community when filling intermediary posts such as cultural attachés, programme organisers, curators, etc. European partners should also pay more attention to the need to develop and participate in funding and creating better infrastructures and to generally develop a healthier ecology in the Arab arts and culture sector. This in turn would improve the nature, scope and quality of exchange programmes.

There has also been loud criticism by European players with respect to the Arab Spring. When engaging with this topic, they tend to follow the long-established pattern of 'art in the service of democracy' rather than in the service of its own freedom of expression.

In the meantime, it is felt by many Arab organisations that it is too soon to draw generalised conclusions from this period, and that most modes of representation cannot encapsulate the ever-changing and mercurial nature of the Arab Spring. While there are enormous possibilities for renewed terms of engagement with Arab artists, they fear the focus shifting from one set of clichés and discursive expectations to another.

**Art as a revolutionary space**

The feeling of the conference was that there is a need for art to be recognised as a revolutionary space in and of itself, rather than being consigned merely to being the conduit for representations of revolutionary-themed content. It is important that this changing reality and the next phase should be recognised as an unpredictable paradigm shift in relations, rather than as the expected 'step forward' that anticipates Western hopes or fears. This also applies to notions of democratic governance that may differ in terms of structure and implementation between North and South.

The conference recommended that organisations in Southern Mediterranean countries should continue to strengthen their independent cultural coalitions in order to consolidate the position of culture within their local context, and work on developing policy recommendations that are then communicated to large sections of the population. Such work would help them to build a position of strength in order to be able to deal with other European NGOs as equal partners rather than as supplicants.

The cultural civil society sector in the South needs to actively seek and develop alternative routes of funding beyond EU and EU Member States, in order for collaboration decisions to be rooted not in funding necessity but genuinely in the goals and interests of specific organisations. Local organisations should aim to stick to their own strategies and resist the urge to react to funding opportunities. They should aim to retain artistic integrity and honesty in the face of the implied values, styles and expectations of badly-informed joint projects and opportunities. Arab NGOS and organisations should use their programmes and position to build the familiarity and trust of their communities for 'the contemporary', to provide a better conduit for the flow of ideas from outside and from around the region and to reduce resistance to them.

Finally, the Southern cultural sector should build bilateral alliances with civil society and lobbying groups in both Europe and the countries bordering the southern Mediterranean, in order to lobby policymakers on both sides at both macro and grassroots level.

**Mia Jankowicz,** *Artistic Director of the "Contemporary Image Collective" in Cairo, is responsible for collating and editing the reports and contributions from the conference.*

# The positive influence of cultural initiatives

Where political conflicts create division, culture can create space for encounters, dialogue and understanding. From organising a puppet theatre in Afghanistan to assisting young activists in Egypt – the members of the European National Institutes for Culture (EUNIC) network are increasing their focus on post-conflict regions and countries that are in transition.

*By Katrin Mader*

For many years now, peace and security policies have focused on civil society processes and their importance for political stabilisation in crisis zones. But to date there has been relatively little collaboration and cooperation between cultural institutes and the conflict management sector. Is this because culture is not yet fully acknowledged as a credible component of peace and security policy and the work of cultural institutes is still not considered sufficiently valid in this respect?

One thing is clear: if cultural and educational work is to be applied effectively in the field of conflict management, then cultural institutes and networks such as EUNIC must make their activities more transparent. They also have to prove that cultural activity can have a positive effect on conflict transformation. It is only in this way that groups can work together more effectively to achieve their goals of resolving cultural, social and political conflict and securing peace.

The European Parliament stated in a March 2011 report that culture should become a more integral part of European external relations. The report is part of a broader recognition of the importance of culture in foreign policy, a recognition that has helped to focus attention on the role of cultural initiatives in conflict prevention, peacebuilding and democratic transformation within the EU. Calling for a role for culture in civil conflict management, the report also placed renewed focus on the potential role of EUNIC in this respect.

EUNIC has confirmed that one of its strategic priorities is the development and enhancement of resources for cultural initiatives in countries that are undergoing transition and instability. Through its cultural activities, the network is keen to place more emphasis on peacebuilding. But it continues to be faced with the problem that – despite all the EU's efforts – the positive influence of cultural and educational work on conflict transformation remains insufficiently recognised or proven. It is important is to start finding evidence and arguments to prove to both national and

EU policymakers that cultural and educational programmes can contribute to conflict resolution.

## *Airy formulations*

In assessing the effects and risks of cultural and educational work in conflict intervention, it appears that cultural institutes often engage in educated guesswork more than rigorous measurement. Outside the cultural sector, it is hard to find voices that recognise the value of cultural initiatives in conflict settings. As Rainer Nolte, head of the Dialogue Programme of Germany‘s Institute for Cultural Foreign Relations (ifa) stated last year in the magazine "Politik und Kultur": "The role that can be played by aesthetic production as the goal of a cultural programme within a systematic framework of actions [of civil conflict management], has so far been left undefined."

What seems to be missing is an overarching strategy for demonstrating the effectiveness of cultural programmes in peacebuilding processes and an answer to the question whether the positive influence of cultural organisations is just an illusion or whether it does in fact have an effect on conflict transformation. Does the culture sector base its actions on concrete knowledge or simply on long-held beliefs and hopes?

> "What seems to be missing is an over-arching strategy for demonstrating the effectiveness of cultural programmes in peacebuilding processes and an answer to the question whether the positive influence of cultural organisations is just an illusion or whether it does in fact have an effect on conflict transformation."

It is time to start finding answers to this crucial question and to close the gap between theory and practice. There is a need to build a stronger, evidence-based case for the importance of cultural initiatives in fragile countries. The field of civil conflict management has made progress in measuring its accomplishments. An exchange of knowledge could be a starting point in better measuring the achievements of cultural groups in peacebuilding.

The nature of global conflict has changed in recent decades, from a bi-polar clash of ideology during the Cold War to a series of smaller intra-state and inter-state conflicts today, triggered by causes ranging from dwindling natural resources to cultural, religious and ethnic differences.

The mainstay of peacebuilding once focused mainly on political, economical and security assistance. However, with no significant decrease in civil conflicts and the number of failed and failing states since the 1990s, a new framework has emerged that focuses on crisis prevention and peacebuilding as means of avoiding wars and de-escalating conflicts. In this way, it is hoped that the causes and consequences of conflicts can be overcome. Work in the area of crisis and conflict increasingly takes the form of long-term projects designed to lead to lasting peace processes.

Currently most of the EU's actions still remain focused on improving state organs such as police departments or bureaucratic infrastructure. However, in recent years the EU has started to focus more on peacebuilding and conflict prevention. In 2007, the EU created the Instrument for Stability (IfS) a fund dedicated to building the capacities of relevant organisations and services that contribute to preventing or mitigating conflicts in crisis zones. Here the recognised concept of 'soft power' also plays its part – the use of influence, persuasion and consensus-building to bring about changes in other countries and as a tool for conflict resolution. This is where European cultural institutes can expand their activities.

In Germany, this process began fairly early on. The federal government's "Konzeption 2000" strategy paper that was first published 12 years ago stressed how foreign cultural policy is an integral part of foreign policy. Foreign cultural policy is aligned with the general goals and interests of German foreign policy in terms of stabilising peace, resolving conflicts and exercising a positive influence on the maintenance of human rights. This can be achieved equally effectively by supporting local cultural organisations as through PR and educational work.

A recently-published paper by the UK's Foreign and Commonwealth Office on "Building Stability Overseas" (2011) states that 'soft power' will play an important role in supporting the UK's efforts to create stability. The paper confirms that the work of the British Council is becoming more significant through its efforts to create transparency and promote acceptance of different systems of cultural values, thus building mutual understanding. The Stability Pact for Afghanistan has also described one of its objectives as being to shape identity through cultural activities and creating opportunities for the potential involvement of foreign cultural institutes in the country.

This new role for external cultural policy was articulated by Hans-Georg Knopp, Secretary-General of the Goethe Institute, at a December 2009 conference in Tokyo: "Culture, not just in the narrow sense which limits it to the arts, but also in a more general sense that includes, for instance, sports or popular arts and crafts, helps to overcome the traumatic consequences of conflict and to promote the idea of co-existence in peace and security."

### *Clear guidelines and responsibilities*

The EUNIC network can play a substantial role in developing a joint framework for the participation of cultural institutes in conflict prevention and peacebuilding. Some national cultural institutes are already running a range of programmes in conflict zones, so only a coordinated approach can guarantee the effective use of resources and skills by bringing together knowledge and perspectives learned from past projects. Fragmented national cultural policies should be integrated and coexist in a European strategy that outlines concrete, clear policies and responsibilities in order to improve individual projects and make them more effective.

One possible action would be the development of a joint European action plan along the lines of Germany's "Konzeption 2000". Another starting point could be to take an inventory of those projects that have successfully used the medium of culture to contribute to conflict transformation. All future projects could benefit from gathering together the experiences of everyone involved in these successful projects.

Coordination is crucial. The multiplicity of governmental and non-governmental actors in civil conflict management (who are all competing for funding and as a result have little motivation to work together) presents a further obstacle for cultural actors. What is necessary is a national or European framework for integrating themselves in a coherent civil conflict management system. Projects need to be designed with this in mind and have specific goals. This is vital if cultural actors are to become credible partners. There needs to be a clear set of parameters and standards to show the success and impact of cultural activities on ending conflict, even though it may take generations for changes to become visible.

How can we possibly know whether watching a play promoting tolerance and mutual acceptance at a puppet theatre in Afghanistan will deter a child from becoming an insurgent? As the German peace activist and confict expert, Dr. Jochen Hippler, recently observed at an ifa conference: "When security and development cooperation fail to enforce peace, we should be realistic enough to see that artists can't necessarily do that either". Or as Fareed C. Majari, director of the Goethe Institute in Ramallah, stated at a conference in Tokyo 2009: "Would you invite a burglar who just broke into your home and is pointing a gun at you while he steals your belongings to sing a song with you?"

"How can we possibly know whether watching a play promoting tolerance and mutual acceptance at a puppet theatre in Afghanistan will deter a child from becoming an insurgent?"

It is clear that culture cannot solve conflict, but it can contribute to peace processes. However, as Jochen Hippler points out, cultural dialogue and bringing people together do not always bring positive results. For example, after the Iran Conference in 2000 organised by the Heinrich Böll Foundation, some Iranian participants were subsequently handed out lengthy prison sentences. This is why a dialogue process has to happen at the right time and be carefully planned and monitored. It must be clear what such programmes can achieve and how effective they are. This is the only way that artists and artistic exchanges can make a worthwhile contribution.

Project funding is also a problem. Cultural institutes often feel their work is inhibited by meagre budgets and the need to find potential sponsors. This does, however, force them to set long-term goals and develop procedures for evaluating their work.

Peacebuilding organisations are facing similar challenges; "How do we know when a peacebuilding project has actually built peace? What indicators are most appropriate? What evaluation tools are most useful in assessing the theories of peace building on which projects are based?" asks Ken Menkhaus in his publication "Impact Assessment in Post- Conflict Peace Building" (2004) for the Swiss organisation Interpeace. However, peacebuilding organisations are now investing much more time and effort in analysing and assessing their work in order to find answers to these crucial questions.

Raj Isar, an independent cultural expert and scholar, argues that established instruments could be useful for evaluating the impact of cultural work in conflict settings. His paper "Artistic activism in situations of extreme conflict – the challenge of evaluation" makes the case for applying methodologies from the humanitarian aid field to culture projects. Peacebuilding evaluation processes such as 'Peace Impact Assessment', 'Do No Harm' or 'Conflict Sensitivity Approach' should be used to ensure the balanced development of criteria and indicators for assessing the impact, results and relevance of a project. The American peacebuilding organisation Search for Common Ground, for example, has compiled a Training Manual for 'Participatory Theatre' in conflict transformation, providing clear guidelines of how to use theatre as a healing process in a specific conflict setting.

Given the complex nature of conflict management, there is a need for an exchange of knowledge across disciplines in order to increase capacities, overcome weaknesses and make use of strengths. The recent ifa and EUNIC roundtable discussion on 'Culture and Conflict' in Brussels in December 2011 brought together experts from the fields of cultural relations, conflict management and EU foreign and security policy to share their knowledge and learn from each other's experiences. The follow-up initiative of setting up a "Culture and Conflict" working group led by zivik, ifa's civil conflict resolution funding programme, could be another good starting point.

From all this, we can draw the following conclusions:

- The emergence of civil conflict prevention and peacebuilding has created new opportunities for European cultural institutes.
- European cultural institutes can help peace processes in crisis regions.
- A unified strategy needs to be developed in this respect.
- Institutes need to be realistic about what they can achieve and what risks their projects entail.
- This process could be facilitated by sharing knowledge with established civil conflict management organisations on how to evaluate the impact, results and effectiveness of projects.
- A good starting point could be to make an inventory of lessons learned from successful programmes and gather possible methods of evaluating the effectiveness of cultural programmes.
- EUNIC can play a key role in this process. As a network-based organisation it offers a platform for knowledge exchange and for building strategic partnerships with experts from outside the cultural sector.

**Katrin Mader** was a scholarship holder at the Institute for Foreign Cultural Relations (ifa), working on the "Culture and Foreign Policy" research programme from July to December 2011. Prior to this, she worked in the area of culture and conflict, including time spent at the UNESCO offices in Kathmandu (Nepal) and Hanoi (Vietnam). She is also involved with the London-based project "Culture and Conflict".

# A question of security It is vital that cultural diversity and intercultural dialogue be moved up the international agenda for the sake of human security. For one of the biggest challenges of all in today's world is the challenge to traditional notions of trust. The trust that helps people cope with diversity in their social relations. How can this trust be created?

*By Mike Hardy and Aurélie Bröckerhoff*

More than ever before, this is a challenging time for culture. It feels that peoples are being thrown together for political, economic or just expedient reasons, and relationships within the resulting diverse neighbourhoods can be uncomfortable and tense. Much seems to depend on the match between the nature and pace of change, at a global level, and the local behaviours arising from peoples' choices about how they adapt to the changes.

Cultural diversity and the issues this brings to identity and to our immediate social relationships is probably the most significant contemporary influence on us as individuals and on our communities. For many, this places cultural diversity as one of the prime responsibilities of our times, and on a par with the fight against poverty and the mitigations and adaptations to changes in climate. These, then, might be the three big issues which we 'should all be in together'!

Our world – and its communities – is characterised by continuous change and by permanent diversity, and the challenge is that people-to-people encounters and engagement within these diverse communities bring either enriching benefits or sustained insecurity. The great Mahatma Gandhi once said that "Honest differences are often a healthy sign of progress". But when such differences are expressed through violence, the carefully negotiated social balance in communities and human development generally is placed at risk.

The social upheavals and disturbances in our cities that have dominated national

"I do not want my house to be walled in on all sides and my windows to be stuffed. I want the cultures of all the lands to be blown about my house as freely as possible. But I refuse to be blown off my feet by any."

[Mahatma Gandhi]

and international news serve to underline the fact that in today's multi-polar, multilateral world, uneasy social relationships are the result of a complex interplay of structures and agents within and between societies that goes beyond local communities.

We have more transient communities as well; the churning within global and regional populations that has been experienced over the last decade has introduced new types of interactions, some more dynamic and some more short-lived. We now live in a world where thousands of unexpected guests can show up to a birthday party, or where one community's revolution becomes another's act of terror, mobilised, facilitated or shared across the globe by social media.

The biggest challenge of all in the contemporary world is the challenge to traditional notions of trust. This is the trust that helps people cope with diversity in their social relations.

## *We cannot rest on our laurels*

As social relations are negotiated and renegotiated amidst global flows and changes, we have learnt that we cannot rest on our intercultural laurels. Natural disasters, the rise of populism, economic downturns, food shortages, unemployment, poverty.... all of these put a strain on relations within and between our communities. The way in which we respond to these challenges may vary greatly, not only from person to person, but also as a result of differences in cultural values. A research project at Yale Law School has analysed how cultural values determine the risks we see in our public environment and how this translates into our belief in 'the right' policies. In a survey, researchers found that it is our cultural values more than any other individual characteristic that help predict people's public risk perceptions, suggesting that culture and cultural issues may lie at the heart of our sense of human security.

Among all the distracting discussions and disagreements – about whether multiculturalism is good, bad or indifferent, or about whether interculturalist approaches would be better or more helpful for communities; about central or local policies for integration or assimilation – lies the essentialism of unavoidable and important social relations which, in a society committed to universal standards and rights, must be relations that provide security.

Co-existence and collaboration are not the same thing; living with similar people and full integration into communities are not the same thing; none of these are really problematic per se – provided that human security is given priority.

Human security is a people-centred concept that focuses on the most critical and pervasive risks to people's survival,

"The challenges presented by dealing with differences diminish over time, and anxiety is replaced with a feel-good factor that can serve to strengthen diverse neighbourhoods."

livelihoods and dignity. The threats include natural disasters and disasters caused by humans – conflicts and violence in families or in societies – massive displacements, health-related risks, human trafficking and war, as well as the sudden economic and financial downturns characteristic of contemporary capitalism. All these risks and threats are more serious in a 21st century where there are unprecedented levels of change. A 21st century in which successful and peaceful relations depend more than ever before on peoples' abilities to share space, resources and understanding; when social relations are subject to multiple influences, complex identities, growing inequality and a total interdependence.

Viewed in the context of the European project, the real paradox may be that throughout Europe's journey, public policy has been simultaneously encouraging and enabling national and economic identities. And these are essentially and meaningfully at odds with each other.

This has created new kinds of social relations within what has helpfully been referred to as post-immigration multiculturalism. Therefore, we may worry about being British or French, or about our heritage as Lithuanians or Dutch, and we cherish our history, culture and language. We may be anxious about assimilation and our rights and so seek out best practice and experience when it comes to integration – both for migrants joining neighbourhoods and for hosts receiving new neighbours.

Because we worry about newcomers and the demands placed on us by the associated new social relationships that follow, we can decide whether immigration policies and the concepts of exclusion through 'gated communities' for long-standing residents should prevail.

The fact is that new European neighbourhoods are no longer predictable; a potential mobile population of some 270 million work-age 'Europeans' can effectively redefine the migration plans or political manifesto aspirations of politicians in Europe's member states. If restricting or slowing down the emergence or consolidation of multicultural neighbourhoods meets the political aspirations (and demands of voters) across Europe, this is simply not recognised as reality in the European Union. So there is a significant disconnect between what so-called democratic voices are saying and what is actually and unavoidably happening.

## *New cultural interfaces*

Be that as it may, the new neighbourhoods in the cities of the 21st century world will encourage and create communities with differences. We are now seeing neighbourhoods characterised by new social relationships, new cultural interfaces, expectations and consequences. According to historians and sociologists specialising in contact theory, the challenges presented by dealing with differences actually diminish over time, and anxiety is replaced with a feel-good factor that can serve to strengthen diverse neighbourhoods. Barely a day passes without us being reminded of the responsibility that we all have to 'deal' with cultural differences and 'create the conditions' for peaceful relations.

This is what makes culture so important in meeting contemporary challenges. Many believe that complex, diverse and ever-changing societies are creating social relationships in contemporary Europe that may not come naturally to people and need to be worked on. The standard analysis therefore juxtaposes the economic inevitability of mobile labour in the economic union of the European project with a social inevitability of threats and risks arising from the confusing identities of new neighbourhoods.

Most studies point to a preference on our part as humans to coexist with people like ourselves, so we have to work at relationships with 'others'. Yet, as we are aware, in the 21st century it is social relations with others that are often more common, partly because of new and ever-increasing mobility, and partly as a consequence of the choices that we are now more able and more likely to make.

Focusing on our cultural values in our approach to social relationships will still be necessary in these new neighbourhoods. Not just because we worry about living with what is different, but also because of culture's prominent role in developing sustainable communities. But we must continue to ask questions of ourselves so that we can do this more successfully. In the myth of Icarus, the father builds wings that will allow his son to escape from exile in Crete. It was not Icarus' lack of ability to fly that led to his fall, nor the construction of the wings per se, but rather his desire to fly higher and higher when the materials his wings were made from were not able to withstand the heat of the sun.

### *A world of differences*

In recent years, 'human security' has emerged as a new approach to the way in which we evaluate human development. Within this paradigm, it is the individual and their environment, rather than systems and communities, which become the main protagonists in assessing the impact of globalisation. It takes community dynamics as its starting point as there is a potential for disorder, threats to peace and stability and raised levels of fear. Our social relationships become the thermostat for our risks and vulnerabilities. And they also embody our ability and potential to build stable communities.

A part of the challenge is to recognise the world we live in and to take it seriously. Of course we live in a world of differences – a world in which increasingly sophisticated communications and transport systems create new and impelling neighbours and neighbourhoods.

New neighbourhoods can, it would seem, create new challenges and totally

"Today's leaders need to work together to develop a new social contract for diversity."

new risks, and we are tempted to suppose that this new context is just too hard, too difficult and much more likely to end in tears than to yield positive benefits. These conditions demand a new and more sophisticated type of leadership to work to bring the global family together and not drive it further apart.

## *A new social contract*

Today's leaders need to work together to develop a new social contract for diversity. And we must do so with conviction and dedication, trying to find a consensus between conflicting interests. Moving cultural diversity further up the agenda on social relations and treating it as just as serious and important an issue as poverty and climate change would be a key requirement of such a new and contemporary social contract. John Stuart Mill in his famous deliberation "On Liberty" says: "men and governments must act to the best of their ability. There is no such thing as absolute certainty, but there is assurance sufficient for the purposes of human life. But on every subject on which difference of opinion is possible, the truth depends on a balance to be struck between two conflicting reasons".

So although we may feel incapable of building wings that won't be soaked up by the sea or melted by the sun, we can get closer to fulfilling the needs and purposes of human life by working together. The social contract for diversity does not spring from a Hobbesian view of the state of nature, nor from Lockes' belief that people living in this 21st century would willingly come together. Great leadership does not manifest itself in knowing all the right answers but starts with asking the right questions. How do we understand the effects of risks and threats in relation to people's vulnerabilities? How do we plan, develop and mobilise people's capacities to respond to risks and threats in an effective, efficient and sustainable way? How does this build resilience? How can we facilitate the use and development of capabilities by utilising new opportunities arising from innovation and development? How can we reduce people's vulnerabilities by mobilising their own capacities? Seeking these answers could provide the 'great leadership' that Rousseau saw as critical to the success of any social contract.

Dialogue between and within cultures is critical if these challenges are to be met. It helps acknowledge that differences exist and addresses the need to encourage mutual trust and understanding between diverse people. The environment in which such dialogue takes place is marked by difference, proximity and interconnectedness.

Placing cultural diversity and intercultural dialogue higher on the international agenda is critical for human security and a prime responsibility of our time as it will promote an understanding of the most critical and pervasive risks that seriously threaten the survival, livelihood

ake. Indian legend tells of
the end, one god dropped
of his victory. The
struggle so it

and dignity of individuals. When the Anglo-American poet W.H. Auden visited the Musée des Beaux Arts in Brussels, he felt so moved by the painting 'Landscape with the Fall of Icarus' that he wrote a poem about the experience. The painting, often attributed to Pieter Bruegel the Elder, depicts an everyday scene of rural life. While in the foreground the world goes about their business, one can see a young Icarus creating a splash as he falls into the sea, unnoticed by those around him. In his poem, Auden expresses how we often don't notice the big moments in time… "the expensive delicate ship that must have seen something amazing, a boy falling out of the sky, had somewhere to get to and sailed calmly on". Let us not, like the people of Bruegel's painting and Auden's poem "turn(s) away quite leisurely from the disaster", but let us have the courage to face our challenges together, head on.

**Mike Hardy** is Professor of Human Security, Social and Intercultural Relations at Coventry University, where he is also Director of an Applied Research Centre on Social Relations research.
**Aurélie Bröckerhoff** is a researcher and PhD student in human security, social and intercultural relations at Coventry University.

# Creative people's advocates

When the rule of law has been eroded, when social services are lacking and there is no free press, the artist often takes on the role of government critic, people's advocate, community organiser, human rights defender or even movement leaders. But more importantly, they can create spaces for encounters. *By Mary Ann DeVlieg, Victoria Ivanova, Rosario Pavese and Ole Reitov*

It may be a truism to state that conflict is a complex and multi-faceted phenomenon. However, there is a tendency to summarily define contemporary conflicts using binary logic as either 'modern' struggles for resources, primordial 'tribal' antagonisms or epic confrontations between the 'civilised' and the 'uncivilised'. As a result, policy is often informed by simplistic assumptions, bolstered by historical amnesia and the inability to grapple with the contextual nuances of contention.

These faux-pas lead to embarrassing situations (to put it mildly) where European states are found to be supporting oppressive regimes, trading financial aid for political leverage, and shielding people from responsibility within their own jurisdictions when they are directly or indirectly perpetrating violence elsewhere.

International criminal justice can also be seen in a critical light. The recent push to selectively tear certain violent acts from their contexts and bring them before the International Criminal Court in The Hague only succeeds in superficially demonising the perpetrators while leaving the victims with little more than their victimhood. This is not to say that the juridical notion of justice is irrelevant, but it should not be the sole mechanism for processing events that occur within and as a result of conflict situations. Juridical justice will always represent a top-down approach to regulating social relationships, and whereas it may be portrayed as a humane substitute for blood-soaked revenge (if we are to believe the French historian Rene Girrard), the people it leaves behind will rarely feel any wiser.

'Culture' is a word that makes Europeans both proud and nervous. On the one hand, there is a feeling of great pride in the importance that Europe places on a robust cultural infrastructure, on its historical significance and its maintenance and development. On the other hand, there is the prickly subject of European member nations having used culture as a signifier of hierarchy (and supplement to violent invasion) during times of colonial subjugation. Both of these 'stamps' continue to exert their force on European attitudes and actions to this day, which means that a truly sophisticated and forward-looking international cultural policy will necessarily have to take into account a balanced understanding of both trajectories.

Despite these foreboding complexities, one thing cannot be denied: bottom-up approaches to social development and individual/group empowerment are essential for sustainable conflict resolution, and socially engaging projects based in the arts and culture are a powerful resource (if not the most powerful) in facilitating such approaches.

For this reason, serious consideration should be given to the development of autonomous and independent cultural movements, spaces and institutions. They offer opportunities for free thinking and dialogue and can even act as safe havens in difficult socio-political environments. For instance, one of the most widespread global challenges today is pervasive social inequality and the violence that results from the inability of governments to control it, or their complicity in upholding it. Individuals are first and foremost citizens, but their formal recognition as equal members of a political body is the first step towards the effective exercising of their political rights. However, wide gaps in social equality, cultural and linguistic differences and political borders hinder mutual recognition between members of an integrated socio-political body. This is where art can make a significant contribution to easing tensions between diversity and homogeneity through the creation of spaces where creative practice intersects with human rights agendas in the interests of a broader notion of social justice, particularly in defence of vulnerable communities. In this context, the recognition of the human rights violations suffered by these communities should be seen as the first step. Different forms of artistic expression can then provide the necessary platform for the second stage: reclaiming these rights.

## *Laboratory for creative collaboration*

A similar dynamic is evident in post-war zones where the scars of conflict remain exposed. A good example is provided by the Cultural Centre REX in Belgrade, which played an important role in mediating the residual trauma prevalent in post-war Serbia. REX provided a safe space for socially engaging, psycho-therapeutic activities, whether through open forum debates as a backdrop to newly opened exhibits, or as a laboratory for creative collaborations, aimed at improving the social conditions of the city and the country. Yet rapidly disappearing public spaces worldwide means that 'open environments' are often hard to find or access, resulting in increased social atomisation and psychosocial alienation. In this sense, cultural spaces often serve as meeting-points for people whose paths might otherwise not cross, thereby fostering a more inclusive approach to social citizenship.

Artists can also play a fundamental role in the peacebuilding process, particularly in societies divided by armed conflict or where open conflict is curtailed by all-pervasive repression. When the rule of law has been eroded, when social services are lacking and there is no free press, the artist often takes on the role of government critic, people's advocate, community organiser, human rights defender or even movement leader. Individuals who use creativity to fight injustice often face direct or indirect persecution for their activism. While frameworks for the support of human rights defenders already exist, these support mechanisms often do not take into account such latent forms of activism and overlook the specific risks faced by artists and culture workers doing the work normally associated with activists.

Nowadays, it is not uncommon for cultural workers who are also active within civil society to work in multiple media, while culture is also a common ingredient in projects striving for social justice and equality. Thus, collaborative relationships between human rights and arts organisations and networks hold great potential for developing alternative support structures for rights defenders that function by accessing under-utilised resources (which often originate in the art world) and occupy interstitial spaces in larger social justice agendas.

"Theatrical improvisation allows people to investigate the root causes of difficult social, political and economic realities, explore personal feelings and relate to the emotional expressions of others through story-telling."

Perhaps the most thoroughly explored artistic methodology employed in conflict situations is the use of theatre with vulnerable individuals and communities. Augusto Boal's famous Forum Theatre method and the work that this visionary creative practitioner initiated in his native Rio de Janeiro and across South America provide an excellent example of the virtues of participatory cultural activities that are built on principles of direct engagement, creative expression and dialogue.

Theatrical improvisation allows people to investigate the root causes of difficult social, political and economic realities, explore personal feelings and relate to the emotional expressions of others through story-telling and spontaneous action. At the same time, they are an active celebration of the strength of their own voices and of mutual, equitable exchange between people. By creating an alternative space for social engagement, theatre for development can educate, empower and even heal. Numerous initiatives of this kind have been launched all over the world, such as the Amani People's Theatre in Kenya, Zwakwane in Zimbabwe, and the Berlin Fountainhead Tanz Theatre in Germany.

Apart from the obvious benefits to those directly involved, there is also great value in the knowledge and understanding that is generated. The people we tend to call 'victims of conflict' rarely have a chance to tell their own stories first-hand. Typically, their stories are recounted by mediators who unilaterally interpret their needs and dictate solutions. However, when human rights and development actors actively collaborate, the specific needs of specific groups can be directly linked to appropriate resources and solutions devised in collaboration with the users. This not only makes the work more effective, but also makes it easier for marginalised discourses to reach the mainstream.

Starting points could also be found in the existing human rights infrastructure. Transparency International, for example, has 45 ALACs (Advocacy and Legal Advice Centres) in 40 countries with different historical, cultural, legal and social backgrounds. These centres are dedicated to encouraging citizen participation in the fight against corruption in particular and the defence of rights in general. Citizens can use the centres to highlight rights violations and lodge complaints. Linking these (or similar human rights organisations) with artists' and cultural networks could create a space where both parties could work together in realising different forms of social justice. Dynamic initiatives of this nature could provide a timely response to today's global conditions where flexibility, creativity and innovation are key to moving beyond the pervasive disenchantment and passivity that can often result from overexposure to conflict.

Often the leading institutional cultures of the different disciplines (arts and culture/human rights/development), including planning timeframes, evaluation criteria, funder management, assumptions on valid outcomes or priorities, can create obstacles to such collaborative experiences. Language is used with different weighting – for example 'development' activities are not the same for those concerned only with economic development as for those who value human development above all. Likewise, freedom of expression advocates do not bend before questions of taste, local sensitivity or controversy: a human right is a human right. And artists often work on less obvious, more immaterial levels of consciousness or self-confidence. While there have been successful cross-disciplinary, cross-sector projects for many years now, NGOs can often be wedded to their own methodologies.

In this context, institutions such as EUNIC and the main human development agencies and foundations could act as catalysts for increased dialogue and mutual understanding between sectors. By highlighting good practice, commissioning joint analyses and bringing key players together, overall perspectives can be created to demonstrate the value and constraints of separate approaches and the synergies created in collaborations, as experimental as these may be.

There is also a need for mapping both the dangers and the resources available to non-professional activists working in the culture sector. 2011 saw an increase in the repression of and attacks on artists and culture workers globally, most notably in the

"While there have been successful cross-disciplinary, cross-sector projects for many years now, NGOs can often be wedded to their own methodologies."

Middle East/North Africa, China, South East Asia and Central America. Systematic and widespread repression of artists and culture workers indicates the need for both global and local mechanisms to support and defend artistic free expression.

The International Coalition for Arts, Human Rights and Social Justice (ICARJ, www.artsrightsjustice.net) has the potential to be a useful and timely platform for local, regional and international networks defending creative activism. A recent proposal by Freemuse, the world forum on music and censorship http://freemuse.org, and others to create a global monitoring system (http://artsfex.org) for freedom of artistic expression is a welcome step in the same direction, as is the new Working Group 'ARJ' (arts-rights-justice) within the EU civil society platform 'Access to Culture', which had its constitutive meeting in Brussels on 13 February 2012.

Potential ways forward should now include the following:

- Mapping existing organisations that support artists and cultural operators whose rights are abused or endangered;
- Commissioning studies on short-, medium- and longer-term actions to improve protection of threatened artists and arts initiatives;
- Collaborating with existing work on more humanistic and cultural indicators for measuring development;
- Creating a clearing house for sharing information, cases and analyses so that cases can be better matched to the appropriate resources;
- Creating a global monitoring system for abuse of freedom of artistic expression;
- Awareness-raising and training projects addressing the arts sector, the human rights sector and policy makers.

**Mary Ann DeVlieg** has worked in the culture sector for more than 30 years. Since 1994 she has been the General Secretary of the IETM international network for contemporary performing arts. In 2010 she founded the International Coalition for Arts, Human Rights & Social Justice, www.artsrightsjustice.net. Co-authors **Victoria Ivanova, Sidd Joag, Rosario Pavese** and **Ole Reitov** are also members of this organisation. Victoria Ivanova works as a strategy coordinator at an arts foundation in Donetsk in the Ukraine and is a member of the art platform Trans Europe Halles (TEH). Sidd Joag is an artist and experimental filmmaker. He is the co-founder of Zero Capital Arts, an organisation which supports low-cost socially and politically engaged creative projects and exhibitions. He is also a member of FreeDimensional, an initiative which supports the freedom of art around the world. Rosario Pavese is a member of the Latin American Network Art for Social Transformation initiative, which is committed to fighting for social justice. Ole Reitov is the Programme Manager at Freemuse, a Danish organisation that advocates freedom of expression for musicians around the world.

# Peace-building: Learning from local experiences

**What are the positive, practical experiences of external cultural policy initiatives in conflict regions? Which ones have been proven worthwhile and what circumstances are needed for their success? Is it possible to successfully transfer initiatives that have shown positive results in one place to another location? Conflict experts and peacebuilders share their experiences, gather examples of best practice and tell us their hopes for the future.**

# Healing from within

When vision and will come together, anything is possible. Even peace. Fearless, strong-willed people are working in conflict zones, undeterred by the day-to-day violence, and dedicating themselves to civil society initiatives. They combine professional strategies for conflict resolution with cultural empathy and are demonstrating how cultural differences can be experienced in a constructive way. *By Michael Gleich*

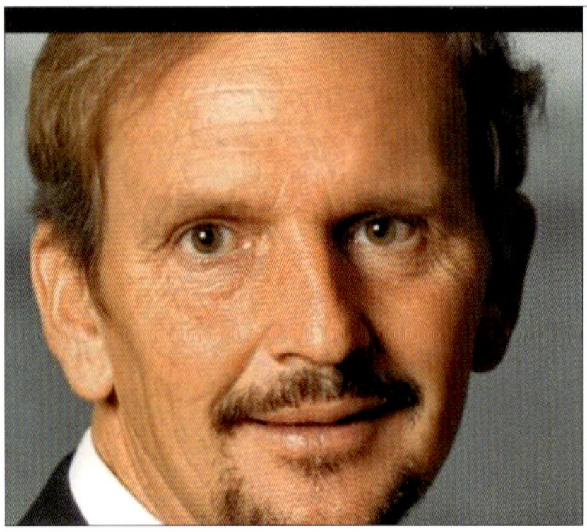

Of all the peacemakers, it was the two murderers who touched me the most. As a young man, Joe had fought for the Catholic armed underground, shot a British officer and been handed a 22-year prison sentence. Peter had long been a career terrorist on the Protestant side and had an even more serious record. As members of two cultures that were battling for supremacy in Northern Ireland, they found themselves fighting a civil war in which everyone was a loser.

At some point, something snapped. When Joe was released from prison he was depressed by what he saw: frustrated young people with no chance of training or a job were inciting mini-revolts in the poor areas of Belfast out of sheer boredom. Peter's life collapsed even more spectacularly. He dropped out when he was ordered to shoot a disgraced member of his own paramilitary group. Out there in the woods, he found he was unable to pull the trigger and asked himself in despair: "What has this war done to me?"

Joe and Peter separately came to the same decision. They wanted to carry on fighting, but non-violently. They both had a difficult path ahead of them as they attempted to escape the orbit of their former comrades-in-arms. They were in constant danger of being denounced as traitors. Today, they are both social workers who work with young people to persuade them to keep their distance from the paramilitary groups. They are putting all their efforts into finding a political solution to the conflict. It is not the 'Road to Damascus' story that impresses me about them so much as their unerring belief that Catholics and Protestants can live together as equals, along with their strong will to begin life afresh in their mid-forties. When vision and will come together, anything is possible. Even peace.

It happens more often than we might think. Since the early 1990s, more than 80 violent conflicts have been resolved: in

> "Logic will get you from A to B. Imagination will take you everywhere." Albert Einstein

Mali, Mozambique, Haiti, East Timor, Kosovo, to name but a few. The situation in these countries ranges from fragile to stable. And there are yet more reasons for optimism. Since 1992, there has been a 40 percent reduction in particularly violent conflicts, and the number of people killed in such conflicts has fallen by 98 percent since 1950. And we should not forget events in places like South Africa, where a country ruled by fear and racism made the transition to democracy with hardly a drop of blood being spilled. This was more than anyone had hoped for. But charismatic leaders such as Nelson Mandela and Frederik Willem de Klerk possessed both imagination and initiative.

## *War is now an event*

So why are we not celebrating? Why is the International Day of Peace not a public holiday? And why does watching the evening news make us feel that the world is increasingly ruled by war, death and destruction? The explanation is simple and twofold. Simple, because we are dealing with the way the media typically distorts reality – the amount of violence in the world has not increased, just the number of reports. Twofold, because the responsibility for this does not lie solely with sensationalist journalists seeking to increase their viewing figures or sell more newspapers.

The public is also to blame for focusing on the negative. We are fascinated by dramas involving life and death, and war brings them into our homes every day. The battlefields are reported like football matches. During the last Gulf War, embedded journalists related what was happening like over-excited sports commentators. War is now an event. Peace is quiet, slow, boring, and reporters soon lose patience with it as they race around the globe.

And they are not the only ones. Research also cultivates its blind spots. There should be nothing more important than finding out when and how peace can be achieved, but unfortunately very few researchers are interested in breaking new ground by exploring the causes of peace. War sells better – even in trade journals and at conferences.

So any kind of exciting changes go unnoticed. In the past, war was declared by statesmen, prosecuted by generals and armies and brought to an end by presidents signing treaties. Nowadays these kinds of wars between countries involving huge numbers of victims have become the exception. This is surely a step forward for civilisation.

But now we are faced with new challenges. The international community is confronted by violent conflicts that emerge from within societies. They are a society's heart attack, its organ failure. Generally, two or more ethnic groups with different cultures come to blows in order to gain power. Or so it seems. But underneath it all, it is about mutual respect and recognition. I would even go as far as to say it is about the desire to be respected and loved by others. Every single one of us yearns for love, and communities are no different.

The healing of such societies that are torn apart by hate also has to come from within. The poet Hölderlin remarked that "where danger is deliverance also grows", and indeed, a new generation of peacemakers is growing up. They do not demonstrate, and they no longer leave it to politicians and armies to take charge of events, preferring to roll up their sleeves and get involved. Doctors and human rights activists, trade unionists and housewives, sportspeople, aid workers, priests and educators – many of them are risking their lives in their desire to find non-violent solutions. They are creative, professional, courageous and, above all, successful.

They count it as progress when rebels lay down their arms, as happened in 1995 in Mali; when minefields are cleared and peasants return to their fields, as in the north of Sri Lanka; when the army removes road blocks, as in Israel; when Catholic children can once again walk to school through a Protestant suburb, as in Northern Ireland; when Ugandan child soldiers are allowed to take up civilian jobs.

## *Project Civilisation*

With every step, peace regains a tiny piece of territory. Behind every step there are social innovators, empathetic people who are perfecting techniques for promoting mediation, active listening and reconciliation. The art of peace requires great skill. All together, they form civil society. It sounds like they are sitting around drinking tea, but in fact they are creating a secret superpower. Alongside national governments, multinational organisations and transnational corporations, they are increasingly becoming the face of globalisation. Whether small circles of activists or large special interest groups, one thing unites them: they are extremely flexible, which makes them difficult to control and even harder to stop. Their strength lies in their global networks. They use the internet and emails to tell each other what does and doesn't work. Suddenly a successful campaign in one place has become an object lesson somewhere else. Working together in a loose alliance, private peacemakers all over the world are advancing Project Civilisation.

These days a good idea needs no time to spread from the Cape of Good Hope to the other side of the globe. In the aftermath of its apartheid regime, South Africa found itself faced with the question: should we allow people who have tortured and massacred to go free in order to maintain peace in our country? Or should we take them to court and once again risk furious uprisings on the part of entire ethnic groups? This is a typical dilemma faced by societies the morning after the night before. South Africa found its response in the Truth and Reconciliation Commission. The main culprits were punished, while lesser miscreants and victims were invited to conciliation talks. This balancing act proved to be successful, allowing wounds to heal and democracy to endure.

Since then, other countries have experimented with similar instruments, as has happened in Rwanda. The village communities organised their own tribunals called Gacaca, which means "sitting in the grass". Lay judges and elders presided over these open-air courts, pronouncing judgement on the main perpetrators of genocide against the Tutsi. This was a desperate, common effort to heal the deep sense of shock caused by the genocide. This grassroots movement in its most literal sense can be viewed as a real success story. It is proof that all peace is created by peoples; otherwise it is not created at all.

Civil wars tear societies apart. The leave in their wake traumatised children, shattered villages and hostile groups that still mistrust each other and contemplate revenge, despite any ceasefire that has been imposed. Ethnic groups often live in separate areas and have no communication with each other.

This is where non-governmental peacemakers have an important role to play. Unlike official diplomats, they can find unconventional ways of bringing the members of enemy groups to the negotiating table. When the German Benedictine abbot Benedikt Lindemann opens the doors of his monastery in Jerusalem for discreet talks, Israelis and Palestinians know that they can come together without fear of spies. The hallowed walls provide a refuge. The monk is the mediator. He does not ask the politicians whether he is allowed to get involved. He just does it. He is inspired by an image that he has never lost sight of: the image of Jews, Christians and Arabs all living together in peace in the Holy Land.

This flame burns inside all successful peacemakers. They are driven by a vision of how they can change their country for the better. They are "unrealistic" in the positive sense of the word. They don't accept things as they are. The importance of this has been shown in Sri Lanka, a country that has been torn apart by a bloody civil war for over 20 years. A young colleague from the shattered north of the country

"They use the internet and emails to tell each other what does and doesn't work. Suddenly a successful campaign in one place has become an object lesson somewhere else. Working together in a loose alliance, private peacemakers all over the world are advancing Project Civilisation."

told me: "The war has been going on all my life. It has poisoned our minds and our hearts. We just can't imagine a life without attacks and bombings." The worst thing about this is that people who have only ever known violence will always turn to violence as a solution when in doubt. Of course it presents a risk, but at least it is a familiar risk, whereas peace is a journey into the unknown, an adventure with an unpredictable outcome.

This is why imagination is so critical. It unleashes energies that – as Einstein said – can take people everywhere. When Singham, a Tamil who had lived a carefree life in Berlin for 15 years, decided to return to war-torn Sri Lanka, his friends told him he was crazy. But he dared to dream: "One day the island will once again be rightly called "Happy Lanka." He didn't just leave it at that, but used donations to build houses for refugee families, set up a school for children orphaned by the war, and looked after street kids. Tamils and Singhalese, supposed enemies, work side-by-side in his organisation. Singham is one of those volunteer bridge-builders who are prepared to risk all in the quest for reconciliation. The very best of them are a charismatic blend of Mahatma Gandhi and Bill Gates. They have that rare ability to think big and act decisively – and be good managers. These new professional peace activists understand that security and stability are also linked to money, jobs, economic growth and development.

It is worth investing in humankind's number one dream. According to experts at Oxford University, the average civil war last seven years. Of course, every year and every victim are one too many, but the good news is that wars do come to an end, sooner or later. But sooner is better than later. If it is not possible to prevent a war, then the international community can at least try to curtail it. United Nations interventions are in fact better than their reputation suggests. According to a study by the US think tank RAND, two out of three peacekeeping missions are successful. And they are cheaper than might be thought when listening to the awkward skirmishes in the Security Council. The total cost of all 16 blue-helmet missions carried out in the last year was just under five billion dollars. To put this into perspective, the USA spent more than this every month on the war in Iraq, and as the world's self-proclaimed sheriff, they have just experienced one debacle after another.

Multinational institutions such as the United Nations and the European Union are the state counterpart to a closely-linked civil society. The UN and EU have made great strides over the last few decades in combating poverty, improving health and promoting human rights. In this way, they have made a major contribution to building 'positive peace': a peace that is more than just the absence of war, a culture that is no longer governed by violence and fear, but by respect and love. In the end, this is what it's all about.

And of course it's about money. It's amazing but true that it makes economic sense to invest in peace. The Oxford experts have calculated that a typical civil war costs around 70 billion dollars. On the loss side, they place lower economic growth, equipment, illness, refugees and organised crime. To look at it another way, every year that such a war can be shortened brings a dividend of 10 billion dollars. It costs just a fraction of this amount to try to end the war by deploying an international intervention force. The new wars need both approaches. They need their societies to be healed from within, with civil society initiatives and peacemakers being the decisive factor in this respect. They also need strong resolve on the part of the international community if it decides in favour of military intervention. In many troubled regions, the fighting is not done by regular soldiers but by militias organised into unruly gangs. Many of them are still teenagers with the emotional maturity of children. And so this is how they behave – wildly, erratically, turning killing into a game. From my own experience of war zones I know that if someone bangs his fist on the table everyone shuts up. There has to be an authority figure to say 'that's enough!', like the strict father that so many of these children in uniform have never known.

Of course, non-violent interventions are in principle always preferable. Europe's present-day unity has been won at the cost of centuries of bloody war and new spirals of violence. It has been a long hard road to reach today's union of nations where cultural differences are valued and seen as a positive enrichment. United in Diversity – the EU's external and cultural policies should spread this motto as inspiration for the rest of the world. There is a good chance that this voice will be heard in places where people are struggling to return to peace. But only if Europe continues to really live its cultural diversity – in a constructive way.

**Michael Gleich** is a journalist and writer specialising in finding understandable and surprising ways of presenting complex issues such as peace, social change and the environment. His works have been translated into several languages and he has won many awards. For his latest project, "Peace Counts", journalists and photographers travelled to more than 30 conflict regions to document the work being done by peacemakers to find peaceful, proven ways of successfully resolving conflicts.

# Fighting trauma and taboo

Cultural production alone is not enough to break down the dominance of ethno-nationalist parties and beliefs, to overthrow corrupt ruling systems and create a tolerant society. But it is able to create niches where alternative debate is possible, and in this way give people hope and encourage them to put into context the omnipotence of the ethnocentric and counter it with other concepts of belonging, tradition, history and identity.

*By Martina Fischer*

For years, German and European cultural institutes, along with political and private foundations, have been doing their best to encourage cultural initiatives in regions that are beset by crises or recovering from wars. In the past, the focus was on regions such as Southeast Europe and the former Yugoslavia, then from 2002 onwards it was on Afghanistan, and now in the wake of the 'Arabellion' it is increasingly on the countries of the Mediterranean that find themselves undergoing a process of transition.

Along with establishing educational institutes and independent media, the main emphasis tends to be on encouraging the development of civil society, with many projects being targeted specifically at young people. The reason for this is the belief that cultural neglect and lack of economic prospects can leave young people open to ethno-nationalist propaganda and make them easy recruits for wars and civil wars. Instead, a country's youth should be inspired to work on rebuilding their society and the processes of democratisation. As part of Germany's presidency of the EU Council in May/June 2007, a Euro-Mediterranean Youth Parliament was created for the benefit of young people. The aim was to encourage dialogue between cultures in the Mediterranean region and to help the participants to gain intercultural skills. Initial funding was provided by the EU Commission, and it is to be hoped that the project can be driven forward by the Mediterranean countries in conjunction with EU bodies.

Initiatives to promote dialogue and bring people together are considered to be very important in this respect. Examples are the European-Islamic Dialogue, or steps taken to promote settlements and reconciliation between rival groups in divided communities and societies that have been devastated by war.

It is generally assumed that cultural initiatives and educational programmes can assist with the peace process. But we still have to ask ourselves the following questions: what potential do cultural initiatives have to aid in conflict resolution?

How can cultural activities be linked to activities that promote peace in a meaningful and lasting way? What conditions are necessary for them to make a contribution to rebuilding and reconciling societies devastated by war?

First of all, if we are to look at ways of promoting culture as a means of promoting peace, we should not forget that culture can be a two-edged sword. This was clearly demonstrated during the escalating conflict in the former Yugoslavia in the early 1990s, when some people in educational institutions and the media worked actively to try to increase political polarisation, marginalisation and expulsion. Intellectuals and journalists from the different ethno-nationalist camps came together with politicians to emphasise cultural differences and prove the superiority of their 'own' culture and religious orientation over that of the 'others'. In this way they provided an ideological justification for acts of brutality and genocide. Historical facts were ignored or distorted in order to construct a false idea of racial purity and to fuel perceptions of religious and cultural differences. An incredible desire for destruction led to the devastation of the cultural treasures of the 'other' enemy camp, and even people in the cultural sector played their part in creating this ethnopolitical conflict. Before the war, and even more strongly in its wake, a folk culture that harked back to historical myths enjoyed a dubious renaissance.

Myths of heroes and sacrifice surround many of the memorials that have been erected to honour the soldiers and civilians killed during the war. In Bosnia and Herzegovina in particular, many forms of commemoration have emerged that run counter to peacebuilding efforts. In divided societies, cultures of remembrance often manifest themselves in very selective ways that just serve to intensify polarisation along ethnopolitical lines. The feelings of people who have been through loss and suffering are ignored and slighted, and relations become ever more strained.

## *Myths of heroes and sacrifice*

So cultural forms of expression can have an emancipatory effect, but in equal measure they can also cause indoctrination and serve to glorify violence. Cultural products can be used to campaign for tolerance, pluralism, multiculturalism and an open, democratic society, but at the same time they can foster intolerance by cementing monoethnic group identities and supporting models of closed societies, or even by providing the aesthetic backbone of dictatorial regimes. Above all, cultural forms of expression serve to forge an identity or identities at individual and collective levels, and this should be borne in mind when considering the potential of cultural initiatives to help promote peace.

The post-war situation in Bosnia and Herzegovina provides a good example of the ambivalent nature of culture. The official cultural policies of the still-hostile political parties focused mainly on using language and their own versions of history for the purposes of creating division. Educational establishments and the media were enlisted to promote these policies, and literature, film and the visual arts did not remain immune. However, at the same time various cultural forms emerged that dealt with the war in ways that were both critical and constructive. With the help of international funding, the cultural and media scene has developed a new dynamic since 1995 and educated a significant section of civil society, providing a contrast to the ethnocratic model that dominates political life in Bosnia and Herzegovina.

Alongside the shallow and nationalistically-tinged 'folk culture', another culture began to emerge that defied the definition of belonging and exclusion along ethnic lines. A creative cultural sector that transcended territorial and ideological boundaries – particularly in youth culture – could have an integrating effect and at least contribute to breaking down the 'us versus them' mentality. International assistance programmes are vital to support these kinds of initiatives.

Cultural production alone is not enough to break down the dominance of ethno-nationalist parties and beliefs, to overthrow corrupt ruling systems and create a tolerant society. But it is able to create niches where alternative debate is possible. In this way it can give people hope and encourage them to put into context "the omnipotence of ethnocentric autism", as diagnosed by Croat writer Ivan Lovrenovic, and counter it with other concepts of belonging, tradition, history and identity.

"Cultural neglect and lack of economic prospects can leave young people open to ethno-nationalist propaganda and make them easy recruits for wars and civil wars."

Cultural initiatives in themselves cannot create a dynamic to resolve deeply-rooted conflicts or reconcile hostile societies. But as one element within a group of policies designed to promote development and peace they can help to stimulate significant change. As long as there is the political will to find compromises, they can help war-ravaged communities to recover from their traumatic experiences and assist them in their journey towards building trust and reconciliation. They can play their part in creating a society based on democratic participation, pluralism and tolerance.

This presupposes that international actors that are involved in war-affected regions will identify areas of potential and take a long-term view by supporting projects in a systematic way rather than just on an ad-hoc and short-term basis. They must carefully seek out suitable partners for these projects because – as previously mentioned – not all cultural productions are designed to encourage plurality but instead can have a strong nationalistic bent.

Everyone involved in the field of culture, educational institutions and the media can help to glorify things that happened during the war, participate in myth-building and prolong exclusion and suffering. But they can also make a significant contribution towards helping societies deal with the violence they have experienced and in the long term they can assist in their regeneration through public debate. On the other hand, there are examples from post-war Bosnia and Herzegovina where victims of the war were often used to fuel a one-sided politics of remembrance but at the same time were offered no protection. The fate of women who were raped or tortured during the war was long ignored and the whole subject was treated by society as a major taboo.

The film "Grbavica" (released in the UK as "Esma's Secret: Grbavica") by Bosnian director Jasmila Zbanic won many international awards and played a part in helping to break the silence surrounding this issue. The film shows the relationship between a Bosniak woman who was raped during the war and her adolescent daughter in post-war Sarajevo. It reveals how the trauma of the war influenced individual destinies and how social taboos served to prolong the suffering and make it difficult to deal with it in a constructive way.

More than 100,000 people went to see the film in the year after it was premiered in Bosnia. Its release was accompanied by a campaign by local and international NGOs to promote the rights of women who had been the victims of sexual violence. The Medica Mondiale organisation played a particularly prominent role. However, political pressure meant that the film was not shown in the Republika Srpska, the Serbian entity of Bosnia.

### *Inclusive forms of remembrance*

In mid-2006, in the aftermath of the film's release, the Bosnian parliament decided that women who had been raped should be legally recognised as 'war victims' and should receive the same compensation as that given to men who had fought in the war. This was viewed as a great success by human rights organisations and women's groups, even though it should be noted that to date many of the victims have still received nothing and a great many others are still fighting for this compensation. The film Grbavica forms part of the artistic growth of a director who has spent years working with the Deblokada group of artists in Sarajevo making documentaries dealing with the war and how people have been affected by it, and also with the fate of people from all sides as they returned to their communities.

In Bosnia and Herzegovina, along with other parts of the former Yugoslavia such as Serbia and Croatia, civil society groups and individuals have over recent years dedicated themselves to finding constructive ways of dealing with the past. Their mission is to establish the facts, influence teaching in educational establishments and to make the wider public more aware of the need to come to terms with the violence of the past. They want to inspire people to face up to the roles played by individuals during the war and the need for politicians to take responsibility for war crimes and human rights abuses. They are making every effort to create new, inclusive forms of remembrance in order to counter the tendency towards a very selective perception of war victims. The creation of memorials is a controversial issue and artists are faced with huge challenges when designing their concepts. They have to proceed with great circumspection and sensitivity and ensure the public at large is involved in the decision-making process.

Under certain conditions, the encouragement of cultural exchange forums can contribute to conflict transformation and reconciliation. But this does not mean that per se that projects promoting intercultural exchange and dialogue between people in opposing camps produce positive results in terms of peacebuilding.

Caution is needed in this respect, at least in regions that are riven by ethnopolitical conflict. In recent years, a series of evaluation reports and impact analyses across various regional contexts have shown that the success of dialogue projects is very much dependent on whether they are carried out at the right time and are focused on the right target groups. During some conflict stages, multi-ethnic dialogue projects between hostile camps can actually have the opposite effect to that intended, that is to say they can increase confrontation and mistrust rather than encourage rapprochement. In certain situations, peace education initiatives within the individual camps can be more effective than artificial attempts to bring people together. And at times insufficient importance is given to the fact that structural aspects also need to be taken into account alongside the time factor. Taking steps towards building trust need a certain level of economic stability and a sense of security within society.

"Cultural initiatives can help war-ravaged communities to recover from their traumatic experiences and assist them in their journey towards building trust and reconciliation. They can play their part in creating a society based on democratic participation, pluralism and tolerance."

However, existing empirical knowledge about the effectiveness of dialogue projects in post-war and crisis situations is as yet insufficient to draw up a list of lessons learned. This would require more comprehensive studies to be carried out, along with active research measures. It is a highly complex task to measure the effectiveness of peacebuilding actions. One of the main challenges when evaluating such actions is how to define the criteria for success and failure. There is also the problem of how to allocate specific results – particular social developments – to specific actions. The duty of accountability certainly demands that the use and benefit of donations and public money should be appraised, along with an evaluation of actions to promote peace and conflict transformation and to support development policies.

But is much more complicated to assess effectiveness in this area than in the field of traditional development cooperation. This is partly due to the limited resources and tight deadlines required by such evaluation activities. The value of such evaluations is also often somewhat dubious because of the difficulty of coming up with conclusive indicators and because the effects of work in the areas of peacebuilding and conflict resolution can only be evaluated in the long term, many years after particular measures and programmes have drawn to a close.

In any case, evaluations need to be set up in a participative way, i.e. those involved need to be constantly included in the process. The results need to be linked back to those whose actions are being investigated, and evaluations have to be integrated into courses of action in the planning stage. This is the only way to ensure they are part of a realistic definition of goals and provide an aid to self-reflection on the part of those carrying out the evaluations, or even help the latter when they are developing methods for reviewing their goals and strategies (self-evaluation). Critical self-reflection and ongoing self-appraisal are essential processes for international actors who intervene in conflict regions. It is also important to avoid undesirable and negative side-effects as a result of their actions.

It is, however, extremely difficult to prove the effectiveness of cultural initiatives in aiding the peacebuilding process. The empirical measurement of educational programmes is an extremely complex and difficult task because the results only become evident in the long term. It is even more difficult to determine the effects of cultural events in the areas of music, literature and the visual and dramatic arts.

Different forms of artistic expression can play their part in exposing the mechanisms of power and violence, in ensuring that forbidden narratives are heard and in stimulating alternative perceptions and ways of thinking. They can help people to process their experiences of violence, but they do not necessarily *have* to do this. Art is autonomous. Only a few artists devote their work to political activism and peacebuilding. At the end of the day, it is not the primary responsibility of artists to actively influence society by having a political agenda. The role of the visual arts, literature, music, film and theatre is rather to anticipate and mirror trends in politics and society. Culture expresses the quest for identity, suffering and the desire for recognition in a wide variety of ways.

At the same time, we should be clear that cultural production can only be influenced to a limited extent by international support programmes, and it normally does not allow itself to be hitched to set agendas. Moreover, these products are often the cultural expression of political and ideological messages that outsiders with little real understanding of the country find difficult to discern and interpret. International actors should therefore guard against excessively narrow categorisations into 'emancipative' and 'manipulative' forms of cultural expression and would do better to focus on looking for areas where a constructive approach is being taken towards the ambivalence of culture.

In extremely polarised societies it is important to focus above all on creating forums where people from all sides can familiarise themselves with and gain an understanding of the cultural characteristics of the 'other' group that provide them with their identity. In this respect, the external role consists of moderating discussion processes rather than making political assessments and categorisations. Readings and exhibitions can help to set in motion this kind of dialogue that highlights the interests and needs of 'others' while at the same time allowing the expression of one's own interests and needs. However, this presupposes that this takes place in an environment of mutual respect and safety for

"The role of the visual arts, literature, music, film and theatre is rather to anticipate and mirror trends in politics and society."

those taking part. Creating these kinds of protected spaces presents one of the main challenges.

International support programmes for post-war and crisis-ridden regions should therefore be less focused on the 'instrumentalisation' of cultural initiatives for the purposes of promoting peace and more on encouraging plurality and providing meeting places for initiating discourse. But in essence they should espouse values and principles that encourage conflict transformation. The most important of these is inclusivity, in the sense of inclusion and openness not only for cultural actors who are clearly dedicated to supporting peace processes, but also for more 'difficult' actors who are indifferent or opposed to these values.

Impartiality towards the opposing camps is also important. However, this should not be manifested in a way that goes against the principle of siding with people who have had their rights abused or whose interests have been ignored during asymmetric conflicts. One of the main preconditions for conflict transformation is exposing and raising awareness of cultures of dominance and structures of inequity.

Ownership is another important principle – the power of people who are caught up in conflicts to determine and shape their lives. Successfully tackling the causes of conflict and setting in motion the processes of reconciliation largely depends on these people, but external support can of course be a great help. These international actors not only need to have expertise in the area of cultural policy but must also possess and put into practice the same high level of intercultural awareness and experience that they expect from their local counterparts. They must display transparency in their goals and strategies and a willingness to create relationships based on a partnership of equals. Collaboration between international and national actors should open the doors to a mutual learning process. International and national cultural actors also need to develop trust, to carry out ongoing needs assessments and have staying power. Cultural studies expert Tina Balla puts it very clearly: "A process that is moved forward with patience and that must involve the agreement of the society involved", and a "planning process that is sensitively adapted to the conflict involved which allows step-by-step progress from one project to the next". If these standards were upheld when sponsoring, planning and carrying out cultural initiatives, then it is much more likely that they would make a meaningful contribution towards building trust, restoring damaged relations and achieving conflict transformation.

**Martina Fischer** is deputy director of the Berghof Foundation for Conflict Research in Berlin. She is co-editor of the "Berghof Handbook for Conflict Transformation" and has carried out research and published articles on the following subjects: peacebuilding in the former Yugoslavia; combining peacemaking and development cooperation; the role of civil society in conflict transformation; the relationship between the military and society; European peace policy.

# Afghanistan and beyond

Cultural activity supported by foreign governments is barely visible in Afghanistan. Why isn't more energy being put into alternative forms of diplomacy and development? When we consider the lack of success that military action has had in terms of establishing peace and security in the country, it would make sense to try to strengthen civil society – and to put more emphasis on initiatives based around art and culture. *By Jemima Montagu*

Vaclev Havel once claimed that if we are to change our world view, images have to change. And this makes the role of the artist especially important: "The artist now has a very important job to do. He's not a little peripheral figure entertaining rich people, he's really needed." Havel's support for the role of the artist, and by extension the role of arts and culture in shaping history no doubt partly derived from his experience as a playwright and activist who was catapulted into politics and was to become one of the most respected leaders to emerge from the 'velvet revolution'. Despite suffering from a long illness, he continued to go his own way right up until his death last year, and he was able to see the truth of this statement being borne out by the events of the Arab Spring in 2011, when writers, musicians and artists were at the forefront of their own 'jasmine revolution.'

March 2012 marked the 11th anniversary of the destruction of the magnificent standing buddhas in the Bamiyan Valley in Central Afghanistan. It was an act that sparked worldwide outrage and many would argue that it was one of the key events used to build public support in Europe and the West in favour of foreign military intervention in Afghanistan after 9/11. There was of course a great sense of international revulsion at the daily violence, the public stonings in Kabul's main sports stadium and the public hangings on street lamps, but it was the abolition of music, the banning of television and the annihilation of 1,500 years of Buddhist heritage that also played a critical role in swaying public opinion towards supporting the military-led intervention. It was culture that aroused empathy for Afghanistan and the Afghan people amongst the international community.

And yet, if this is true, if international intervention in Afghanistan was indeed mobilised by empathy through culture, then it could also be said that the role of culture in this foreign adventure has not really been explored or exploited to its fullest potential. Cultural activity supported by foreign governments is barely visible in Afghanistan – although when I was living there I did see examples of enlightened initiatives – and makes up a fraction of the foreign billions spent there since 2001. Why, as the military action and the state-building project floundered, wasn't more energy put into alternative forms of diplomacy or development, specifically the support of civil society initiatives, and its poorer siblings, arts and culture?

## *Feel-good actions*

We know the answer, of course. Culture still barely registers on the agenda of international diplomacy and development, and is regarded, at best, as 'soft power' but more usually as 'touchy-feely' or 'feel-good' – phrases that belittle both the activity and the participants, along with under-estimating the real value of culture. It may be a promising sign, however, to see that the UK Foreign and Commonwealth Office's 'Building Stability Overseas Strategy', published in July 2011, includes the following statement:

"Soft power will play a significant role in support of our efforts. The work of the British Council is important in building engagement and trust for the UK through a mutual understanding of values and the role of citizens, governments and civil society worldwide."

Although this may promise a new commitment to the value of 'soft power', it is dispiriting to see that the word 'culture' is still considered off-limits. Yet, by contrast, there was an almost embarrassing over-use and abuse of the phrase 'winning hearts and minds' in the coalition's counter-insurgency strategy in Afghanistan. 'Winning hearts and minds' consisted of quick-win development projects, such as building wells, but also emphasised 'face-to-face' contact between soldiers and Afghans. Soldiers in full body armour sporting a range of automatic weapons were advised to go and shake the hands of local people and say 'salaam aleikum' – inevitably appearing threatening to most Afghan men, let alone women and children.

It is not my intention to mock the coalition soldiers, nor to undermine genuine attempts at cross-cultural engagement, but to query why more wasn't – and still isn't – being done to support cultural initiatives,. There are many proven examples that not have not only demonstrated that they have real value but that are also 'locally embedded' – that is to say, initiated and run by Afghans. It is impossible to describe the culture of a nation as complex as Afgha-

"Soldiers in full body armour sporting a range of automatic weapons were advised to go and shake the hands of local people and say 'salaam aleikum'."

nistan on two sides of a smart card – surely more lessons could have been learned from Iraq regarding the need for committed and well-informed cultural engagement?

Last year I was one of the co-founders of a new agency called Culture+Conflict, building upon three years spent working on cultural projects in Afghanistan from 2006 to 2009. Culture+Conflict is responding to the lack of knowledge and understanding about the role that culture plays in conflict and post-conflict areas around the world. We are building up a body of examples of outstanding cultural projects, and will be promoting them to many different stakeholders in the 'conflict business' – from government departments dealing with foreign relations, defence and international development, to human rights organisations and NGOs already working in conflict zones.

We also want to create a platform for artists and cultural organisations to promote their work and connect with their international peers. We know that some outstanding work has already taken place but these projects are rarely documented and, even if they have been, there is no central place where such examples and write-ups can be found. Given the number of conflicts around the world today, surely there is no shortage of places seeking new approaches to peace-building?

I am not, of course, going to claim that arts and culture are any kind of universal panacea, or that they alone can resolve many intractable world conflicts. Culture and cultural life, however, do continue, despite the daily disruption of war and conflict: culture can be a touchstone for normality (reading a book, listening to music), or a refuge from the surrealism and pain of conflict. Art and culture may offer a space for reflection, to digest the experiences of war, or a means to communicate the incommunicable. There are many extraordinary examples of projects where theatre directors, artists, writers, musicians, film-makers and others have worked with people traumatised by war, using the arts to bring people together, "locating a common humanity", as Michaela Crimmin, co-founder of Culture+Conflict, describes it, "using art as a frame to play out realities too difficult to put into words, and thereby beginning a process of rehabilitation."

### *Theatre or therapy?*

But, as the above examples demonstrate, cultural activity, whether sprouting from the roots of the people and places afflicted by conflict or facilitated and supported by external players, is notoriously – and wonderfully! – hard to pin down. Theatre or therapy? An exhibition or a public engagement project? Or simply 'art' for its own sake? Even here, as I fall back on well-worn words such as 'culture' and 'art', I am aware that there is a wide spectrum of possible interpretations for these terms alone. And here begins the problem of definition, measurement and evaluation, which too often thwarts official support and the funding of cultural activity, whether at home or abroad. The arts and culture rarely fit into the tick-box evaluation matrices expected by donors and tax-payers.

But can, or should, the arts be subject to the same frameworks for evaluation as other disciplines? The challenge of evaluation is a question that Culture+Conflict intends to examine more closely. We would like to see if there are ways to develop robust and yet more flexible frameworks for assessing cultural activity in the context of development or conflict.

We know that opening up the arts and culture to conventional evaluation methods could unlock the door to much more funding and support, to greater recognition from the foreign relations and development sectors; but we also value the independence of culture – the ability to be critical, experimental, and sometimes open-ended. Art, as with any other sector, sometimes fails in its attempts.

There are, however, other forms of cultural activity that have a directly practical, some might say, 'instrumentalised' nature: heritage preservation and regeneration, jobs generated by the craft industry, festivals that bring communities together, the creative economy. These examples relate

"Culture can be a touchstone for normality (reading a book, listening to music), or a refuge from the surrealism and pain of conflict. Art and culture may offer a space for reflection, to digest the experiences of war, or a means to communicate the incommunicable."

to culture and the arts, but they also fit neatly into the funding objectives of government departments for international development or NGO mission statements.

In Afghanistan I once worked for a charity called Turquoise Mountain, an Anglo-Afghan NGO which developed an integrated model of working that linked heritage and regeneration, education and skills development, income generation and enterprise – with culture as the central pivot. Turquoise Mountain was established as a result of a conversation between HRH Prince Charles and President Karzai about heritage in Afghanistan. It was founded by Rory Stewart, now a UK Member of Parliament, and focused on the restoration and regeneration of Murad Khane, a historic part of the old city of Kabul; training in traditional arts skills (calligraphy, miniature painting, carved woodwork, ceramics and jewellery-making); and economic development by supporting traditional craft businesses and marketing Afghan craft skills internationally.

I joined the NGO in late 2006 as one of the founder-directors, after first visiting Kabul at the beginning of that year and seeing Murad Khane in the rain of a February day, when it could best be described as a slum. The streets were submerged in compacted rubbish, and were over-run with filth and waste. I hardly believed it would be possible to bring these tumble-down houses and filthy streets back to life.

Today, the whole district of Murad Khane has been completely transformed, and with it, the quality of life of the people living there. From what was a dwindling immigrant population, the community has now re-established itself. There is now a local public school, clinic, and the Abu Fazl shrine – the most important Shia site in Afghanistan – has a refurbished mosque, courtyard and elaborately carved doors.

The success of the Turquoise Mountain old city project rests partly on ownership of the project within the local community, and 'policing' by local power holders. But the benefits to the community have also been very tangible – cleared streets, waste disposal, a health clinic and school. Last year, the craft training centre moved into the beautifully restored buildings in the old city, and concerns about local resentment have proved unfounded. Although 'building a tourist offer' may be a statement too far in this war-torn city, small craft businesses and traditional Afghan restaurants have already started moving in to capitalise on the new 'heritage zone'. Sceptical local politicians are now competing to be associated with the project, and threatened urban developments on or around the site have been halted. The major donors, USAID and CIDA (Canadian International Development Agency), have also promoted the charity as a flagship project in Afghanistan.

## *In local hands*

The regeneration has taken place over 5 years, and has not been cheap – over $25 million USD has been spent in this period. Once Turquoise Mountain could be justly criticised for having a large imported international staff, but numbers have gone down from about 25 foreign staff in 2008 to only 2 in 2012. International operations have largely closed down and the charity is now managed almost exclusively by Afghans. This alone is something to be proud of: the 'completion' or 'conclusion' of an NGO project that remains a sustainable enterprise is rare in Afghanistan where NGOs tend to grow exponentially with the money available from donors, only for activities to halt abruptly when the agencies move elsewhere.

Turquoise Mountain ticks a number of boxes in terms of concrete development results: urban regeneration, economic development, building livelihoods, providing community facilities and infrastructure, providing education and skills, supporting new businesses – and yet all of these were directly related to the arts and crafts sector. The project has also produced some more intangible benefits that are no less important but much more difficult to measure, such as restoring a sense of civic and national pride. The often repeated statement of Turquoise Mountain staff and students goes along the lines of "I am proud of our country and our heritage, and I want people all over the world to know about this, to know about Afghanistan's beautiful arts and crafts."

The story of Turquoise Mountain, which – inevitably – had its failings along the way, demonstrates that not only can a cultural project deliver hard and soft outcomes, but it also plays into the wider and more impactful narrative of building national identity and pride. I use 'national identity' in a qualified sense because ethnic divisions are so pronounced in Afghanistan that it is always hard to speak of a collective national identity. But what this project did prove is that all Afghans, whatever their ethnicity, can be united by a sense of pride in their shared cultural heritage.

These 'touchy-feely' qualities are of course the essence of 'soft power', but could they have been supported by foreign governments and foreign aid budgets without being attached to the tangible, measurable benefits of training and skills development, a community health clinic, and so on? This is doubtful, but surely it should not be impossible in the future when other opportunities arise?

Another example is Kabul University. All faculties at the University have an academic partnership with a foreign university (or two) except the Faculty of Fine Arts. Yet it too needs help to develop its curriculum, facilities and teaching. As yet, none of the foreign governments operating in Afghanistan or their counterpart cultural institutes have thought it worthwhile to intervene. What are the cost benefits, they might say? How can our investment be measured? We want to encourage a new generation of economists, businessmen and engineers, not artists, actors and musicians…! But let's not forget Vaclav Havel, the unlikely president.

So this brings me back to the original question of what motivates and justifies foreign intervention in war and conflict areas, and what sort of intervention should this be? The slippery words 'foreign intervention' allow many different, and potentially opposing, interpretations from the harmless to the harmful. I would like to co-opt this phrase for culture. Investing in culture, I believe, is investing in the bedrock of a society, the terrain from which many tangible benefits may sprout; and from which many less tangible, but no less significant benefits grow – the roots that bind people together on an emotional level. If we are to 'intervene' at all, and the politics of this question should be the subject of a separate study, then I believe that it is through culture that we can achieve the most lasting and successful form of international intervention.

**Jemima Montagu** is a freelance curator and cultural advisor. She is co-founder of Culture+Conflict, an initiative that addresses the role of art and culture in conflict and post-conflict situations.

## Wars begin in the minds of men

Whether it is Catholics in Northern Ireland or Basques in Spain, cultural arguments have been used to reject what is seen as foreign rule. Culture plays a key role in the way conflicts between different groups and ethnicities play out and it must play its part in resolving conflicts. But how? Cross-border cultural and educational programmes have powerful potential for promoting peace in many places around the world. *By Raphael Vergin*

When understood as a dynamic, multi-faceted and often unconscious vehicle for identity and meaning, culture can shape perceptions, judgements and ideas about what constitutes 'us and them'. It can separate the 'normal' from the 'strange' and unfortunately in this way can engender an 'us against them' mentality. As a result, cultural devaluation and identity crises amongst marginalised ethnic groups are often the root cause of internal conflicts in many countries.

Secessionist movements often dispute the right to rule of 'the others' on the basis of their cultural differences: the Catholics in Northern Ireland, for example, or the Basques in Spain and the Palestinians in Israel. In one of the forgotten conflicts of our time, the independence struggles in the Casamance region of Senegal, nation-building and ethnicity are central to the conflict. In simple terms, the ruling elites are rejecting the cultural otherness of those on the periphery.

The creation of the African Union in 1963 provided the continent with a territorial/nationalist model. This led to political elites in nation states such as Senegal trying to absorb different ethnic patterns of identity and specific cultural characteristics in order to create national unity and integration. This national unity was to be achieved through homogeneity and through assimilating the 'otherness of peripheral groups'. In order to gain access to the political and economic resources of state power, those on the periphery (as in Casamance) find themselves forced to give up their own identities in order to become part of the dominant model. Stereotypes and disparaging descriptions such as 'noble savages', 'anarchists' or 'forest dwellers who eat monkeys and palm oil' have created a sense of inferiority among the ethnic groups involved, especially the Diola people, and sparked a desire to escape such taunts. In its extreme form, opposition to such political and economic marginalisation leads either to social and cultural assimilation or to violent conflict and rebellion.

By looking at a specific conflict in context and focusing on the cultural dimension, we can start to understand the potential and limitations of culture in conflict transformation. Despite the relatively high importance of ethnicity in the conflict mentioned above, the political and socio-economic prerequisites for providing equal opportunities for all ethnic groups and peoples also need to be guaranteed in terms of universal human rights, democracy, security and the rule of law. It is also vital to progress the multi-track negotiations with the fragmented rebel group Mouvement des forces démocratique de la Casamance (MFDC). After nearly 30 years of conflict, some of the group's factions are still calling for independence and keeping the struggle alive with the help of transnational financial support.

## *Geopolitical implications*

But the cultural dimension has much more than just a niche role to play in the complexity of the Casamance conflict – it has geopolitical implications. How, for example, do we deal with the fact that unified cultural areas can exist homogeneously across national borders but not maintain a symbolic bond with the centralised state?

When the German writer and thinker Gottfried Herder wrote that "the wild mixture of various races and nations under one sceptre" is in conflict with the aims of government, then it seems fair to ask just what governments can do to create a sense of integration in spite of and on the basis of cultural diversity. I interviewed the Senegalese historian Abderrahmane Ngaide in 2007 as part of a field study on the Casamance conflict. He believes that the solution lies in cross-border regionalisation, saying that this would help increase the legitimacy of the nation state and ensure that people still feel they are maintaining their ties to their ethnic roots, while at the same time seeing the effects of economic development within the nation.

Along with improvements to infrastructure in order to increase people's mobility and expand trade as part of creating regional economic areas, cross-border culture and education programmes also offer huge potential for promoting peace. Fostering an appreciation of the culture of previously denigrated ethnic groups, promoting the maintenance of traditions, customs and cultural heritage, and creating a regional centre of excellence can all help the people of the region to develop a new, more self-confident sense of identity that is of benefit in the process of nation-building.

Africa's past is of course totally different from that of Europe with its recent experiences of military conflicts and the redrawing of borders. Lack of political will and the fear of losing power mean that many African governments are (still) inclined to reject these kinds of transnational proposals. It may also remain too unclear what unintended consequences there might be on the fragile states and war economies of West Africa. This is where European cultural institutes and cultural policies could help in the medium-to-long term by offering advice and helping with implementation. They can also bring to bear their experiences relating to hybridity, transculturalism and identity on the delicate balancing act created by globalisation, regionalisation and nation building. Transnational cultural projects are already booming in Europe and can surely be adapted to suit the needs of other continents.

If we look more closely at current projects, we can see that cultural activities are being supported as a means of exercising soft power to deal with the consequences of protracted violence in the Casamance conflict and as part of other peace processes. Inter-ethnic festivals, peace radio, interactive theatre, films and photography all offer the potential and opportunities to overcome feelings of deprecation, division and difference between ethnic groups and to create opportunities for dialogue between formerly hostile parties. Suddenly rehabilitation, trust, humanity, reconciliation and healing start to emerge and there is the discovery of a commonality amid diversity that does not rely on a common language. It is important to be inclusive, particularly by involving people living in remote regions and not simply focusing on urban centres or elite groups.

Issues such as sustainable growth (in this instance the creative economy), gender, human rights, education, health and environment need to be addressed as part of projects dealing with culture and conflict – at the point where the link to non-violent conflict resolution is justified in the regional context and above all is triggered by the suggestions and initiatives of the local people themselves.

Overall, it is a good idea to predominantly support and promote existing local structures based on a participatory assessment of needs. Before launching projects – and not only those in the area of culture and conflict – it could be worthwhile to invest in some cultural reconnaissance in order to get a better picture of intercultural competence and sensitivity to cultural differences and needs.

The Arab Spring has made it even more obvious that it is worth focusing on digital media and its potential to support the processes of social change by increasing pluralism. Digital media also offer an innovative way of strengthening ties between sponsors and donors and specific projects, in as much as they provide additional ways of documenting project activities and progress in a transparent way and promoting direct and interactive dialogue. Finally, from the perspective of grass-roots initiatives, it is important to find ways of creating dialogue between policymakers and the main actors in conflicts, so that these key individuals can appropriately adapt their attitudes, positions and approaches to meet the calls for peace and international understanding on the part of local people and communities, and also, quite simply, so that they talk to each other. This kind of advocacy work could well benefit from the creative methods such as the use of audio-visuals to influence the awareness and decision-making process of the key players concerned. Community radio is a widespread discussion platform that is generally well-accepted by the local population. Radio programmes and radio plays are often much more successful than conferences and round table discussions at keeping people informed across wide geographic areas, irrespective of their level of education, and can influence them much more profoundly at an emotional and symbolic level.

If "wars begin in the minds of men" as suggested by UNESCO's charter, then the reverse must also be true and overcoming violence and hostility must also start with people's minds. This is where cultural activities have a potential role to play in helping to change people's attitudes and behaviours. However, it is not always the case that culture is used to help prevent violence and war. As Martina Fischer and others point out in this report, it can actually contribute to violence and hatred as well. The ambivalence of culture in conflicts therefore makes it imperative to look more critically at calls for independence and freedom for the arts, at least from the point of view of culture's practical role in conflict transformation, and even to put forward counter-arguments in favour of more control and a greater sense of responsibility.

Here, we are talking about responsibility in the sense that projects undertaken within the context of civil conflict management efforts always serve an external and interventionist function, in spite of all right and proper attempts to ensure participation, self-determination and ownership. By taking into account not only the interests of sponsors, donors and tax-payers, but also our own motivation, responsibility and willingness to learn, it is imperative that we assess whether our projects might not also have the potential to actually intensify the conflict. The principle of 'do no harm' must be respected.

We need to work on the basis of the lessons-learned principle so that people on the ground can be guided in a more effective way. To do this we need specific criteria, frameworks and indicators that are developed, continuously tested and enhanced in a dynamic way through dialogue and the exchange of ideas and experiences amongst all the key players from both the culture and conflict camps, in order to promote the maximum amount of peace and the minimum amount of violence.

"Transnational culture projects are already booming in Europe and can surely be adapted to suit the needs of other continents."

We have to accept that it is currently very difficult and time-consuming to quickly or accurately measure progress towards peace. Having said that, it is important to focus on best practice examples that show how potential outcomes can be both devised and evaluated.

"How senseless is everything that can ever be written, done, or thought, when such things are possible. It must be all lies and of no account when the culture of a thousand years could not prevent this stream of blood being poured out, these torture-chambers in their hundreds of thousands."

Erich Maria Remarque – All Quiet on the Western Front, 1929.

It is precisely this question we have to ask ourselves in relation to post-conflict Nepal, a country where we have for some years been running a number of projects as part of an initiative called culture4peace. Working with representatives from Nepalese civil society, we have been supporting dialogue and reconciliation processes through workshops, training sessions and community radio initiatives that build upon the success of each other. Interactive theatre, film and radio plays are all integrated as components of follow-up projects.

In this example, it is relatively easy to quantify the effects of these initiatives in terms of the numbers of people informed about civil conflict resolution; the number of participants at training sessions on the subject; the number of actors; the topics addressed; the estimated number of listeners to radio programmes or audiences at films shown in villages. Age, sex, social status can all be measured and quantified. What is much more difficult to quantify is their effectiveness, the intensity of the dialogues or the transformative nature of what is said and heard.

However, in terms of monitoring and evaluation, it is possible to gather important qualitative feedback from participants (and random samples of audiences in various communities) using questionnaires, group discussions, telephone interviews and participative observation, and also to provide these people with qualitative feedback from our side. The interpersonal aspects involved in the implementation and evaluation of projects, such as trust building, non-violent communication, readiness to embrace dialogue and conflict resolution, can all be observed and assessed in the field. However, people often pursue their own interests and egotistical goals, so answers to surveys and questionnaires can be deliberately biased. Nevertheless, despite these potential shortcomings or inadequacies, and despite a lack of resources, we have had some success in terms of monitoring effectiveness and in gathering useful data based on experience, and we can build on this.

The kind of practical information gathered in the course of project work (and in this case underpinned by the experiences gained in a project that has been running since 2009 under the auspices of the Nepali Civil Peace Service, in which training seminars on interactive theatre play a key role) could and should be continuously added to, expanded and made more transparent through inter-organisational dialogue. But how can we now even think about more flexible frameworks for cultural activities in the area of conflict transformation? How can we reconcile the apparently insurmountable differences between the desire to honour the 'temple of art' on the one hand and specific peace agendas on the other?

If the causes of conflicts are infinitely complex then so are the potential solutions. For example, it is undeniable that freedom of expression is a fundamental principle of human rights, democracy and pluralism. According to democratic peace theory, these in turn can, under certain circumstances, help to foster non-violent conflict management and so promote peace. It could also be argued that every form of conflict, even the most violent, can at first be necessary, sensible and right.

### *Stirred to action by artists*

A society that is moved and stirred to action by artists and that denounces the current state of affairs and identifies solutions, effectively shapes its conflicts and determines their form. Building stable nations and achieving national unity within Europe was a long, slow progress that often involved violent altercations.

It could be argued that independent artists should simply be given a bag of money and their freedom (within the restrictions imposed by their society at least) with our best wishes, without worrying about other issues, such as a sense of awareness. The consequences could be either positive or negative.

The fact is, those who are primarily interested in promoting a peace agenda rather than artistic freedom would need to impose strict criteria in order to ensure they have the maximum amount of control over the success of this approach. In this way they would follow an intrinsic logic that is also designed to make them less vulnerable and legitimise their own peace efforts. This could result in much creative potential being lost, but could also prevent some damage occurring, the consequences of which might be much more severe than the potential success envisaged.

Having said that, this does not mean that it is impossible for artists to be given the maximum amount of freedom in a conflict transformation situation. Various organisations, such as the Dutch Prince Claus Fund, are already supporting culture and conflict initiatives in a more flexible way. Other initiatives, such as the British Culture+Conflict programme, are making a valuable contribution in terms of gathering, evaluating and publishing valuable data through their approach to documentation and best practice. What is clear is that the resulting lessons learned should be evaluated in as transparent a way as possible and widely discussed in order to be able to use the success of a more flexible approach as a key bargaining point when dealing with more conservative donors.

In principle, cultural activities should not be subject to any more restrictions than the general peace process itself, whatever the potential outcome paradigms, for it is just as difficult to effectively and quickly measure the impact of, say, a symposium, as it is to foresee in detail the potential impact of setting up a peace museum. The fact that in terms of peace work both can be equally well conceived, implemented and evaluated and that local target groups can also give important qualitative feedback on these and other similar activities should be sufficient reason to pursue both options.

There may be a benefit in shifting the discussion away from specific positive outcomes towards reflecting on potential unintended negative consequences. In this way, background checks and trust-building within the framework of freedom for the artist could help to prevent unwanted potential damage. As a result, artists would have freedom of choice in the creation and presentation of their work and would simply be 'assessed' through regular monitoring and a final evaluation for documentation. Workshops on awareness and responsibility could also be integrated into the programme.

In general, there is a need to gather more data based on experience and to increase funding and resources aimed at the practical and analytical management of the cultural dimension of conflicts. The exchange of ideas and experiences within Europe could and should be actively promoted by the European cultural institutes and pursued in international and cross-discipline forums, as is the case with the informal working group Culture and Conflict, coordinated by the Institut für Auslandsbeziehungen (Institute for Foreign Cultural Relations, ifa). This provides clear evidence of the important role played in conflicts by art and culture.

**Raphael Vergin** was a trainee at the Society for International Cooperation and also worked for several years for the peace and human rights organisation Peace Brigades International in Nepal and Germany. In 2009 he set up the project culture4peace which focuses on intercultural aspects of peace processes. As part of his political science studies, he carried out research into "obstacles to constructive conflict resolution in the Casamance conflict (Senegal)".

**A voice for the voiceless** The South African government uses culture and art as a way of achieving togetherness, mutual understanding and respect and as a means of overcoming the long and heavy legacy of colonialism and apartheid. In Brazil, music is commonly used to lure youth away from drugs and crime. Percussion, in particular, seems to offer the additional side-effect of channelling frustration and aggression into harmony. What else can culture do?

*By Bernd Reiter*

For many social scientists, cultural phenomena are peripheral – a mere reflection of the really important factors that determine life: economics, assets, the ownership of the means of production, and the political power that has its roots in this material base.

According to Karl Marx, it is material conditions that determine the society and culture of an era. For Marx and his followers, whoever holds the money and power can define what is right, beautiful and just, and cultural life is a mere reflection of these basic power and wealth constellations. There are countless examples of how powerful and influential elites have radically restructured the 'lifeworld', and this framework is still able to provide us with many revealing questions and answers. However, like any theoretical framework, it provides just one way of looking at reality.

Another was developed by Antonio Gramsci (1891-1937). In his Prison Notebooks, he pondered the autonomy of culture that at one time was established and defined in a certain way. Later authors, in the tradition of the German/Austrian Edmund Husserl (1859-1938) and the Austrian Alfred Schütz, gave more detailed accounts of how culture, once institutionalised, can become autonomous and withstand some of the direct changes in material conditions.

It was Gramsci who introduced the idea of 'cultural hegemony' – a situation where one version or definition of culture is imposed on material conditions, influencing, structuring, and restricting people's actions and thoughts. For Gramsci, the content of cultural hegemony was almost always shaped by the ruling classes and it restricted the opportunities of poor and working class people. Schütz, in particular, set out the conditions under which certain behavioral patterns become institutionalised, thus gaining some degree of autonomy from material living conditions. Thorstein Veblen (1857-1929), who was writing around the same time as Gramsci, believed members of the "leisure class" only engaged in conspicuous and unproductive consumption in order to set themselves apart and reconfirm their elite status. According to him, elite culture was empty and meaningless, and it was mostly aimed at maintaining and reinforcing status rather than contributing to general welfare. It did not merely grow out of and reflect material conditions, but rather culture and customs affected these material conditions.

"Art, however, is social not only because of its mode of production, in which the dialectic of forces and relations of production is concentrated, nor simply because of the social derivation of its thematic material. Much more importantly, art becomes social by its opposition to society, and it occupies this position only as autonomous art."

Theodor W. Adorno

Norbert Elias (1897-1990), a German sociologist of Jewish descent, took this analysis a step further by demonstrating that the upper classes constantly invent new cultural forms and manners in order to set themselves apart from the rest – who then seek to imitate these latest mannerisms. This starts an endless game of cat-and-mouse that results in forms of behavioural and cultural expression that are ever less practical, rational, and functional.

"Such a public sphere, we believe, creates a space whereby the critical models of artists, theorists, philosophers, historians, activists, urbanists, writers, and others working within other intellectual traditions and artistic positions could productively be represented and discussed. The public sphere imagined by these collaborations is to be understood, then, as a constellation of multifaceted platforms in which artists, intellectuals, communities, audiences, practices, voices, situations, actions come together to examine and analyze the predicaments and transformations that form part of the deeply inflected historical procedures and processes of time."

Okwui Enwezor

All these theories and frameworks point to the autonomous power of culture. Culture, once created and institutionalised, has an effect on people's thoughts and behaviours, determining what they perceive to be right, beautiful, and proper.

Furthermore, all the authors mentioned above agree that culture tends to be biased towards the ruling classes, but also that it influences the lives of ordinary people by channelling and restricting their options in their efforts to achieve upward mobility because they emulate the habits of the rich. In other words, status maintenance is to a large extent performative, and cultural forms allow it to create, maintain and reinforce its separation.

Such a framework also allows consideration of the liberating potential of culture and cultural production. If culture is to some degree autonomous and if it affects people's options and values, then it also has the potential to impact and change their lives in negative and positive ways.

The key factor in this equation is the content of culture and the values and preferences that it transmits. If it is normally the rich and powerful who load culture with their own preferences – preferences that are in themselves not genuine, but driven by the need for distinction – then a progressive or revolutionary culture and art aimed at producing social change, more democracy, more participation, more self-determination, and more justice, liberty, and equality can use culture and art to disseminate and instil values and preferences associated with these values. The resulting utopia is one of a 'culture and art of the people' – one that provides incentives for a deeper and more meaningful democratic praxis. After all, democracy renews itself through associations formed in the public sphere, as Jürgen Habermas has so insistently asserted, and culture and art are the public expressions of this par excellence.

This is a utopia because, in reality, public spheres and the media that influence, inform, and even uphold them tend to be privately owned, thus representing particular rather than general interests, mostly of a commercial nature. But utopia or not, if it is recognised that culture and art can be autonomous and constructed by society, then they have the potential to bring about social change, and it also explains how and by which means such a change can come about.

In a truly democratic system, public spheres and the media that create and influence them should be geared towards democratic – meaning general – aims and they should focus on issues of citizenship, democracy, justice, and equality. If they were to do this, they would have the potential to create a democratic public sphere that actively disseminates and spreads a democratic culture, not least through the production and dissemination of democratic and educational works of art.

### *A world of democratic culture*

In such a world, democratic culture has the potential to influence all those who are exposed to it and who engage with it. In this way it has an impact not only on their thoughts and actions, but also on

> "The Rwandan civil war clearly attests to the power of culture and the media in mobilising people and imposing analytical frameworks to guide people's thoughts and actions."

their norms, values, and preferences.

We can grasp the power of culture and art by looking at its influence in most market-driven societies, where its main and hegemonic function is the dissemination of consumerism, individualism, and materialism. The culture of the market is indeed so pervasive and powerful that it ensures the continued working of market systems, constantly instilling new wants and needs and a restless drive towards consumption. Without it, markets could not work and constantly expand.

But what can culture achieve in situations of conflict? In a poignant article entitled "Civil Society, Pluralism, Goldilocks and Other Fairy Tales in Africa," Leonard Markovitz (2002) argues that in situations of civil war and conflict, civil society (and as a consequence culture and art) are toothless. Where weapons speak the loudest, the often ephemeral voices of artists, neighbourhood associations, and civic activists are drowned. Similarly, where public spheres are emptied out by fear, hatred, and mutual suspicion, democracy cannot renew itself. Like other political realists, Markovitz, shows that states and state power need to uphold, enforce, and protect the basic civil rights of free speech and association, without which democratic culture cannot thrive.

Although this argument is certainly illuminating and explains many situations where culture and art are pushed to the fringes by guns, fear and violence, there are still many empirical examples that contradict it and perhaps provide an exception to this general rule. Taken all together, these examples allow for some tentative deductions and generalisations about the autonomous power of culture and art in conflict situations.

One of the most telling negative examples of the power of culture and the media is the civil war in Rwanda. Here, radio stations were able to fall back on old resentments and actively disseminate a culture of hatred that was ultimately channelled into genocide. The Rwandan civil war clearly attests to the power of culture and the media in mobilising people and imposing analytical frameworks to guide people's thoughts and actions. With the support of their organisations, ethnopolitical entrepreneurs were are able to use and manipulate the media in order to advance their own agenda and spread dissent and hatred.

## *Platforms for encounters*

Beyond Rwanda, we have witnessed the brutal power of the media in shaping and forging cultural norms in Nazi Germany and everywhere else where particular frames of reference and ways of seeing things are propagated to the point where they become the new mainstream. However, this power does not have to be directed towards such negative ends, as media content is not in any way predefined.

A very positive example that points to the power of culture, media, art, civil society and the public sphere in overcoming division is that of post-apartheid South Africa. Here, immediately after the dismantling of apartheid, the new Department of

Arts and Culture set out to promote cultural and artistic events with the explicit aim of bringing together the different groups of South Africa who had previously been kept divided by law.

I remember meeting a representative of the new South African government in the late 1990s who told me that for the first time, South Africans of different ethnic backgrounds were able to come together. Culture and art provided the main platforms for these encounters. So it should not come as a surprise that in a society that is still strongly divided, culture and art are perceived as stages or platforms for the practice of togetherness, the exchange of ideas, mutual learning and respect. In June 2012, the South African Department of Arts and Culture presented a "National Strategy for Developing an Inclusive and Cohesive South African Society" (pdf available at: http://www.dac.gov.za/reports.htm). The first line of the report reads: "This is a draft National Strategy on Social Cohesion and Nation-Building of the Department of Arts and Culture (DAC)." Under the concept of ubuntu, which involves interconnectedness, sharing, and commitment to the greater social good, this report states the vision of the Department of Culture and Art as: "To develop and preserve South African culture to ensure social cohesion and nation-building." It goes on to say: "This mandate derives from its role as public custodian of the diverse cultures, languages and heritage of the people of South Africa and as the national leader in providing public support for the development of innovation across the full spectrum of the arts as creative, economic and social practices, and as bearers of a dynamic society. As a consequence, the department's programmes cover the administration of arts and culture in society, language, heritage promotion, national archives, records, libraries and heraldry."

The South African government is therefore using culture and art as a way of achieving togetherness, mutual understanding and respect and as a means of overcoming the long and heavy legacy of colonialism and apartheid. In doing so, it highlights the importance, relevance and power of culture and art. This power is considerable, as is shown by the example of integrated sport in South Africa. The symbolism and lasting impact of playing football, rugby or cricket together goes beyond the players themselves. It sends a powerful message to the rest of the nation and even to the global sports audience. It instils values of togetherness and celebrates unity, and in doing so it forges a new democratic, hegemonic culture that has a positive effect on people's values, norms, and motivations and influences the material conditions of their lives.

There are many other examples of how culture and art have the power to instil democratic values that provide the direction and motivation for democratic action. Such values have the potential to influence material conditions. In Brazil, music is commonly used to lure youth away from drugs and crime. Many well-

"The symbolism and lasting impact of playing football, rugby or cricket together goes beyond the players themselves."

known NGOs, including Viva Rio, Afro Reggae, ISER, Pracatum and Bagunçaço, offer after-school music education as a way of engaging urban youth in positive and constructive activities. Music has proven to be a powerful tool in the struggle for Brazilian citizenship. Music is a way of increasing the self-esteem of groups that have historically been mistreated and disrespected: the victims of a deeply-ingrained institutional racism. As musicians, poor urban youth can gain a voice and a public platform, or in this case, a stage. By making their voices heard, they are able to break their imposed silence and overcome their invisibility. Their voices enrich the Brazilian public sphere in important and consequential ways, making it more diverse and a reflection of Brazil's multicultural society. Percussion, in particular, seems to offer the additional side effect of channelling frustration and aggression into harmony. The Brazilian impromptu percussion formation "O Zarabe", created and led by the Bahian musician Carlinhos Brown, provides a good example of this. In a TV interview given in the late 1990s, Brown explained that the 200 men who were running, drumming, and singing with him as they roamed the streets of Bahia could be using this energy to rob and steal in an "arrastão," that is, a mass robbery orchestrated by a band of thieves sweeping up whatever is in their path. Instead, Brown explained, O Zarabe was a peaceful, musical arrastão that channelled youthful male energy into music (O Zarabe  is made up exclusively of young black men).

"Art has to do with life. Only from art can a new concept of economics be formed, in terms of human need, not in the sense of use and consumption, politics and property, but above all in terms of the production of spiritual goods."

Joseph Beuys

The power of music to heal divisions and overcome separation can also be seen in the United States, where racial divisions and segregation are among the harshest in the world. In cities like New Orleans and Memphis, where African Americans dominate the music scene, we can see how integration is at work in bands and carnival floats. White Americans – who are normally the main orchestrators and beneficiaries of American racism – take part in forms of black cultural expression and in doing so become as one with their fellow black band members. New Orleans and Memphis both have a long history of black music and are unique in providing a kind of contact between black and white that is rare elsewhere. This contact seems to spring from their music scenes but it ends up characterising their societies, setting them apart from other American cities. New Orleans and Memphis show us how culture, music and art are able to bring together people and groups who are normally divided to take part in a joint project, whether it is playing in a team, forming a band or simply coming together to enjoy cultural events such as carnivals. Whenever this happens, cultural praxis provides orientation, motivation, and practical examples of joint actions that bring together those who are so often separated.

## *Culture becomes political*

The Argentinian philosopher Enrique Dussel (2000) and his French colleague Jacques Rancière (2007) both argue that we need to rethink what constitutes "the political." While Dussel argues that everything is political, Rancière suggests that most political problems are actually of social origin, but that they can be addressed by political means. In this essay, I have expanded the notion of the social to include the cultural. Most political problems are indeed rooted in social and cultural problems, but political solutions are not enough to address them successfully.

When culture is used as a tool to tackle social division, suspicion or even hatred between groups, then indeed it becomes political, as Dussel suggests. Enwezor Okwui, artistic director of the Dokumenta 11 exhibition in Germany (2002), explains this in his book The Short Century (2001), saying that culture and art have the power to make, unmake, and redraw divisions among people and groups. At a very basic level, inter-group conflict is the result of portraying certain people as different from, or better than, others, and thus justifying their privileges. Government action is often called for in crisis situations, but such action cannot change the very definitions and frames of reference that pitched people and groups against each other in the first place. However, culture and art can do this.

**Bernd Reiter** is Associate Professor of Comparative Politics and Latin American Studies at the University of South Florida, Tampa. His research topics include democracy, citizenship, participation, civil society and education. He has spent time in Colombia and Brazil working on projects to aid street children and at-risk urban youth and to increase the participation of favela dwellers.

**References**

Adorno, Theodor W. 1997, *Aesthetic Theory.* Minneapolis: University of Minnesota Press.

Beuys, Joseph, 1997, *The Multiples*, Cambridge: Busch-Reisinger Museum.

Dussel, Enrique. 2000, *Democracy in the "Center" and Global Democratic Critique.* In: Okwui, Enwezor, Okwui 2000, Democracy Unrealized: Documenta 11_Platform 1. Ostfildern-Ruit: Hatje Cantz Publishers, pages 267-284.

Enwezor, Okwui. 2001, *The Short Century*, Munich: Prestel Verlag.

Markovitz, Leonard, 2002, *Civil Society, Pluralism, Goldilocks and Other Fairy Tales in Africa*, In: Bond, George Clement and Nigel Gibson, Contested Terrains and Constructed Categories. Boulder: Westview, chapter 5.

Rancière, Jacques, 2007, *On the Shores of Politics.* New York: Verso.

# Setting the truth free

Northern Ireland is only just beginning to emerge from a painful and destructive period characterised by sectarianism, isolationism, armed conflict and murder. In common with so many conflicts, the roots of 'the Troubles' in Northern Ireland were arguably as much cultural as they were political and economic. Can culture also help to create lasting peace? *By Peter Jenkinson*

In common with many other European nations, the United Kingdom has a legacy of imperial and colonial adventure and misadventure on every continent that stretches back hundreds of years and that redrew the maps through the use of force. This complex British history and practice of invasion, plantation, human trafficking, slavery, exploitation and repression in multiple locations across the world led, in many instances, to enduring violence and conflict and finally to struggles for peace, justice, autonomy and independence. The lessons of this long imperial period continue to cast long shadows and are still being unravelled, unpacked, assessed and disputed through to this day. Without doubt this critical debate on rights and wrongs will and should continue long into the future, as new narratives emerge, injustices are corrected, histories are retold and as new and more positive and more equitable relationships and alliances are made and remade between the former colonisers and the colonised, and with those who inhabited ambiguous positions in between.

Yet for the United Kingdom there is one conflict much closer to home, in fact right on the doorstep, which has deeply affected national life for centuries and that today is only in the earliest and most fragile stages of the long journey to eventual peace and reconciliation: the conflict in Northern Ireland.

The painful, bitter and destructive period of sectarianism, isolationism, armed conflict and murder from the 1960s onwards, that became known as 'the Troubles' and which was witnessed on television screens across the world for decades, is one from which Northern Ireland is only just emerging. In common with so many conflicts, including many in the Middle East at this moment, the roots of 'the Troubles' in Northern Ireland were arguably as much cultural as they were political and economic.

The crucial question for us now is: if the roots of 'the Troubles' were as much cultural as they were political and economic, is this also true of the potential solutions? And if so, what exactly is the role, or even responsibility, of culture in rebuilding, reconnecting, reshaping and reimagining Northern Irish life and society? What is it specifically that culture can do, or make possible, that nothing else can? And why? Alternatively should culture even be employed in so 'instrumentalist' an agenda as conflict management and resolution and the re-creation of a strong and purposeful civilian and civic life for all? Or might culture continue to prove to be a malign force, slowing or blocking the path of reconstruction and 'normalisation'? And finally, in a broader European and international context, what lessons might be drawn from the ongoing Northern Ireland experience?

> "Human beings suffer,
> They torture one another,
> They get hurt and they get hard.
> No poem or play or song
> Can fully right a wrong
> Inflicted or endured."
>
> Seamus Heaney Nobel Laureate From 'The Cure at Troy'

I should stress from the outset that – although I have shared Irish and English family heritage – I am from England and not from Northern Ireland and so my perspective here is very much that of a more distant, or even consciously naïve, observer who has not been directly involved in the vast sweeps of history that have affected this troubled place on the very western edge of Europe in recent times. But I have had the great privilege of being involved with Northern Ireland over the last five years through being appointed as a deliberately 'outsider' expert advisor on the 'post-conflict' art programme in the ancient city of Derry~Londonderry and latterly on its successful bid to be the first 'UK City of Culture' in 2013. It has been a fast-moving, exciting, inspiring, puzzling and troubling experience and, as so many 'outsiders' do, I have become fascinated with the people, the place, its multiple unresolved stories and myths and the huge energy and wit that is being brought to bear to create a more positive future for all.

The roots of the Troubles in Northern Ireland lie in the long and complex history of the frequently antagonistic relationships between the islands of Ireland and Great Britain and specifically events almost 400 years ago that dramatically changed these relationships forever. In 1613, under the instructions of King James I, the wealthiest Guild Companies of the City of London, (many somewhat reluctantly) made settlements in the province of Ulster in the north of Ireland. Ulster at that time was regarded as the most Gaelic and the most troublesome of the Irish provinces in the eyes of the English Crown and therefore needed to be brought under control, lest it make alliances with England's enemies in Continental Europe.

The London Guild Companies divided up the best land between themselves and established 'plantations', often replacing the Irish names of the towns and villages with English names. They built the walled city of Derry at a key defensive position on the River Foyle in the North West of Ireland, renamed it Londonderry and established new 'English' forms of political and civic administration across Ulster. From this moment of the English (and subsequently Scottish) Protestant and Presbyterian settlement of an Irish and predominantly Catholic territory – an event that many living in Ulster regarded rather more negatively as an unjust and unjustifiable English 'invasion' – the seeds were sown for division, discord and conflict along practically tribal, ethno-political lines in the four centuries that followed.

## *Laboratory of Empire*

This northern Irish colonial adventure would influence British overseas expansion from this period onwards. The many lessons learned from the 'Plantation of Ulster' were to be exported to Britain's rapidly-burgeoning colonial, and latterly imperial, territories across the world, making Ulster an early 'Laboratory of Empire'.

Whilst strife and conflict were, almost inevitably, constant over the centuries that followed, the most sustained period of systemic violence and sectarian bloodletting – the Troubles – engulfed Northern Ireland from the late1960s. What started out as civil rights protests were rapidly accelerated by the events of 'Bloody Sunday' in 1972 in which, as the subsequent UK Government 'Saville Inquiry' concluded only in 2010, British soldiers murdered 14 innocent civilians in Derry. Whilst the Troubles were most often all too neatly and conveniently characterised, not least in Britain, as a distant battle between two conflicting sides on another island – Catholic v Protestant, Nationalist v Unionist, Green v Orange – the truth is that from the beginning the third partner in this battle was Britain itself, or at least British political and military leaders, though few of them acknowledged this at the time or even since.

As they ran their course over the next 30 years, the Troubles would result in the deaths of more than 3,600 people – 2,000 civilians, 1,000 members of the security services and 600 paramilitaries. Many others were permanently wounded and, in such a small province in which communal and familial bonds were extremely tight, everyone living there could not but be directly and deeply affected by the debilitating conflict that raged on an almost daily basis.

The Troubles attracted unprecedented national and international media attention. Year by year, toxic words and images of hatred, pain, cruelty and breakdown were flashed across the world, accompanied by narratives that were often far from objective, if not avowedly partisan. For most outsiders this dramatic conflict is all that the reality of Northern Ireland represented and for many this is still the case today. But, as always in conflict territories, there were many other realities than those presented by the outside media.

As is the case in most conflict situations, as the violence deepened across Northern Ireland many people chose to leave, in-

"Year by year, toxic words and images of hatred, pain, cruelty and breakdown were flashed across the world."

cluding artists, creative practitioners and intellectuals, exiling themselves and moving to other parts of the island or to other parts of the world, in particular to North America where the diasporic connections were especially strong. Some would never return. But many of those who stayed in Northern Ireland felt a strong responsibility to play a part in contemporary events. As the artist John Kindness stated, "The Troubles changed the agenda – a lot of us felt a need to bring what was happening on the street into our work."

The most famous and vibrant examples of this were the murals and frescoes that were painted on buildings and walls in both Catholic and Protestant communities across the province, drawing, quite literally, the battle lines to come. Often featuring extreme and violent images depicting 'paramilitary' fighters, children in crossfire, Orange marches, drive-by shootings and fallen heroes, the murals reflected and underscored, and arguably boosted and glorified, the rapidly growing separation of the two conflicted communities: art simultaneously in the service of cohesion and division. But these intimidating and celebratory murals were not and are not the only cultural story.

Many mainstream and official cultural and academic institutions remained frozen, almost paralysed, by the Troubles, unable to respond for fear of being perceived as taking sides. For example, the exhibiting or collecting of directly Troubles-related contemporary art by the primary public institutions in Northern Ireland was minimal during the period, nor did the art market beyond pay much heed to art that was often perceived as too socially and politically engaged for elite tastes at the time.

### *An upsurge in creative energy*

However, despite the conservatism of most institutions, there was, simultaneously, an upsurge in artistic, cultural and creative energy as immediate, on-time account was taken, through art, photography, literature, poetry, music and film, of the ongoing conflict.

The work of Brian Friel and Stephen Rea at the Field Day Theatre Company, the writings of Nobel Laureate Seamus Heaney, Seamus Deane, Michael Longley, Tom Paulin and Pulitzer prizewinner Paul Muldoon, the exuberant punkish songs of The Undertones and Stiff Little Fingers, the works of visual artists including Willie Doherty, Rita Duffy, Paul Graham, Victor Sloan, Conrad Atkinson and Richard Hamilton and the films of Paul Greengrass, Ken Loach, Pat O'Connor, Alan Clarke and Neil Jordan bear witness to the fact that, during the darkest years, the Troubles were also characterised by cultural output that directly connected with the realities and complexities of the region in multiple ways. This work reflected the conflict back to the people living through it and bore testimony to their struggle and suffering, whilst importantly drawing British and international attention to, and placing a sharper focus on, the intensity, volatility, violence and vibrancy of what was happening in, and to, Northern Ireland.

This three decades of work touching upon the Troubles – by artists and cultural activists of every kind, using every type of art form, from street artist collectives to now internationally renowned creative figures – significantly had no one common role, purpose or manifesto. Throughout these years the artists' work fulfilled various different functions – it bore witness, protested, interrogated, affirmed and celebrated, quietly reflected, angrily denounced, gave voice to the voiceless, called to action, made connections and reconnections, took sides, encouraged empathy, contested the foundation myths and stereotypes at the root of the conflict, healed, inspired, scrutinised, sanctioned ambiguity, satirised, proposed novel answers to ancient questions and asked new questions of old answers, memorialised and mourned, opened up the wider world beyond Northern Ireland and, for some at least, sought the elusive truth of the situation everyone was living through.

The brother of the youngest civilian killed on Bloody Sunday in 1972 claimed, throughout the decades that followed, that all he wanted all along was to "set the truth free". Whilst there may not have been a common artistic purpose, this – setting the truth free – may arguably have been one of the common artistic motivations.

Today it is not possible to imagine the Troubles in Northern Ireland without this astonishing record of work created by, and the agency willingly and passionately provided by, artists. Nor indeed to imagine any conflict without the record and agency provided by artists and cultural activists. Certainly art and culture did not stop the battle that raged for decades – and perhaps this should never be expected. But what did it do or make possible? Even now it is perhaps too early to assess precisely what its impact was, across Northern Ireland and across the world. But is it not critical that we reach this understanding, not least to be able to pass on this knowledge and painfully-acquired wisdom, openly and with generosity, to people living in and with current and future conflict situations?

Northern Ireland is now described as being in a post-conflict situation. I'd like to speculate that whilst culture played a vital, multi-levelled, multi-constituency role during the conflict – as witness, as protestor, as connector, as provocateur, as memorialist and so on – it is perhaps during this so-called post-conflict period that culture can play its most powerful and purposeful role yet.

40 years on, there is at last the space for reflection, for reassessment, for compassion, for openness, for peaceful pause and for slowness and patience. Now at last there is time for conversations that were previously deemed out of the question, for new relationships and partnerships, not least with the world outside and, crucially, for the weaving of new generations, who never knew the Troubles but who will be shaping the future into the ongoing story (and stories) of Northern Ireland so that it becomes 'their story', a 'shared' story, connected with the difficult past but not trapped or frozen by it. The truth can and will at last be set free.

History says, Don't hope
on this side of the grave.
But then, once in a lifetime
the longed for tidal wave
of justice can rise up,
and hope and history rhyme.

Seamus Heaney From 'The Cure at Troy'

The stories of Northern Ireland are about to be presented on a new global stage. The crucible of the Troubles, the city of Derry~Londonderry, is to step up to lead the Northern Irish renegotiation of its past, present and future. In 2009 plans for marking the 400th Anniversary of the connection of the two cities of London and Derry~Londonderry in 2013 through new cultural partnerships and collaborations were well underway when the UK government, intending to build on the success of Liverpool's year as European City of Culture in 2008, announced a competition to become the first UK City of Culture in 2013. Designating itself as the City of Derry~Londonderry (thereby signalling the inclusion of both 'traditions' in the city from the outset), the city entered the competition with great drive and passion and in June 2010 was declared the winner, marking yet another highly significant milestone in British-Irish relations. The headline of the city's bid was 'Telling a new story' with the foundations built on the twin philosophical pillars of 'Purposeful Inquiry', boldly looking afresh at the past and present in order to inform the future, including the revisiting of the culture of the Troubles, and 'Joyous Celebration', marking the energies and achievements the city and its people sustained even through the darkest and most painful years of the past. If there is an answer (or likely answers) to my speculation on the power of culture in peacemaking and renewal in the post-conflict period, it is likely to be found in this city on the edge of Europe in the year, and the decade, ahead, starting with the London Olympics and Paralympics this summer.

The opening concert, the 'Peace Concert', of the 2012 Cultural Olympiad, produced in collaboration with the agency Peace One Day, will be held not as would be expected in London but rather in Derry~Londonderry on 21 June 2012. This will signal to the world the intention of the London Olympics to return to the modern Olympics' original focus on truce and peacemaking when it was reinvented in the late nineteenth-century by Baron de Coubertin in a Europe torn apart by war. Equally it will signal yet another dramatic moment and shift in British-Irish relations. Following this concert, the UK will initiate a conversation about culture and peacemaking that will move from the London Olympics and Paralympics of 2012 to Derry~Londonderry in 2013 and then on to Glasgow when it hosts the Commonwealth Games in 2014, before the conversational baton is passed on to Rio de Janeiro when it hosts the Olympics and Paralympics in 2016 and, it is to be hoped, onwards from Brazil thereafter.

Northern Ireland will thus play a key role in the global conversations still to come. So, looking to the future it is clear that, whilst the collision and contestation

"So hope for a great sea change
On the far side of revenge.
Believe that a farther shore
Is reachable from here.
Believe in miracles
And cures and healing wells."

Seamus Heaney From 'The Cure at Troy'

of cultures – English v Irish, Protestant v Catholic, Loyalist v Nationalist, Orange v Green, insider v outsider – were at the root of the centuries of conflict in the north of Ireland and particularly of the Troubles of the last century, in the twenty-first century it is most likely to be culture, from within and, vitally, from without, that is set to play an ever more critical, deeper and more sustained role than ever before in the rebuilding, reshaping and the reimagining of this damaged but now optimistic province, in ways that will undoubtedly provide inspiration, encouragement and hope to the rest of the world. It will not be easy or quick. It will take several generations. There will undoubtedly be setbacks. There are still militant minorities, hooked on conflict, that do not accept the current version of peace and will do all they can to disrupt it.

But the positive course is now set and unstoppable. It is about putting the negative past behind us, whilst at the same time never forgetting it and trying to better understand it from all possible perspectives. Looking ahead through a new culturally-enabled lens will ensure a more peaceful, empathetic, creative and inclusive future that – importantly and at long last – is for everybody.

**Peter Jenkinson** OBE is an independent cultural broker based in London UK and a co-director of Culture+Conflict (www.cultureandconflict.org.uk), an initiative started in 2011 that supports art and culture in conflict and post~conflict situations through programmes of research, projects, events, advocacy and network development. Culture+Conflict works with artists and creative practitioners and with local, national and international organisations. More information on Derry~Londonderry UK City of Culture 2013 can be found at www.cityofculture2013.com and at Peace One Day www.peaceoneday.org

# The power of the artist: the search for common ground

Whether during the Middle East conflict, the Chinese Cultural Revolution or the collapse of Yugoslavia, culture always has a special role to play. And each different location needs individual approaches when it comes to cultural initiatives and conflict resolution. Is there any common ground? How can music, literature, the fine arts and remembrance culture really exert an influence on society? We can learn from different experiences around the globe.

CLOSED

# The political in the poetical

There is rarely conflict between two vital cultures that are animated by creative individuals. And vice versa: a culture that is no longer vitalised by "humanity's desires" takes on the rigor mortis of an instrument that can be only too easily abused. Such 'cultureless' conflicts are in fact struggles for power and vested interests. But literature can combat this, because all classics are imbued with one essential meaning: the aesthetic resistance of the individual in adversity. *By Yang Lian*

In 2012, I was made a Fellow at the Institute for Advanced Study in Berlin, and immediately upon taking up the position in October I translated into Chinese a poem by the exiled Uyghur poet Exmetjan Osman (see box). I was inspired to do this by its beauty, but even more by its depth. Its title is a play on the famous Arabian tale of the "One Thousand And One Nights". The cruel Persian king has taken Scheherazade as his wife in order to kill her the following day, but the clever heroine of the story has thought of a way to delay her execution. She tells the king stories that are so exciting he has to keep her alive for another night in order to hear more. At the end of 1001 nights he has fallen in love with her. Life is born of creativity and wisdom defeats death.

This directs us to the deeper meaning of the poem. As a poet who shares with Osman the pain of exile, I can understand only too well how, when he describes a peaceful, sunny day sitting in a small park in a foreign country, he is on the one hand living in the here and now, "more or less enjoying the daytime" as he observes the shade cast by the tree, the grass and the faces passing by, while on the other hand he feels with total clarity how this here and now is opening up a crack. He makes out a shadowy Scheherazade among the passersby, and seeping through the sunlight are all the nights lived on a knife-edge. As the charming words fall from her lips, no-one knows more painfully than Scheherazade how widely the abyss of death is yawning beneath her, ready to swallow her up the instant the Persian king tires of her.

Densely poetic, the phrase "the meaning of the murder" encompasses "the nights passing endlessly" and his own "pondering". Reality instantly breaks in two, into light and darkness, the changing nature of which provides the complex structure of the poem. The day is filled with night; reality is permeated by an imaginary past. No matter where finds himself, an exiled poet can never escape the pain that lies deep within. But here too lies the meaning of exile: those "unhearable voices" and "unseeable lights" are "my life's dark mirrors" that "illuminate" "my fate" – and the fate of all humanity.

At the end the poem takes another unexpected twist. Just as Scheherazade wins the love of the Persian king with her wisdom, the poem too comes to an end on an affirmative note. But this affirmation is not simplistic nationalism or religious dogmatism; rather it is "humanity's desires". Even in the "nights passing endlessly", the cracks in the asphalt can be penetrated – by the sun or by the grass that "rings from our shining steps". Exmetjan Osman is a Muslim poet, but his poem goes beyond all external theological doctrines ("what even God and Satan can't divine") and achieves fulfilment in its belief in humankind. The power of this poem far exceeds our initial expectations. Because of the way the Uyghur independence movement has been brutally suppressed by the Chinese government, we find ourselves anticipating a nationalistic poem or a poem propagating Islam, or at least a poem that denounces persecution. But the poem does not conform to any of these collective forms of expression. Its poetic content is very familiar to me. By affirming "humanity's desires"

**The Nights Passing Endlessly Through Scherezade's Mouth**

In a public park
where I like to sit
in the thick shade cast by the branches of a tree
i was more or less enjoying the daytime
I was watching grass sprout from cracks in the asphalt
and the sun as it shone in the faces passing by
as I pondered the meaning of the murder taking place
in the nights passing endlessly through
Scheherazade's mouth
when a fortune-teller woman approached me
and asked permission
to illuminate my fate
from my life's dark mirrors

Staring in silence
at her sly eyes
I must have been lost in thought a long time
When I looked up
she had moved away from me, quickening her
steps like the nights passing endlessly through
Scheherazade's mouth
These steps
Like bells hung round the necks of people
strolling by
rang out in an unhearable voice
These steps
as if celebrating the sprouting of grass
from cracks in the asphalt
shone with an unseeable light

Right then
I wanted to know
if that fortune-teller woman could find out
what even God and Satan can't divine –
humanity's desires,
ever since we've strolled in public gardens
more or less enjoying the daytime
watching the sun from endless passings of night
as the grass rings from our shining steps

Exmetjan Osman

it is questioning Islamic culture and opening up resources so that this ancient tradition can step forward into the modern world. This kind of critical self-reflection is the real driving force of poetry. Collective mentalities and slogans of any kind are far removed from Exmetjan Osman, but I feel that he and I – a poet who began writing as a result of reflecting on Chinese cultural traditions – share a real closeness. In the fight for autonomy between Chinese and Uyghurs we find ourselves on opposing sides, and yet we are united by our affinity of mind and spirit.

It is no exaggeration to talk about our "affinity of mind and spirit", as we are bound together by similar experiences that have been both painful and enriching. When the Cultural Revolution ended in 1976, it left behind a wasteland: not only politically and economically but also in terms of culture and language. No other era in the history of Chinese civilisation has thrown thought into such a state of confusion, even disintegration. When viewed against the 'cultural self-reflection' that lasted throughout the 1980s, our writings found an outlet in one utterly simple question: "Who is to blame?" Who should take the responsibility for this deeply barbaric catastrophe that went beyond all normal common sense and understanding? If the overwhelming majority considered themselves to be victims, then where were the perpetrators? Was reality in fact even more absurd than the literature of the absurd with countless victims but no perpetrators? The only possible conclusion must be that every victim was also a perpetrator. We hid behind masks that we decorated with the fine-sounding rallying calls of 'Communism', a word we had imported from Europe. But deep within we were permeated with the legacy of a thousand years of authoritarian thinking. This legacy had particularly extinguished our ability to create an individual consciousness of ourselves on the path to reflection. So the 1980s became known, with good reason, as the 'age of self-reflection'. With our critical questions, we penetrated deep into many different layers – from external reality, history and culture, to language and the psyche. The political catastrophe that we had lived through had been fuelled by a thousand years of authoritarianism and an aberration of thought for which the Confucians had paved the way with their ideal of a 'Great Unity". The thought control of the traditional Chinese educated classes became part of the fixed structures of family and state.

## *Every victim was also a perpetrator*

In the 20th century, the Chinese then gave themselves over to fanatical dreams of modernisation; indeed they tried to destroy their own traditions. In doing this, they overlooked the fact that 'modernity' is not a commodity that can be imported but has to have its roots in a culture's creative self-transformation. Anyone who rejects clear self-knowledge is unable to modernise and will simply sink ever deeper, afflicted with blindness and ruled by the dark side of tradition. This is what happened in 20th century China. If only two words fall from our lips – "Long live ..." or "Down with ..." – then we are all followers of authoritarian thinking. And we have simply parroted increasingly convoluted foreign terms – in the past: "Communism", "Capitalism", "historical dialectic" and "dictatorship of the proletariat" and today: "post-Cold-War-era", "post-colonial", "post-revolutionary", and everything that is "post" just because they are fashionable slogans, without thinking about their meaning. But who can evade the responsibility of being a co-creator of 'Newspeak'? We can say everything without it having the slightest shred of meaning! The inevitable result is that words lose their connection to meaning until in the end we are left with nothing more than a linguistic cynicism that causes language to disintegrate. The emptiness of words promotes naked power and vested interests. All the prevailing hollow political phrases have already become an organic component of commercial globalisation.

But then we have to ask ourselves whether this sentence only describes the nightmare of the Cultural Revolution or whether even more than this it actually illuminates today's worldwide spiritual crisis: "Anyone who rejects critical self-reflection becomes a 'perpetrator'". The more I try here to discuss 'contemporary Chinese culture', the more I find myself faced with the questions: Does culture actually exist? And if so, what does it consist of? And what should we call it? I have to admit that of all the world's many foreign cultures, classic Chinese culture is perhaps for me the most foreign – precisely because I have no geographical distance from it. The continuity of Chinese script awakens in me (and even more so in the rest of the world) the illusion that there is a direct line connecting the old and the new China. But this is purely a chimera. In reality, 20th century China – and particularly 'contemporary' China since 1949 – is a monstrosity standing on the ruins of traditional Chinese culture.

The clash between its own culture and Western culture that China has experienced since the first Opium War (1839-1842) dealt it a major blow that toppled the Chinese from their position of excessive self-conceit and landed them in the middle of an inferiority complex. Unwilling to come to terms with their 'backwardness', they imported European culture en masse, and radicals even went as far as to utter the battle cry: "Down with the Confucian shop!" All the many foreign and borrowed words that I mentioned earlier have penetrated the Chinese language via Japanese, which has reproduced European words in Chinese script. These second-hand European words now make up more than half of the vocabulary of Chinese urban-dwellers. The aforementioned clash of word and meaning has therefore become characteristic

"The emptiness of words promotes naked power and vested interests. All the prevailing hollow political phrases have already become an organic component of commercial globalisation."

of so-called contemporary Chinese culture. When the word for 'people' (renmin) is made up of the general word for 'person' (ren) and the word for the lower rungs of society, the 'ordinary people' (min) as opposed to civil servants, then when should we speak of 'people' and when of 'ordinary people'? What is the difference? And who decides this? This semantic void can be filled by the country's rulers as they see fit. We only have to look at how much political persecution of the people has been carried out in the name of the people since the establishment of the 'People's Republic of China'.

This kind of baleful influence is not just a Chinese idiosyncrasy. Which Communist country during the Cold War did not subject its people to similar empty words? Is this now 'Chinese culture'? Or should we simply talk about 'Communist culture?' It is a mechanism used by the state to misappropriate all kinds of concepts – 'nation', 'fatherland', 'culture', 'history' and even 'international'? A ' future' embellished with evolutionary phrases and based on economic logic sparked an enthusiasm within more than two generations of Chinese people that was blind to the inherent contradiction in the slogans 'fatherland' and 'international'.

Millions of young people, like my father, came from well-off backgrounds, but nevertheless considered capital to be corrupt. They came together to form the Communist Party, fuelled by a desire to build a society of equals in China, and in this way – and with the best of intentions – they committed themselves to the destruction of their own class. Even today, many of them are still considered idealists of the highest order. But whatever respect we have for their idealism, we cannot close our eyes to the fact that the catastrophe of the Cultural Revolution had its roots in precisely these empty 'ideals'. Looking back, we are dismayed to see how a country whose civilisation dates back five thousand years could lose its humanity and common sense to such an extent that fundamental issues such as respect for private property have to be relearned and a system of law and morality has to be painstakingly rebuilt.

## *A shock awakening*

I call China a 'monstrosity' because, although we have to admit that it has undergone a transformation into modernity, this transformation has been fuelled solely by debased sources from West and East and has failed miserably. The modern Chinese culture that was dreamt of by our fathers' generation has not materialised.

In one respect, I am grateful to what I call the 'nightmarish inspiration' of the Cultural Revolution, because without it we would probably still be trapped in a state of stupefied indecision. This shock awakening was necessary to create a chain reaction of critical questioning. It is only now that we recognise the full extent of our affliction: we are unable to carry on the legacy of a 'Chinese cultural tradition' but we also cannot simply engraft Western culture.

When everything around us is 'alien', then we are left with no other choice but to become 'voluntary aliens'. By allowing our individual potential to blossom once again and by bringing together the different resources from past and present to create a new synthesis, we can create our very own contemporary Chinese culture. To take one of the leitmotivs of the 20th century discussion on modernisation – treating traditional Chinese culture as the 'substance' while modern Western science is the practical 'function' – then we should consider independent thinking as the 'substance' and turn the cultures of past and present, of China and elsewhere, into the 'function'. For as long as we fail to create an open tradition that is part of growth we will have no tradition at all and will just be left with a past that never wants to end.

When analysing Chinese culture in such detail, I do it knowing that this is not an idle undertaking but that without a deep knowledge of my own culture in all its complexities I can never hope to understand other cultures. The world may have shrunk in this era of economic globalisation, but this 'closeness' has nothing to do with greater understanding. On the contrary: conflicts are generally on the increase. Since the end of the Cold War, hatreds and tensions between peoples and religions all over the world have not diminished but instead have amplified. Since the end of the First Gulf War in 1991, the world has become even more mistrustful of the question of whether a war is 'just' or whether it is just profitable. And since the Arab Spring we would of course like to know *from* what we are 'liberating' ourselves but also *to* what?

Samuel P. Huntington tried to define the world after the Cold War as a "clash of civilisations", but this theory is highly simplistic and stereotypical. First of all, it does not explain the contrast between rich and poor that permeates every civilisation in a capitalist world; and secondly, by stressing the cultural conflicts, it conceals the benefits that groups from different cultures can gain from each other. A well-known Palestinian writer once said to me: "They've got nothing against mongrels, as long as they're the ones who have brought them up".

One of my most fond memories is the time I met the poet Adonis in Jordan in 2003. In the course of our conversation he spoke about how religion benefited the authoritarian system of Arab rule. In this respect, he stated quite clearly: "I am against Islam." I was deeply shocked by this statement because – compared to the ideological control that I personally experienced – the religious and spiritual control that Adonis was rejecting stretched way back,

> "This shock awakening was necessary to create a chain reaction of critical questioning. It is only now that we recognise the full extent of our affliction: we are unable to carry on the legacy of a 'Chinese cultural tradition' but we also cannot simply engraft Western culture."

long before the first signs of any kind of Arab Spring. And what affected me even more was how the power of self-reflection that Adonis brought to his own Arab culture was so similar to my own experiences with China.

And what is more: we are bound together by an 'affinity of mind and spirit'. A deep sense of trust has grown up between us based on personal integrity. We are the first of our Chinese and Arab literary contemporaries to engage in a direct exchange of ideas. We are both in the same situation: we are both fighting on a dual front. On the one hand, we are confronted by the complex difficulties of our present culture as it moves towards modernity (and also by the enrichment that results from this), while on the other hand we have to deal with the way the rest of the world (and particularly the West) generally simplifies us by reducing China to mere ideology and the Arab countries to nation and religion.

We are also similar in the way we react to these challenges. We both have an internal conviction that cultural change can be driven forward through independent thinking and creative individuality. Outwardly, we both reject all simplifications that lower the level of the discussion. And we both adopt an attitude of universal critical reflection when looking at the world. The lesson that we have learned from 20th century Chinese history is that every civilisation has to base its modern self-transformation on a creative assimilation of the positive elements of its legacy. Otherwise this civilisation will go the same way as that of the Chinese: instead of truly adapting Western ideas, we simply imported the Soviet model of 'Communism' – a Communism that no-one in the West wanted anything to do with.

Adonis is also wrestling with a similar problem. In Sufism, he has found a legacy that allows the fruitful modernisation of Islam from the inside out. When I took a first superficial look at the ideas of Sufism I was amazed to find that as far back as the 10th century, Mansur al-Hallaj proclaimed: "I am The Truth!" According to Sufism, man has the internal capacity to gain the highest level of spirituality and become one with Allah through love. This deeply anthropocentric version of Islam led to al-Hallaj's public dismemberment and execution. And yet he paved the way for an incisive and dazzling spiritual path – a path that has led through ten centuries to Adonis, and even to Exmetjan Osman! What is even more remarkable is the fact that the Muslim community in the Chinese province of Xinjiang (also known as East Turkestan) has developed and spread under the influence of Sufis that were seeking refuge from persecution. As followers of an anthropocentric Islamic tradition, they should not be seen as the enemy of all those Chinese that are also striving towards Chinese modernity. Quite the opposite: the two groups should be fellow-travellers who inspire and encourage each other in their journey.

Now it should finally be possible to resolve the issue of 'cultures and conflicts'. A culture that has the vital capacity for self-reflection will not only avoid the emergence of conflicts but will also resolve conflicts; it will not create enmity but understanding. When I say "the vital capacity for self-reflection", I mean the capacity for self-examination in every culture. This ability not only paves the way towards independent thinkers in other cultures, but also towards other cultures that have been labelled as opposing parties in a conflict.

## *'Cultureless' conflicts*

In the centre of every culture there is the goal of creating an individual consciousness – just as the meaning of democracy rests in the Enlightenment. A majority that closes itself off from independent thinking and personal choice is susceptible to being dominated by an extremist and authoritarian system. We can say that there is rarely conflict between two vital cultures that are animated by creative individuals. And vice versa: a culture that is no longer vitalised by "humanity's desires" takes on the rigor mortis of an instrument that can be only too easily abused by those in power. How many examples are there in the world of such 'cultureless' conflicts that are in fact struggles for power and vested interests?

The monstrosity that was China's official 'Communist culture' over the last fifty years and more was a common dictatorship suffered by over a billion Chinese – Han Chinese, Tibetans, Uyghurs and Mongols alike. Official rewriting of history meant that this 'China' was simply set alongside the empires of the many different preceding dynasties, and particularly with a China under the rule of the Manchurian Qing dynasty whose territories stretched into Tibet, Xinjiang, Mongolia and large swathes of land to the north of the Great Wall as far as the Stanovoy mountains.

"A culture that has the vital capacity for self-reflection will not only avoid the emergence of conflicts but will also resolve conflicts; it will not create enmity but understanding."

When making this equation, the historical complexities were deliberately ignored. The Qing rulers divided the people into different social classes – Manchurians, Mongols, Muslim Hui Chinese, Tibetans and Han Chinese – and joined together with other minorities to keep the Han Chinese under control, despite the fact that the latter outnumbered them one-hundred-fold but still found themselves reduced to the lowest social stratum. This is why the Dalai Lama, the head of Tibetan Buddhism, became the emperor's spiritual instructor at that time. And the Hui Muslims in Xinjiang enjoyed a social status that was much higher than that of the Han Chinese, despite their uprisings being put down by the Qing dynasty.

Early in the 20th century, with his rallying cry of "Drive out the Tartars, establish the Republic!" Sun Yat-Sen laid the ground for the way the concept of democracy was subsequently confused with the fight between the different ethnic groups. The inherent contradiction in this – the fact that Sun used ethnic prejudices for the purposes of pure pragmatism while propagating a democracy based on overall human rights – cast a dark shadow over a whole century of Chinese history and created confusion in the minds of the rest of the world. The conflict between the Chinese people and their authoritarian rulers was falsely considered to be a conflict between different ethnic groups. This erroneous belief contributed in no small way to a lack of serious historical thinking and, worse still, allowed the rulers to give the appearance of legitimacy to their suppression of supposed 'ethic conflicts'.

Similarly, the current dire situation in the Middle East cannot be blamed on 'cultural conflict' between Palestinians and Israelis but is the historical product of egoistic and irresponsible Western colonialists.

Have Western intellectuals looked at this issue in sufficient depth? I mean, really looked at it, rather than just staying quiet out of politeness (or self-preservation?). Politeness has to be put to one side when thinking. For example, the slave trade has been exhaustively studied, but what about the First Opium War, one of the dirtiest chapters in human history? This war marked the beginning of modern Chinese history with all its twists. I once asked a well-known British historian the question: "Is there a detailed monograph on the Opium Wars?" For a moment, the man simply looked blank. This is another example of the lack of critical self-reflection within a culture. It is not only the Arab lands and China that need to develop this capacity for exhaustive self-reflection, but also to a lesser extent Europe and the USA. In today's era of globalisation, political correctness and profit are the only hard currency. They have long ago eroded the differences between cultures and united humankind in egotism and cynicism. We are now faced with a single conflict: look, here's the profit – do you want to grab it with both hands or run away from it? But where can you run to? Faced with this ever-present reality, the individual has never been more helpless.

## *A world full of chanted slogans*

But perhaps I have missed the point here? Once a conflict has reached this stage, what use is a poem? Can it resolve anything or change anything? Let's be honest – a Chinese poet who translates a poem by an Uygur poet is not going to change anything in reality. Exmetjan Osman is still living in exile. The world is still full of chanted slogans. The bright desert of commerce still bears witness to the spiritual crisis of humankind. In the end there remains an everlasting desolation that all the world's poets know only too well, regardless of the bounds of time and language. No true poet can escape it.

And yet, wonderful things do happen. However strongly a supposed conflict is raging, we only need the poets of different ethnic groups to come together for a rea-

"The current dire situation in the Middle East cannot be blamed on 'cultural conflict' between Palestinians and Israelis but is the historical product of egoistic and irresponsible Western colonialists."

ding – Han Chinese and Uyghurs, Iraqis and Americans, Turks and Kurds, Russians and Chechens, Poles and Lithuanians, and yes, even Israelis and Palestinians – and we soon see that they are all exactly the same in the way they lay bare their perceptions of existence, strive for deep poetic understanding and their efforts to push themselves to the furthest limits of their language. This bond creates a common 'grammar' that allows a poem to go deeper than mere language, transcending the battlefield and speaking from one heart to another, and in doing so we recognise the classics of other cultures as our own. For all classics are imbued with one essential meaning: the aesthetic resistance of the individual in adversity. The "Heavenly Questions" (Tianwen) posed 2,300 years ago by Qu Yuan have established this poet from the ancient state of Chu as a 'questioner'. He was later to drown in a river while in exile. Similar fates were suffered by Ovid, the creator of "Metamorphoses", who also died in exile; by the Tang dynasty poet Du Fu, who sublimated the pain caused by his unsettled migratory life far from royal courts by transforming it into incomparable verse; and by many others, including Dante, Celan, Mandelstam and Tsvetaeva. For these poets, the earth was never a paradise. Anyone who seeks after meaning inevitably lives in exile.

This is what is revealed to me by "the nights passing endlessly" in Exmetjan Osman's poem. "Endlessly", because we cannot believe in any promise of some illusory 'progress'. Every poem (indeed, every line) ends with an 'impossible', but the poet begins unremittingly with the impossible and makes himself the 'poetical other'. Here, the word 'poetical' takes to an extreme the intellectual content and dynamic that is naturally inherent in the concept of 'poetry'. I don't write my poems in normal 'Chinese', (because such a thing doesn't exist), but rather in my own 'Yanglish', and in the same way I have discovered Exmetjan Osman's 'Osmanisch' in his poem "The nights passing endlessly through Scheherazade's mouth". This poem has not disappointed me. It is so calm and yet so powerful in the way it moves from light to night to light again. Its brilliance illuminates its Uyghur author and also enlightens me. And I am convinced that any Chinese person who reads it will be deeply moved. Poetry lends depth and clarity to the vision of a lyrical self and also affects its attitude towards nations, states, languages and religion. This is why I give my unconditional support to Osman's fight to save the Uyghur language and culture, just as I work whole-heartedly to preserve the purity of that of the Chinese. At the same time, I am committed to the transformation of Chinese civilisation as it modernises, so I am inevitably opposed to the absolute rule of a Communist Party that denies minorities their rights.

One of the things I like the most is when poets sit together side-by-side and translate each other's work, conveying it image by image and line by line into another language. Aided by their fulgurous poetic understanding, they can penetrate deeply into the other's work, in such moments feeling a sense of inner connection and the absence of all conflict. In 2006, also in Berlin, I had an opportunity to talk to the South African poet Breyten Breytenbach, who has first-hand experience of the suffering caused by conflict. We discussed the meaning of the phrase "poetry is our only mother tongue". This phrase succinctly sums up the beauty of poetic 'boundary-crossing'. In 2012, at the annual conference of PEN International in Gyeongju, South Korea, we – Chinese, Uyghur and Polish poets – all agreed that we should no longer wait for 'political solutions' that rely on obscure negotiations, but instead we ourselves should roll up our sleeves and get involved. With every poem that we write, we resolve conflicts and cast a soft, shimmering net of understanding. This is the attitude that we as poets take towards the challenges of today. By its very nature, the 'poetical' is always political.

Compared to the tumult of 'conflicts', poetry speaks with a quiet voice, and yet its 'No' comes across loud and clear. In this way, like Exmetjan Osman's light of wisdom, it can break through the darkness of the "nights passing endlessly".

**Yang Lian** is a Chinese poet who is currently a Fellow at the Institute of Advanced Study in Berlin. In 2012 he won the renowned International Nonino Prize for literature. The son of diplomats, he was born in Switzerland in 1995 and grew up in Beijing. In 1979 he joined a group of poets who published the "Jintian" magazine. At the time of the Tiananmen Square massacre he was in New Zealand and took part in the protests against the actions of the Chinese government. Shortly afterwards his works were blacklisted in China and his Chinese citizenship was revoked.

# Reconciliation is not just going through the motions

Since the war in Bosnia ended in 1995 there has been much talk of reconciliation. A great deal of money has been spent on garnering the opinions of international experts, almost as if reconciliation were a branch of rocket science, rather than being about "settlement, understanding, compromise" between neighbours, as defined by the dictionary. But what does it really come down to? *By Slavenka Drakulic*

There was a flurry of media attention when Serbian president Boris Tadic visited Vukovar in October 2010, where he was met by the Croatian president Ivo Josipovic. Tadic visited the mass grave near Vukovar and asked for forgiveness for the massacre carried out by the Yugoslav National Army and Serbian paramilitaries in the autumn of 1991. It was the first time that a Serbian president had expressed his profound regret for this crime.

Josipovic , who in the first year of his presidency had done more than any of his predecessors to promote reconciliation, then visited the village of Paulin Dvor, where Croatian paramilitaries had killed eighteen Serbian civilians and one Hungarian in December 1991.

These were impressive gestures by the two heads of state, designed to bring the vicious cycle of war to a symbolic close. A few days later, the Bosnian tripartite presidency also joined in by calling for reconciliation. Bakir Izetbegovic, the newest member of the presidency, said he apologised "for every innocent person killed by the army of Bosnia and Herzegovina".

While this frenzy of reconciliation activities attracted a large share of praise from the international community and the people of the region, many voices were also raised in criticism. Weren't all these well-meaning gestures and expressions of remorse simply political theatre for the benefit of the world community? Where were the lists of prisoners of war who had disappeared? When would stolen cultural property be returned to Croatia? When would refugees return to Krajina?

It has always been difficult to believe politicians in the Balkans, even when they seem to be acting with the best of intentions. But we must start to believe them if we are to progress down the path of reconciliation. We need to start taking their words seriously and assume that their gestures indicate a serious intention to change perceptions and attitudes towards each other's countries. The political willingness to bring about reconciliation demonstrated by Tadic and Josipovic was as clear as that of former Croatian president Stjepan Mesic when he officially apologised in Belgrade in 2003. In March 2010, the Serbian Parliament also passed a "Declaration on Srebrenica". Although it stopped short of using the word genocide, it clearly acknowledged the responsibility of the Serbian army for the massacre of 8,000 Bosniaks in July 1995.

## *Capitalism 1, patriotism 0*

Ever since the war in Bosnia ended in 1995, there has been much talk of reconciliation – first and foremost from abroad. A great deal of money has been spent on garnering the opinions of international experts, almost as if reconciliation were a branch of rocket science, rather than being about "settlement, understanding, compromise" between neighbours, as defined by the dictionary. After endless rounds of meetings, the experts came to the conclusion that what was needed was for people to work together. Well I never. They came up with a whole series of recommendations on how this might be achieved – as if the people of Croatia, Serbia, Bosnia and Kosovo need to be told. They only have to look at the region's criminal scene to see that there is already a certain amount of bottom-up collaboration going on. Undeterred, people are calmly carrying on with the kind of criminal activities that had been normal before the war, from the smuggling and trading of fuel, weapons, people and tobacco to contract killings. Businessmen at all levels are also working together, sometimes overtly, sometimes behind the scenes. The Slovenes were the first to start exporting their products to Serbia: capitalism 1, patriotism 0.

When Tim Judah, a journalist for The Economist who knows the region very well, published an article about the "Yugosphere" in 2009, he unleashed a huge storm of protest, especially in Croatia. He wrote about the unbroken collaboration and cooperation going on at all levels, which shows that the former Yugoslavia is still effectively functioning as a single entity, despite the fact that nationalist ideology condemns such collaboration as "anti-patriotic". "Times are hard", writes Judah, and it is natural that people try to exploit the advantages of a common language and the fact that consumers are used to having certain products.

Judah tells how in the last few months alone numerous new initiatives have been announced: the founding of a railway company jointly owned by Slovenia, Croatia and Serbia; a meeting between the national lottery companies of Macedonia, Montenegro, Slovenia, Kosovo, Serbia, Bosnia and Herzegovina and Croatia, with a view to agreeing a merger; the signing of an agreement on the extradition of criminals between Croatia and Serbia and between Bosnia and Croatia; and an agreement on military cooperation between Serbia and Croatia, to name but a few.

It was clear from the criticisms levelled at the article that it was not so much the examples of collaboration that people found offensive, as the use of the word "Yugosphere". Yet not even the most hard-line Croatian nationalists (who, it should be noted, also condemned Slovenia for blocking Croatia's entry to the EU) could deter Croatian businessman Emil Tedeschi from expanding his market into Slovenia, Bosnia, Montenegro, Macedonia and Serbia. Tedeschi prefers the term South Eastern Europe, while others prefer Western Balkans – anything, so long as it doesn't include the prefix 'Yugo'. Nothing illustrates more clearly how nationalist sentiments and values withstand the test of time, regardless of how collaboration works in reality.

The main difference between reconciliation efforts over the past fifteen years and today is that for a long time there was no real political will behind the endeavours. The new impulse has come from a new generation of politicians who are much more committed than their predecessors to seeing their countries join the EU. Long considered a rogue nation, Serbia has now stepped up and signed a number of important agreements. The country has become a member of the RCC (Regional Cooperation Council, formerly the Stability Pact) and signed up to the CEFTA (Central European Free Trade Agreement) and the PFP (Partnership for Peace), a military cooperation programme established in 1994 between NATO and, to date, 23 European and Asian countries.

"Undeterred, people are calmly carrying on with the kind of criminal activities that had been normal before the war, from the smuggling and trading of fuel, weapons, people and tobacco to contract killings."

This should serve to strengthen Serbia's negotiating position on the issue of abolishing the need for visas to enter the EU and help to forge closer ties to the EU itself. While the EU's attitude towards Serbia joining the Union can hardly be termed enthusiastic, it is recognised in Brussels that stability in the region is inextricably bound up with each country's hopes of joining the EU one day, irrespective of when that might actually be.

When business people continue to collaborate, Croatian publishers take part in book fairs in Belgrade, national football teams play each other and ordinary people visit their relatives across the border without being suspected of treason, is there even a need for an official policy of reconciliation? Or should it be left to spontaneous, bottom-up initiatives, as a few prominent commentators have suggested?

If we look at the Croatian press, we still find someone like Tim Judah being accused of "Yugo-nostalgia", or a Croat businessman being called a traitor because he sold his factory to a Serb. There is still opposition to the idea of a hotel or shipyard being bought with Serbian capi-

DISTRICT L.
Nº9
SHANKILL

tal. According to surveys, the majority of people in Serbia, Croatia and Bosnia are far from being reconciled with the idea that their neighbours are no longer their enemies. Is it not reasonable to believe that, were citizens left to their own devices, reconciliation would take at least a few more generations?

## *No justice without truth*

Neither war nor peace simply happen spontaneously. Wars are the result of political will, primed by inflammatory rhetoric that creates a concept of the 'enemy' and justifies aggression. The same goes for peace and reconciliation processes. They need to be initiated and conducted from the top, spreading values downwards that are the exact opposite of those promoted in war, namely tolerance and collaboration. If reconciliation between France and Germany, for example, had been left to the ordinary man in the street, a united Europe would still be a hundred years off.

The precondition for reconciliation, and the fundamental principle that underlies it, is justice. But there can be no justice without truth. Without a legal system for trying war criminals – in which the truth about crimes committed in recent wars is revealed – every attempt at reconciliation is bound to fail. In Croatia, the main obstacle to reconciliation is the absurd conviction, cultivated and nurtured over nearly two decades, that the Croatian army cannot be guilty of war crimes because it was acting in defence of the nation, with the result that war criminals are regarded as war heroes. For this reason, the International Criminal Court in The Hague is seen as an enemy institution – and not as a vehicle for uncovering the truth.

If a culture of denial existed at both public and political level in Serbia before the Declaration on Srebrenica was issued, then Reconciliation in Bosnia and Herzegovina has also made much more difficult by its special status as a divided country. Not just divided administratively, but psychologically and emotionally: victims and perpetrators live together in the same states, the same towns, maybe even in the same village on the same street.

Promoting different values means constructing a different psychological framework. It is no longer necessary to persuade citizens to collaborate across state borders: they are doing that already. What is needed now is to send out the message that collaboration – visiting, trading, working together, breaking down negative perceptions of each other – is not only politically correct but also politically desirable. It should be possible for a Croatian writer to publish a book in Serbia, or for a Croatian musician to put on a concert in Serbia, without being pilloried in the media, as was the case until very recently.

But how does a government get such a message across? Perhaps indirectly, such as by supporting common initiatives, from regional agreements like the Regional Cooperation Council or the Partnership for Peace, to smaller-scale initiatives such as singing competitions or the much-trumpeted school exchanges. Not surprisingly, the mass media has an important role to play. It is from the mass media that values seep into everyday life, not the other way round. If the government were to start systematically promoting anti-nationalist values, public TV channels would probably follow suit. Not necessarily because they felt that they had to, but it is not unreasonable to suppose that broadcasters would soon recognise that reconciliation was the order of the day rather than nationalism and hate. In any case, private TV channels are less prone to spreading nationalist propaganda and always concerned about their ratings, so they would be very likely to jump on this particular trend.

Sending out positive signals to the neighbours is a useful, but short-term strategy. A new government, a new dominant political will, can still quickly swing public opinion back towards nationalism again – which is precisely what happened in the 1990s. In order to really establish different values, we need a long-term approach, with a primary focus on teaching an understanding of history. If the process begins by trying war criminals, it needs to continue with historical research and the publication of history books and textbooks. Teaching an understanding of history needs to be based on fact, not myth and ideology.

"If reconciliation between France and Germany, for example, had been left to the ordinary man in the street, a united Europe would still be a hundred years off."

## *Living with contradictions*

A glance at today's history books provides all manner of contradictory information. For example, 65 years after the end of the WWII, the Croats are still struggling to come to terms with the fact that the only time in history when Croatia was ever independent was when it also happened to be a fascist puppet state, the Independent State of Croatia (NDH). Indeed, the first president of the newly established state of Croatia, Franjo Tudjman, never tired of insisting that the new Croatia was built on the foundations of the old one. The Croatian constitution, however, says just the opposite, that the new state is founded on anti-fascism – showing that Croatian society is still divided over its past.

In all post-Yugoslavian societies, people are used to living with such contradictions. During communism, their memory was usually at odds with history. It is easy to disseminate propaganda in a country that is ruled by communist ideology, folklore and myth, and where there is a dearth of concrete historical facts. After 1945, it was claimed that 700,000 civilians had perished in the Jasenovac concentration camp during the NDH era, while some four decades later a more realistic 60,000 became the accepted figure.

The precise number of NDH soldiers and civilians executed in Bleiburg just after the war ended is still a matter of dispute, but it runs to the tens of thousands. It was hard for people to imagine that Tito's glorious army could have committed war crimes. Generations of Yugoslavians grew up with the contradiction of not being able to question the 'truths' contained in school textbooks, while being told very different stories at home. It was easier not to challenge the dogma.

## *Too little history, too much memory*

So far, there has been too little history and too much memory: this is one reason why people were so quick to take up arms in the 1990s. History books and textbooks are as much a part of the problem as they are a part of the solution. Historians should stop behaving as slaves to the current ideology and start presenting facts.

But education is a long drawn-out process. Any education process aimed at bringing about some form of reconciliation has to be about much more than simply correcting textbooks. To bring about reconciliation, society needs a consensus. To articulate the truth, there needs to be a public forum. Any responsible society interested in reconciliation should be able to do this, as was the case in Germany. Culture can serve as the forum for this debate.

The question is: how can arts and culture foster reconciliation, while mainstream culture and its institutions – for example the Serbian and Croatian Academies of Science – promote nationalism? Like mass media, culture serves as a vehicle for nationalist propaganda before and during wars. It would be wrong to talk of the reconciliatory role of culture and arts as if they were independent of political will.

Our expectations of culture generally tend to be too high: we hope that culture will help us create a better, more peaceful and more just society. Underlying this idea of the potential role of culture in the process of reconciliation is a belief that artists and intellectuals, and educated people in general, are somehow beings of a higher moral order. Because they are educated, they should by definition know better than the rest of society. However, this is not necessarily the case.

It has been proven time and time again throughout history that culture is ideally suited to being used for propaganda purposes, especially in totalitarian regimes. Why? Because the morals of artists and cultural bureaucrats are in fact no different to those of anybody else. Moreover, in the former Yugoslavia (but also elsewhere), there was a tradition of cultural servility to the regime – indeed there was barely any other type of culture worth the name. Then again, this can be understood as a kind of survival strategy, where self-preservation forced artists and intellec-

"It has been proven time and time again throughout history that culture is ideally suited to being used for propaganda purposes, especially in totalitarian regimes."

tuals to effectively become employees of the state. So it is no surprise that it was precisely this group of people who were disseminating nationalism in the 1980s. Writers, academics, journalists, members of cultural institutions – educated people became cogs in the nationalist propaganda machines. Their task was to create a sense of 'others' within society in order to persuade people to commit to the idea of armed conflict, to war. They did their job very well.

An emblematic image from 1993: Radovan Karadzic – poet, psychiatrist and the president of Republika Srpska – standing in the hills above Sarajevo. Alongside him stands the Russian poet Edward Limonov, shooting a machinegun in the direction of the city.

When talking about the role of culture in the reconciliation process, we should not ignore its capacity to produce ideology and propaganda, to manipulate people, to prepare for and justify mass murder. However, the opposite is also true – if culture can be turned into a nationalist propaganda machine, then, in a democracy that allows the free circulation of ideas, it can also be a key element in the reconciliation process. But this can only happen if projects supported by the state are free from political abuse. Compared to other activities, such as arms procurement, culture can achieve a great deal with relatively little cost. Only a fraction of a country's budget is normally allocated to culture. It might just be worth investing a little more.

## *A process of reconciliation*

To a greater or lesser extent, a process of reconciliation is already underway and has been for some time. It is almost two decades since the wars, and a whole new generation has grown up. But if this new generation is to be the one that should consolidate the progress of reconciliation, then the news is not good. In a recent opinion poll among high school students between 17 and 18, only 27% think that the NDH was a fascist state, while more than 40% think that Croats in Croatia should have more rights than citizens belonging to national minorities. 40% are against prosecuting Croat soldiers for war crimes and every second one of them (49 percent) is against Croatia joining the EU. Even if this opinion poll is not representative of all Croatian youth, it serves to remind us that nationalist values are still highly influential. This mini-snapshot of the new generation offers little in the way of hope to a government that wants to demonstrate its political will. However, it should also motivate us to act quickly and decisively if we truly want to achieve lasting reconciliation before the end of this century.

Ultimately, one cannot but notice a kind of paradox at work within the territory of the former Yugoslavia. First came independence and then the destruction of Yugoslavia in a series of bloody wars. Tens of thousands of lives were lost. A conservative estimate for Bosnia alone suggests that some 100,000 people died.

Hundreds of thousands of people were displaced or resettled, not to mention all those who were maimed and orphaned. Between 30,000 and 50,000 women, mostly Bosniaks, were raped. Now, a mere decade since the tragedy, all the newly established independent states want to join the EU and live in union with neighbours who, historically speaking, they were killing only yesterday.

Why fight for independence? Why go to war? Was it a civil war? Was there only one aggressor? How many victims were there on each side? It is hard to find answers to these kinds of questions, and convincing the public to accept them is even harder. But in order to succeed, reconciliation programmes must deal with these questions at all levels, and this will require the necessary political will. Reconciliation does not come easily and it takes time, but it might take less time and be easier if there is real political will, starting with governments, that leads to a top-down process of reconciliation. At least, one would like to imagine that such an approach is worth trying, given the failure of the last 15 years of laissez-faire. The latest news is that the Serbian President Boris Tadic has visited Croatia for the second time in a month – this time accompanied by more than 70 Serbian businessmen.

**Slavenka Drakulić** is one of the best-known Croatian writers and journalists. Her novels and non-fiction books have been translated into many different languages. She writes for various publications, including the New York Times Magazine, the Süddeutsche Zeitung and La Stampa. She lives in Vienna and Istria.

# Europe's problem zone

Today it is still difficult to come to terms with the fact that, of all things, it was representatives of culture, literature, journalism, theatre and film who were the first to set off down the nationalistic route. One of the first victims of Serbian nationalism was the tiny province of Kosovo.

*By Beqë Cufaj*

On 30th January 2012, an Albanian man doused himself with petrol and set himself on fire outside a shopping centre in the Kosovan city of Prizren. Fortunately an off-duty policeman was among the many passers-by who jumped in and managed to save his life. This incident is worth mentioning because in another January – on 14th January 1968, to be precise – the Czech student Jan Palach set himself on fire in Wenceslas Square in Prague as a protest against the Soviet invasion, triggering protests throughout the whole communist bloc. The 'Prague Spring' remains one of the most memorable events of recent history. And just over a year ago, on 4th January 2011, the self-immolation of Tunisian street vendor Mohamed Bouazizi in the town of Sidi Bouzid set in motion the series of popular revolts that were to change the face of North Africa and that are now referred to as the 'Arab Spring'.

Of course it would be naïve to set the failed self-immolation attempt of the citizen of Prizren alongside such historical events. It is very unlikely that a successful attempt would have set off mass protests in Prizren, Pristina and other towns and villages across Kosovo and triggered an 'Albanian Spring' that would affect the entire Balkan region. Or at least this is how the newspapers reported the event.

## *A place in the European family of nations*

On 17th February of this year Europe's youngest nation, the Republic of Kosovo, celebrated the fourth anniversary of its independence. Before this, the Albanians and particularly the Kosovar Albanians – who, to put it somewhat melodramatically, lived in a state of subjugation – were fighting for their freedom and for a chance to become 'normal' members of the European family. In this respect they were little different from their neighbours.

However, the striking difference is the long time they had to wait before their efforts finally bore fruit. The reasons for this go way back in history and can be found in the random restructuring of the political landscape of Southeast Europe early in the last century after the collapse of the region's two dominant powers, the Ottoman and Austro-Hungarian empires. The Balkans were left a minefield that decades later was to result in massive bloodshed, with the main victims being the Kosovar Albanians, who found themselves plunged into a serious conflict with the Serbs.

Although Albanian political and cultural circles are reluctant to admit it, during their centuries of subjection to the Ottoman Empire and to a certain extent during their colonisation by Serbia over the last eighty years of the last century, the Albanians were prepared to adapt themselves to these regimes. Their survival probably hinged on the fact that they accepted the Islamic faith and major portions of the mythology, traditions, language and culture of their Ottoman and Slavic rulers. However, the more ethnically self-contained Albanians living in the craggy and remote northern highlands clung on to their original language, culture and firmly-rooted patriarchal tribal society and formed a strong nucleus for potential future resistance.

After World War I, Albania set out on its erratic path towards becoming an independent state, facing many setbacks along the way. In the meantime, the Albanians who had been left in Kosovo, which had been separated by the Great Powers at the London Conference of Ambassadors, were largely ignored by the rest of Europe and were left to try to hold out against the Slavic oppression of the Serbian-Croatian-Slovenian monarchy. As the most underdeveloped region of the southern Slavic state structure, and faced with the constant threat of reprisals, it was difficult for Kosovo to make any progress. The burning of countless Albanian villages in Kosovo during the 1920s and 1930s was viewed as a legitimate act of state force. This explains the sad fact that many Kosovar Albanians welcomed the conquering of the Balkans by troops from Nazi Germany as they hoped it would lead to the creation of a national entity – an area that to this day is generally referred to by the somewhat alarming name of Greater Albania.

A brutal revenge was taken. The communist victory after the Nazi troops were driven out of the Balkans led to the Yugoslav monarchy being replaced by a socialist state headed by Josip Broz Tito. Kosovo was awarded the status of an autonomous socialist province within the Republic of Serbia and the Yugoslav Federation.

During the first twenty years of the Tito regime, Kosovo was very clearly the poorest region in this state of 20 million people and was faced with difficulties on every front. This is demonstrated by the fact that in 1945 around 90 percent of Ko-

"The more ethnically self-contained Albanians living in the craggy and remote northern highlands clung on to their original language, culture and firmly-rooted patriarchal tribal society and formed a strong nucleus for potential future resistance."

sovar Albanians were illiterate. Enormous challenges and social dramas played themselves out after the dream of unification with Albania (now also under communist rule) was shattered. In the 1950s, pockets of Albanian protest in certain areas were easily suppressed by the Yugoslav police and army.

Kosovo's Albanians gradually began to adjust to the need to find some sort of accommodation with the Tito regime without necessarily considering themselves to be a normal part of the state structure.

## *School integration*

Under Tito, Belgrade also began to treat the Albanians somewhat differently to under the pre-war monarchy. Attempts to integrate Albanians into schools had some success. Children were allowed to learn in their native language and then go on to higher education in Belgrade, Sarajevo, Zagreb, Ljubljana or Skopje. Back in Pristina, they began working as doctors, journalists, writers and film directors, or they entered politics.

The first Albanian-language newspaper appeared as early as 1945. Ideologically, it was strongly in favour of the direction being taken by the Communist Party of Yugoslavia. The first Albanian literary magazine "Jeta e Re" ("New Life") followed on its heels in 1949. The first Albanian-language university was established in Pristina on 18th November 1969, at the time of the huge wave of student protests that swept across Europe. However the political reprisals of this time stand in stark contrast to the progress made in the areas of education and culture. These included the mass expulsion of Albanian Muslims to Turkey and the arrest and imprisonment of young Albanian intellectuals on the orders of the head of the notorious Yugoslav security service known as the OZNA or UDBA, the Serb Aleksandar Ranković, one of Marshal Tito's closest colleagues. This period of more than 20 years highlighted two issues. Firstly, despite the fact that the Serbs considered themselves to be in the vanguard of socialist equality, this was largely ignored when it came to the Albanians. The Albanians for their part felt justified in their belief that the Serbs were an occupying and colonising force, irrespective of their political hue. To date it is still not clear whether Kosovo and the oppression of the Albanian people was the reason why Tito distanced himself from Ranković.

But in any case there is no denying the fact that towards the end of the 1960s and particularly in the 1970s Kosovo gained greater autonomy within the Yugoslav Federation. Not only did the Albanians have their own newspapers, TV stations, universities, journalists and writers, film directors and theatre, but they also had political representation in the Federation through the regime, the ruling ideology and Albanian politicians loyal to Marshal Tito. This led to a first cautious opening of the border between Kosovo and Albania. Students and academics, artists and cultural actors from both countries came together; films and books were shared; and Kosovo's Albanian writers could finally proudly declare that their work was also being published in the "Motherland".

The Enver Hoxha regime in Tirana also involved Kosovar academics in the process of standardising the Albanian language. This cautious rapprochement between two countries that after the Second World War had first embraced each other and then fallen out was maintained until the death of Josip Broz Tito on 4th May 1980.

The immediate aftermath ushered in a new chapter in relations between the Slavic peoples of the Yugoslav state and the Kosovar Albanians. Despite being designated a minority, in terms of their numbers the Albanians of Kosovo, Macedonia, Montenegro and Southern Serbia all together formed the third-largest population group after the Serbs and Croats, outnumbering the Slovenians, Montenegrins, Bosnian Muslims and Macedonians. The reasons for the mass protests of Albanian students in Pristina in March 1981 have still not been completely explained, but the slogan that they chanted as they marched through the streets remains etched in people's memories: "Kosovo – Republic!"

The result was a tightening of Belgrade's policy towards Pristina and the Albanians. The Albanian politicians who were part of the nomenklatura left behind by Tito made some efforts to balance the interests of the communist federation and the demands of the Kosovar Albanians. Albania's leaders were shaken by the sickness and eventual death of Enver Hoxhas, leading them to close the border and refuse to support those who sought to disrupt Kosovo's ossified status quo. This suited the Yugoslav communists, who believed the increased openness with Albania was the main reason for the unrest. Small Marxist-Leninist cells and leftist groups had emerged in Pristina and amongst the Kosovar Albanian diaspora in Germany, Switzerland and Austria who were opposed to the Yugoslav regime and disseminated the idea of uniting all Albanian areas of the Balkans. The prominent Albanian journalist and author Jusuf Gërvalla, who had fled to Germany in 1979, was shot to death in the small southern German town of Untergruppenbach on 17th January 1982, along with his brother Bardhosh and a co-worker, Kadri Zeka. This murder has never been officially explained, but there was and is no doubt that it can be attributed to the Yugoslav secret service, who had already assassinated a whole series of Croatian political émigrés. Gërvalla's murder made it clear to Pristina that there was no going back. The freedoms enjoyed under the 'socialist autonomy' before 1981 gave way to a climate of tension and squabbling amongst the Albanians, egged on by Belgrade. Everything was policed, including the press, art, theatre, film and, of course, literature.

In a state where Tito's absence was felt more and more with every day that passed, the Serbs and Croats also increasingly began to express their political disaffection. Now the conflict had shifted, so no-one any longer spared a thought for the Kosovar Albanians, who in the 1970s and 1980s had made appreciable progress in their infrastructure, economy and culture and who had been gradually turning away from their patriarchal and extended family structures. And now the nationalism of the Serbs – the largest and most powerful section of the Yugoslav population – had descended from the realms of mythology and religion to take root in the politics of Belgrade. Today it is still difficult to come to terms with the fact that, of all things, it was representatives of culture, literature, journalism, theatre and film who were the first to set off down the nationalistic route. It was they who lamented the role of Serbs as supposed victims during the Second World War and particularly during the communist rule under Tito, who they variously denounced as being Croatian or Slovenian.

### *Memorandum of the Serbian Academy of Sciences and Arts*

The fact that the political elites in Yugoslavia set off down the path to hate-filled nationalism, chauvinism and war at a time when the foundations of the red empire were rocking and starting to collapse in Eastern Europe can be attributed to this malign ideology. And of course Kosovo was once again the first to suffer.

The notorious Memorandum of the Serbian Academy of Sciences and Arts called for compensation and reparation for the victimisation suffered by the Serbs, along with the establishment of Serbian rule over people's lives, religion and souls in every corner of the earth that held a single Serbian grave. In the wake of this Memorandum a former communist apparatchik by the name of Slobodan Milošević appeared on the scene. After ordering the murder of his political mentor Ivan Stambolić, he quickly ascended to Belgrade's political throne and turned himself into one of the most terrible dictators seen in Europe since the Second World War.

Kosovo's autonomy was quickly and firmly swept aside, accompanied by Albanian protests and the murder, torture and imprisonment of hundreds of young people. Milošević deployed the whole political and military apparatus that he had inherited from Tito to push forward a bloody campaign that today is viewed as all the more intolerable because of its blatant absurdity.

The collapse of talks aimed at finding a peaceful disbanding of the former Yugoslavia led to war and bloodshed that particularly affected the civilian population. The break-up began in Slovenia and Croatia, but it was the particular brutality of the events in Bosnia and Herzegovina that brought the dawning realisation that peace would never be established without milita-

"The political reprisals of this time stand in stark contrast to the progress made in the areas of education and culture. These included the mass expulsion of Albanian Muslims to Turkey and the arrest and imprisonment of young Albanian intellectuals."

ry intervention on the part of NATO. The pictures of refugee convoys and Sarajevo in ruins, along with words such as 'mass graves', 'Vukovar' and 'Srebrenica', sparked public support for military operations to be undertaken against Milošević's regular and irregular troops.

## *Dr. Rugova's pacifist movement*

During this period, the Kosovar Albanians were setting up parallel institutions under the leadership of the pacifist writer and scholar Ibrahim Rugova, with a view to countering Serbian attempts at forcible assimilation. In hindsight there were two positive aspects of this 'state within a state': its clandestine maintenance of an Albanian-language educational system and the way it raised international public awareness of the oppression of Albanians by the Milošević regime. At the end of the 1990s, a whole nation within Europe was being ruled and oppressed by a (Serbian) minority that made up barely 10 percent of the total population, supported in classic fashion by the police and military.

After 1989, the Kosovar Albanians were to all intents and purposes excluded from the administration, education system, political structures, media, economy, health system and cultural production of the state that ruled them and hence were forced to rely on parallel institutions or improvisation. Thousands of young men and women fled the country to seek refuge in Germany, Switzerland, Austria and the USA. It was largely the financial contributions of this new diaspora that ensured the 'parallel state' could function in an adequate fashion. The 'government' and political parties had sufficient funds to send representatives abroad in order to draw the problems of Kosovo to the attention of international public opinion.

Dr. Rugova and his cohorts could certainly consider themselves to be true statesmen. The fact that they had to show their Serbian passports during their travels and on their return home did not detract from their sense of their own importance. After all, Kosovo's parliament had declared a republic in 1991, though this remained unrecognised except by Albania, which at the time was desperately trying to keep its head above the stormy waters of democracy. Europe had never before been home to this kind of virtual state.

The USA and the countries of Western Europe had honestly believed that the Dayton Accord would halt the bloodshed in the former Yugoslavia, even if the Kosovo question could not be resolved. But after the demonstrations by the Serbian opposition in 1997 they were finally forced to admit that Milošević only had one option if he was to cling to power, and that was to return to the place where he had begun his political career a decade earlier: Kosovo.

In Kosovo, people had gradually begun to lose faith in Dr. Rugova's pacifist movement. The emigration of thousands of

"During this period, the Kosovar Albanians were setting up parallel institutions under the leadership of the pacifist writer and scholar Ibrahim Rugova."

young Albanians to countries where conditions were very different, along with the discovery that US, British, German, Swiss and Austrian TV channels could be received via satellite, brought home to them the illusory nature of their own republic. It also served to bolster hope amongst Albanians that the West would not simply stand by while they were being ripped apart by the claws of a Serbian tiger that simply wanted to provoke a new conflict in order to keep at bay the opposition that was being so energetically led by Zoran Đinđić.

The timing was perfect. Young Albanians from Kosovo who had saved a few deutschemarks or US dollars during their time abroad were at the same time gathering in an Albania that had been brought to the brink of civil war in 1997 by the autocratic regime of Dr Sali Berisha. A Kosovo Liberation Army, or KLA for short, suddenly appeared on the scene in the same year, setting up bases and creating flashpoints in various regions throughout Kosovo. The response from Milošević's military machine was brutal and uncompromising. It was to be the beginning of yet another war in the Balkans, but this time it was also the last, because the brutality of the actions taken by Milošević's soldiers and paramilitaries in the villages of Drenica and Dukagjini forced the West to attempt mediation between the two warring parties.

The Rambouillet Conference in France was attended by the full political spectrum of Kosovar Albanians together with Milošević's own representatives, but it achieved little or nothing. The West then had little choice but to try and underline the seriousness of its attempts to bring about a peaceful resolution by launching an air campaign against Milošević's troops in both Serbia and Kosovo.

## *A new war in Europe*

In the final year of the twentieth century, Europe had once again been dragged into a new war: a war that would stir up emotions and divide public opinion, but that, above all, would create an enormous amount of suffering. During the bitter debate on NATO's intervention, the well-known German philosopher Jürgen Habermas spoke of "a need to intervene in an emergency based on a legitimisation by international law". Milošević took his revenge by driving a million Albanians out of Kosovo: more than 10,000 people of Albanian nationality were killed. The West felt it had a clear responsibility to try and bring this tragedy to an end. After 78 days of aerial bombardment, Milošević admitted defeat and pulled the Serbian troops out of Kosovo, a retreat that included many Kosovo Serbs and members of minority groups who feared reprisals at the hands of the Albanians who had returned to Kosovo in June 1999. The fear felt by the Serbs and other minorities was not unjustified. Albanian acts of vengeance were more than just brutal. Both the NATO KFOR soldiers stationed in Kosovo and the biggest mission in UN history, known as UNMIK, formed as a result of UN Security Council Resolution 1244, found themselves in a difficult position. The Albanians hailed them as liberators, while the Serbs condemned them as an occupying force. The international troops not only faced the task of overseeing the return of those had been driven out and rebuilding the country, but also of ensuring that the rights of the Serbs and other minorities were protected. In the months and years that followed the end of the war, Kosovo had to deal with countless traumatic experiences. Hundreds of humanitarian organisations flooded into the country to lend their support, including animal protection groups, technical aid organisations, groups involved in searching for missing persons and mine-clearing organisations. It should not be forgotten at this point that those members of the Kosovo Liberation Army who had come down out of the mountains and occupied the towns and cities when NATO troops entered the country had changed their one-time slogan "We are ready to die for our country" to "Steal and plunder as much as you can".

The consequence of this was that those parties that grew out of the military groups concerned had a very bad showing in Kosovo's first free elections, while the pacifist Dr Rugova – thought by many of his international allies to be politically dead in the water – enjoyed a revival in fortunes. With support from the UN mission, Rugova's Democratic League was called upon to set up provisional government institutions with responsibility for rebuilding the country from nothing. In fact, after a decade of neglect, it would be fairer to say that they were starting from a position of less than nothing. In the 1990s, Rugova's party had controlled the 'parallel' government and were no strangers to corruption. Bearing in mind the adventurism of the UN and other agencies, combined with their obvious ignorance of the true state of affairs in the country, it can come as no surprise that embezzlement and large-scale abuse of Western aid money became common practice amongst many international aid workers and Kosovar politicians.

## *A heroic war of liberation*

In order to divert people's attention away from what was really going on behind the scenes, politicians in Kosovo invested a great deal of effort into fostering the notion of a heroic war of liberation, all served up with lashings of pathos. The Albanian politicians fed the hungry population a diet of media outpourings: the main thing is that you have survived thanks to our heroic efforts and are now reasonably free; the rest will come, all in good time! Let's call on the writer Thomas Bernhard for help: "There is nothing to praise, nothing to condemn, nothing to lament, but there is much that is ridiculous, everything is ridiculous if we but ponder death".

The massive influx of aid workers from the UN, the EU and all manner of NGOs provided the people of Kosovo with a massive culture shock that they are still trying to digest. And all the great tragedies in the rest of the world – September 11, Afghanistan, Iraq – do not alter the fact that people are still worried there could be further conflict in this southernmost part of Europe. The Albanian majority in Kosovo have on numerous occasions come close to believing they might follow the example of other peoples and lose their newfound freedom.

Their disappointment runs particularly deep because they feel they are being let down by both sides. The international community has spent huge amounts of money and sent in a whole army of people to help, but it has not even been able to provide households with sufficient electricity, let alone satisfy other basic needs. Meanwhile, local politicians have simply sat on their hands. It was this that helped foment what have become known as the "March riots" in 2004. Barely five years after freedom had finally been achieved, violence broke out on the streets of Kosovo once again, and this time the main victims were the members of ethnic minority groups, especially the Kosovo Serbs.

The international community continued to apply pressure in Pristina and Belgrade to get all sides around the negotiating table to discuss the status of Kosovo. By this time, Milošević was in the Hague facing trial, Đinđić had been brutally murdered on account of his more open attitude towards the West and Serbia's neighbours, and yet nothing had changed in the negotiating positions of either side during the Albanian-Serbian talks.

"The massive influx of aid workers from the UN, the EU and all manner of NGOs provided the people of Kosovo with a massive culture shock that they are still trying to digest."

Chaired by the ex-president of Finland, Matti Ahtisaari, and the diplomat and top Balkans expert, Albert Rohan, a two-year marathon of talks took place between Pristina and Belgrade in Vienna. Their only possible outcome could be the independence of Kosovo as proposed by President Ahtisaari. Although he envisaged a considerable amount of international oversight and far-reaching rights to self-government and autonomy for the Kosovo Serbs, the Albanians finally accepted the compromise as being a prerequisite for an eventual breakaway from Serbia that was sanctioned by the international community.

And so on Sunday 17 February 2008, the parliament in Pristina, with the backing of the European Union and the USA, proclaimed the independent Republic of Kosovo, heralding the end of one of the bloodiest conflicts in European history. Serbia, however, refused to recognise the independence of Kosovo, a position it maintains to this day. There are still problems between Serbia and Kosovo, especially in the northern part of the country, and EU-mediated negotiations between Pristina and Belgrade continue. The hopes of reaching a settlement have still not been totally dashed, but it will require substantial pressure to get the message across to the Republics of Serbia and Kosovo that only those countries that can meet the necessary democratic criteria can become part of the European family. Paradoxically, the border conflict actually suits the political leadership of the both countries. It is easier to keep the Serbian or Albanian people supplied with long-standing conflicts than it is to provide them with good government!

After four years of independence, Kosovo is still a long way from meeting all the criteria that have been set. Although it managed to make a successful transition to independence with the help of its international allies, the new state soon fell prey to corruption and organised crime, with electoral fraud and maladministration becoming part of everyday life.

Despite Eulex, the EU's largest rule of law mission, Kosovo is still considered to be a problem region, with an under-developed judicial system that is struggling under the weight of corruption and undue political influence. Kosovo is the only country in the Balkans whose citizens are not allowed to travel in Europe without a visa. The situation cannot be sugar-coated. The final two decades of the last century may have been unbearable, the 10 years of UN involvement may have been chaotic, but since independence the Albanian Kosovars have been faced with an even thornier dilemma. It is time for them to take a long hard look at themselves and face up to the reality of their situation. If they are to become valued members of the Western family of nations, they need to free themselves from political, economic and cultural clientelism, but so far there has been little sign of this happening. The grinding poverty (Kosovo's GDP per head of population is similar to the average in Africa); the corruption that pervades all areas and all levels of society; the terrible image that the country has in Europe and around the world are not causes for great optimism.

The people of Kosovo continue to live in a kind of virtual reality created by television, the internet, the media and a somewhat battered dream that their future lies in Europe. Their dissatisfaction is palpable, yet there is no sign of a revolt against the corrupt political classes, who, while being pressured by the international community because of their corruption, are also being supported by them in order to maintain stability.

Let us now return to that attempted self-immolation in Prizren. The stimulus for this dramatic act was the fact that a shopping centre had refused to take back a plasma screen TV that the man had bought a couple of days earlier. He was so incensed that his protest almost ended in tragedy.

The big question for Kosovo now is: what will happen if the Albanian people wake up one day from their virtual reality world and realise that the whole thing is just an illusion that is not going to provide people with their basic needs any more than it is going to fulfil their desire to be a part of Western civilisation and thinking?

**Beqë Cufaj** (born 1970 in Deçan/Kosovo) is a Kosovar Albanian writer. He lives with his family in Stuttgart. He studied linguistics and literary science in Pristina and now writes for various Balkan and Western European newspapers, including the FAZ, the NZZ and Courrier international. He has published several volumes of essays and prose and his novel "projekt@party" was recently published by Secession Verlag.

# Seeing with both eyes

The attitude of the West is all too often based on interests rather than on empathy and objectivity. Serious cultural dialogue and acceptance of the other's culture form the foundation for culture as an effective element in resolving international conflicts and clashes between different groups. But this dialogue has to be fair and we need to be seeing with both eyes, not just one, writes Egyptian author Salwa Bakr. *By Salwa Bakr*

It was not by chance that ancient Egyptians worshipped and sanctified the animals around them, such as eagles, crocodiles and the white 'Beno' bird whose power lies in its bitter-tasting meat that other animals cannot chew or swallow. The power which lies at the root of feelings of superiority serves as the justification for rising above other nations and also for 'correcting' it when required. Many wall paintings in ancient Egyptian temples point to this in their depiction of the captivity of the Jews in Babylon.

The idea of superiority over others lies at the centre of all ethno-cultural racism. It is often fuelled by the fires of sedition, whether within local societies or at international level. This idea of superiority justifies violence and aggression and is linked to cults of worship and the use of power in an inhumane way.

Every political, economic or military conflict is driven and fuelled by cultural ideas. Aggression against others can be based on the idea of being different from them. And even though religion is a part of culture, it can once again stir up violence and adapt it to its own requirements because it is holy and absolute.

I remember how in the 1970s the Egyptian government used to import live sheep from Bulgaria to be sold and slaughtered as a sacrifice during the Islamic sacrifice festival, as ordained by the prophet Ibrahim and his son Ismail. But the Egyptian people refused to buy or slaughter these sheep, despite the fact they were so cheap, because Bulgaria was a communist country and its people were infidels. People made fun of these sheep because they looked different to Egyptian sheep.

Another example: apart from during the Second World War, when the British had Indian troops in their army and Egypt and India were part of the British colonies, most Egyptians had never had any contact with Indians. They soon began calling Indians stupid once they discovered that they were pagans who believed cows were holy. This situation seems to be religious, but in fact it has a cultural core – the hostility towards British rule. This seemingly religious aspect is in actual fact of a cultural nature.

Cultural reference points formed by religion provide the perfect example of how conflicts are fuelled. The Jews thought they were God's chosen people, while the Muslims took pride in the fact that they were the nation that reached out to people, but they still termed as 'strange' anyone who could not speak Arabic. The Persians were also called strange, despite their cultural superiority over the Arabs in the Middle Ages.

Arab historians categorise the revolutions and conflicts caused by economic and social problems that were triggered by the Persians against Arab Islamic states as racist revolutions against Islam. They claim that these revolutionaries were morally degenerate, having sexual relationships and accepting public relationships that were prohibited by Islam, and were themselves infidels. Centuries later, the British occupiers used these exact ideas to stir up the Egyptian people against communism and communists.

And this is still going on today: after the protests erupted in Egypt on 25th January 2011, political Islam used these arguments against the civilian secular movement during the subsequent first parliamentary elections and the referendum on the constitution. Anyone who was secular or civilian was an infidel and therefore morally degenerate by nature. During the elections, the Islamists made it clear that anyone who voted for the constitutional articles that were in their interests would go to heaven, and anyone who voted against would go to hell.

In some regions of the world where illiteracy and ignorance are widespread, the popular culture that is infused with religion still provides the fuse for igniting conflict. Conflicting powers usually play on the elements of this culture to stir up the masses and convince them that they are the side that represents them and that it is in their interests to fight against the other camps. During the civil war in Sudan which resulted in the division of Sudanese lands into two countries, the war and subsequent partition was given a cultural justification. But the fact that Sudan is a multicultural country does not justify this partition. The problem was and remains the authoritarian government that is based on the fallacy of religious rule. This is responsible for the problems and tragedies that have beset this country that is so rich in natural resources. The ruling regime did and still does not only persecute people in the south, but all citizens. Muslims and Christians all continue to suffer oppression. Everyone turned to cultural differences to fuel the conflict and conceal the economic reasons that lay at its core.

## *A culture infused with religion*

During the protests on 25th January, official media loyal to the Mubarak regime ran a campaign against the revolutionary and liberal movements that was based on popular cultural references. One media representative specifically focused on attacking Dr Mohammed ElBaradei, the former director of the International Atomic Energy Agency, saying that ElBaradei was out of touch with the Egyptian people. He had lived most of his life outside Egypt and worked for the United Nations. He knew nothing about how farmers have to sit on the ground and lame their ducks, force-feeding them with beans or corn and pouring water down their throats to fatten them up because there is no time for the ducks to feed themselves naturally.

This was how the media tried to make fun of ElBaradei, making out that he lived in an ivory tower far removed from the real lives of poor Egyptians. Then there were the virginity tests carried out by some army officers on girls who had been arrested for protesting in Tahrir Square during the 2011 uprisings. In this way, the army tried to incite public opinion against the demonstrators, as popular culture equates moral virtue with virginity. It damaged the reputation of these girls, meaning that most families then prevented their daughters from joining the protests against military rule and calling for democracy.

This calls to mind how, during the student revolution in Egypt in 1972, many illiterate young men clashed with the central security forces after some protesters claimed that soldiers had been molesting and harassing female demonstraters. This aroused a great deal of public sympathy and support for the student protesters, as molesting young girls is viewed as a very serious crime.

It is clear that cultural issues are constantly being used to fuel conflicts. Another example is the first Iran-Iraq War during the time of Saddam Hussein's rule. The roots of the conflict go back many hundreds of years to the rivalry between Mesopotamia (present-day Iraq) and Persia (Iran). A primary ideological and cultural reason for the outbreak of the war was the desire to control the resource-rich province of Khuzestan – the battle between Arabs and Persians to liberate the majority Arab population of Arabistan from their foreign rulers. On the Iraqi side, this ideology was so successful that even Shiite Iraqis made a significant contribution to the war against Shiite Iranians.

However, culture can also be a positive weapon for ending or mitigating conflict, but lack of cultural knowledge about the 'other' can lead to a great many mistakes being made. In the past, many young people have left the Islam world to study in the western countries, living for some years in the West, getting to know the way of life and the local people. This produced generations of people who had an understanding of others and escaped from intolerance.

This culture of getting to know the 'other' by travelling and gathering personal experience led to greater knowledge of the West, its art and its culture. But today it seems that this kind of curiosity about the West has been subordinated to a gre-

"During the civil war in Sudan, everyone turned to cultural differences to fuel the conflict and conceal the economic reasons that lay at its core."

ater project of national renaissance, and the time of returning home with direct experience of other cultures is over. Fewer and fewer young people now have an opportunity to get to know other cultures through direct daily contact. This is a totally different situation from those people who move to the West specifically in order to bolster their cultural prejudices and further convince themselves that the West should be feared.

### *From the Crusades to modern Israel*

Those who carried out the 11th September attacks on the World Trade Center in New York were these new types of people who come to the West to confirm their prejudices. Many of these people believe the West is evil, only looks after its own interests and has hated Islam and Muslims since the time of the Crusades. This stance is intensified by the bitterness caused by the history of Western imperialism and its support for the state of Israel. Such people feel that violence is their only form of expression, and their religious and cultural points of reference lead them to fight with the Taliban in Afghanistan or become pirates in Somalia in the name of religion. They believe they are fighting a just war against the (Western) infidels, seeing it as a struggle for God and religion.

Unfortunately, the practical steps being taken to combat what has become known as international terrorism are not enough. The problem is rooted in culture. It arises from a desire to obliterate the 'other' because the cultural significance of the 'other' should be obliterated.

Many years ago, I met an Egyptian in Zurich who worked at the Swiss cultural institute Pro Helvetia. He was happy to meet an Egyptian writer who was been hosted by the institute. But he told me that he was going to send his 11-year-old daughter to Egypt because he was worried about her growing up in Swiss society. He believed Swiss society was morally degenerate and that sexual relationships were widespread between boys and girls. I said to him: "Yes, but you live in the West, and your wife, the mother of your children, is Swiss. You met her and married her for love, so why can't you allow your daughter to do the same?"

This is a common example of a Muslim man who should be a role model because he is part of a modern culture. There are also many examples of girls, the daughters of third- and fourth-generation immigrants, who wear the veil but do not speak Arabic. They live in the West but retain their Muslim identity and culture. They are accepted by open-minded Europeans.

Many students who attend American and foreign universities are not anti-Western, but they retain their religious culture. They are keen to find an alternative Islamic culture in the West. They are living examples of a Western style with an Islamic identity: wearing jeans and make-up does not mean they cannot also wear the veil. They also do not find it a contradiction to speak English or French at home while fasting and practising their religious customs. Political Islam also produces thinkers who not only reject the 'other', but also hate it and are prepared to use violence against it. This was the case when a Danish cartoonist made a drawing that insulted the Muslim Prophet, or when a member of the Danish parliament for no obvious reason chose to demonise Islam and Muslims. There is no serious cultural dialogue that provides explanations for this behaviour.

## *Absence of dialogue*

This Muslim anger that is rooted in Christians' hatred of Muslims and their hostility towards them during the Crusades will produce nothing but more young volunteers from Egypt, Saudi Arabia, Yemen, Pakistan and other Arab countries for the war with the Taliban. The absence of dialogue provides a foundation for cultural and religious fanatics who believe there is no hope for the West; there is then no reasonable thinking or understanding about others.

Those who favour political Islam ask themselves why the West is remaining silent about the massacre of Muslims in Myanmar but was outraged at the genocide in Rwanda. The only explanation the Islamists have for this contradiction is that those being massacred are Muslims, and the West hates Islam and Muslims. And perhaps some of these Islamists think it is a good idea to plant a bomb or carry out an act of violence in order to protest against the West's hostile attitude to Muslims. We remember violent acts such as the attempt to burn down the Danish embassy in Beirut as part of the protests against the Danish cartoons that insulted the prophet. The absence of dialogue and lack of understanding of other cultures brings nothing but more violence and more destruction in the world.

> "Their religious and cultural points of reference lead them to fight with the Taliban in Afghanistan or become pirates in Somalia in the name of religion."

The talks about Nile water that were held after the revolution of 25th January show that this problem is basically a cultural issue. The attitude of ignoring black Africa that was prevalent among Egyptian diplomats and civil servants and their cultural discrimination against the countries of the Nile basin was the reason why these countries reconsidered how the waters of the Nile should be distributed, and particularly Egypt's share. Egypt, the country with the largest share, seemed to be indifferent to the problems faced by these other countries. A good result was only finally achieved after an Egyptian delegation that included some of the 25th January revolutionaries travelled to these sub-Saharan countries and assured them that the Mubarak regime and its representatives had not only discriminated against the countries of the Nile basin but also against the Egyptians themselves. Egypt is an African country, but the Mubarak regime treated Black Africa, and particularly the countries of the Nile basin, as though they were a group of totally different nations.

Serious cultural dialogue and acceptance of the other's culture form the foundation for culture as an effective element in resolving international conflicts and clashes between different groups. But this dialogue has to be fair and we need to be seeing with both eyes, not just one. Looking at the problems of others with a sympathetic eye is essential for constructive and productive dialogue.

Some people wonder how the West can criticise human rights in China while still supporting repressive and dictatorial regimes, as was the case with Mubarak. They also ask why the West has remained silent about the revolution in Sudan and the oppression of the opposition by the Sudanese regime, while concentrating on the Syrian opposition and the massacres committed by the Bashar Al-Assad regime. The attitude of the West is based only on interests, not on empathy or objectivity. This precludes the kind of cultural understanding that can bring to an end conflicts all over the world.

Yes, the cultural element is important and effective. And perhaps it can be the basis for resolving some international conflicts – but only if it is used objectively and fairly.

**Salwa Bakr** lives in Cairo and is one of Egypt's leading writers. She campaigns in the media for intercultural dialogue between the Arab and Western worlds. Her novels and short stories focus on the situation of women in Egypt.

# Heckling from the balcony

All too often, art and culture are helpless in the face of violent conflicts. Nobody is going to write a book or carry out an academic study while bullets are flying around their ears. But it gives us the ability to bear the unbearable, not by simply accepting it but by thinking about it and living it. Austrian writer Andrea Grill gives an account of her own experiences. *By Andrea Grill*

People who write about armed conflicts without being part of them risk being viewed as ridiculous or at best entertaining onlookers by those who are actually living in fear of their lives. They are like the two hecklers on the balcony in the Muppet Show: their mouths open and close, but what use is any of it to someone who is actually living in the midst of a violent, armed conflict? Is anyone going to wave the white flag because of something they've read?

I know that the task I have taken upon myself here is doomed to failure. As someone who lives and grew up in a safe and prosperous corner of Central Europe, what can I add to the art of retrospectively describing conflicts that I only know from watching the news and reading reports? Doesn't everything I have to say sound totally superfluous, coming as it does from an onlooker? How can I have anything to say when I was not there and have never experienced danger?

I could study the word 'conflict' and reveal that it comes from the Latin confligere, meaning 'to collide' or 'to fight'. I could draw on the reflections of philosophers over the last two thousand years. I could emphasise the positive potential of conflict and stress the importance of conflict per se for every kind of artistic endeavour and for human existence itself.

Culture, politics, business? What is the best way of eradicating violent conflict? I find I have two trains of thought that are colliding and fighting within me. The first of these is culture – another of those words that comes from the Latin and reveals something about itself. 'Cultura': treating, nurturing, cultivating. Culture is everything that needs humans in order to exist: fields, conifer plantations, vineyards, orange groves, motorways, cable cars, reservoirs, the moon landing, the satellites circling Mars, technology, fine arts, literature, law, politics, morality, religion, business, science. Everything that is not nature.

Culture can be something that brings groups of people together in the ways that they cope with their lives; culture can be the common element that sets the human species apart from animals. Culture also encompasses politics and the economy. Politics is concerned with public issues, with establishing and managing the state and society, while the economy distributes resources. Art is also part of culture. And even conflict is part of culture.

The economy can distribute art like a scarce resource. Politics can ban art when it wants to force everyone in the country to think the same way. But all three are the result of culture, they are its offspring. They are siblings that cannot exist without each other, that are mutually dependent, but that fight as only siblings can fight. Because they know their relationship is forever. Even if they fall out, they will always be related.

### *Unexploded mines lurking in society*

Children don't have conflicts, children quarrel. Quarrelling is an active form of conflict that settles the fight, and – ideally – only words may be used as weapons. Ideally, a quarrel is a form of fighting that leaves behind no physical wounds. It is closely related to argument, but the latter tends to remain in the academic sphere.

Adults too get involved in quarrels, but they also experience latent, simmering conflicts. They lurk in society like unexploded mines and no-one knows when they will go off. There is no danger so long as nobody moves. One false step could set them off, so instead we'd rather stay put.

In his book *Time of Disorder*, Petros Markaris writes that when he asked a Belgian Green party MP why someone who was unknown to the European public like Herman Van Rompuy was elected as President of the European Council, he immediately replied: "Because he's nice, good-natured, avoids controversy and above all he doesn't attract attention". This book looks at the crisis in – or in fact with – Greece and investigates the causes. "I nearly added "poor thing!" in Greek. When the Greeks say something good about someone they often add "poor thing!" on the end, such as "He's a very genuine person, poor thing!""

"Art thrives on contradiction", writes Petros Markaris. Contradiction implies disagreement. Literature provides a nature reserve where conflict can live in the wild; a conservation area for conflict. Writers and philosophers allow themselves an internal encounter and fight with themselves, which means they are taking themselves seriously. They are quarrelling with others because they take them seriously. Without contradiction, without conflict, there would be no art and no science: there would only be arts and crafts.

A little further on, Markaris adds that in the EU it is an advantage to be inconspicuous and to disguise tensions. In Europe, we, poor things, find that conflict is smothered. Conflict decomposes and we hold our noses in the silent hope that one day it will be carried off by ants, worms or other hard-working creatures.

### *Culture is like a cleaning product*

But that's not the issue here. The issue is the role of art within violent conflicts. Does it have the power to promote peace? Or reconciliation? In my mind, culture is like a cleaning product such as Cif – a thick white cream that wipes away conflict like a stain. Or I see it as a fire engine racing along with sirens blaring and blue lights flashing to extinguish the blazing conflict with foam and water. Or it simply beats it to death with a shovel – there, it's stopped twitching.

In the play "Allegretto Albania" by Albanian author Stefan Çapaliku, one of the characters is called "Reconciliation". She is the most ridiculous character in the play. She always brings her charges useless objects that are the last things they need. A family that has been trapped in their house for months because of a blood feud receive an X-ray machine that nobody knows how to use. Reconciliation is also a TV presenter and every evening on the news she reports on the success of her humanitarian aid programme. In order to resolve the vendetta, she installs a computer and internet connection in the family's house so that the two families can thrash out their problems by e-mail. The family in question don't mind what she does because it brings some variety to their lives. But that's all it brings.

"In the play "Allegretto Albania" by Albanian author Stefan Çapaliku, one of the characters is called "Reconciliation". She is the most ridiculous character in the play."

Concrete help is finally offered by a money-grubbing builder who just wants to get them out of the house so that he can make money by putting up a tower block. He arranges for them to escape to the EU – at least so it seems. They check the route on Google Earth and leave the house.

The play is a good demonstration of how outsiders – unfortunately all too often – simply fall into the role of someone who is at best entertaining while trying to as a mediator.

When I was young in the 1990s, every day hundreds and thousands of people were being killed in an area that was closer to my home than my country's capital. I am of course talking about the wars in the former Yugoslavia that later became known as the 'Balkan conflict'. I met people who had managed to flee to Austria and I tried to help them and translate for them. But I was still an outsider. Children sat around on the steps in my town, looking at the sky for hours on end, jumping and ducking every time a plane flew over. "Bang! Bang!", they shouted, suddenly jumping around in circles. "A bomb, a bomb's landed on his head", they cried. I have to write about them, I'm so sorry for these children, their dead parents, the raped women. I can't forget their eyes – no-one should ever have to see the things they have seen. But how do we go beyond simply feeling sorry for them?

In his book "Infancy and History", the philosopher Giorgio Agamben discusses the destruction of experience. It finds its "necessary correlation not in knowledge but in authority; that is to say in the word and in the story", he writes. "Nowadays nobody seems to have sufficient authority to guarantee an experience, and if they do, they do not think to build the foundations of their own authority on an experience." So a characteristic feature of our times would be inability to experience. And I am a child of my time, so this way of looking at things doesn't seem strange. But I still want to create my own experience. I am trying to tell the story of a violent conflict that had a concrete effect on my life. When a friend's elderly grandmother grabbed a Kalashnikov and fired into the air from the terrace of her house in Tirana, I knew I could no longer carry on writing my planned thesis. A small thing in itself, but it had a very real effect on me at the time. And this is what I want to write about here – real experiences.

## *Albania in 1997*

One of these happened in Albania in 1997, when the collapse of several huge financial pyramid schemes led to countless Albanians losing all their money. The country quickly descended into anarchy and gang warfare and the Albanian people armed themselves en masse. Their weapons came from huge arsenals that had been built up during the communist era. It was important to have a gun – like my friend's grandmother – in order to avoid being summarily robbed or killed. Suddenly the country seemed to have been plunged into a period of history where local rulers could ruthlessly exploit their *rayon*. But this time the difference was that everyone could be a king (and to some extent this is still true of present-day Albania). It's just that some kings were stronger than others.

My research project was funded by a grant from the Austrian government. Once the unrest in Albania came to light, I quickly received a letter withdrawing my grant and prohibiting me in the name of my country to carry on with my research because it was dangerous to life and limb.

During those months, I had a great deal of telephone contact with my friends in Albania. Sometimes I could hear shots in the background. My friends kept telling me it wasn't so bad, I shouldn't worry, they were not themselves in any danger, that things were "just" chaotic. Some of my friends made a name for themselves as journalists or translators and accompanied visiting foreign journalists as they travelled around the country.

I switched my research project to neighbouring Greece, and focused on an ecological study of the biodiversity of Mediterranean butterflies. As far as the study was concerned, it didn't matter whether or not I was carrying it out a hundred kilometres to the north-east. But for me it really mattered. I learned Greek, suddenly found myself living in a country that I barely knew and where I had never intended to live, just a few hours' drive from where I really wanted to be. But it was quiet and peaceful – a good place to work.

## *The helplessness of art and culture*

So why am I telling you all this? Because I'm afraid it is an example of the helplessness of art and culture in the face of violent conflicts. Nobody is going to write a book or carry out an academic study while bullets are flying around their ears. During the First World War, many writers lined up to romanticise the war. Some of them volunteered to go to the front, and without fail they created within the German-speaking world an ideological superstructure for the war linked to the kind of courage, bravery and honest combat that did not exist. Even great writers such as Robert Musil and Thomas Mann, to name just two, did not speak out against the war – quite the opposite, in fact. Their enthusiasm for the war cost some of them their lives. Georg Trakl, the expressionist poet from Salzburg, was posted to Galicia as a pharmacist (despite reporting to go to Albania). After being forced to tend to ninety wounded soldiers, he died of exhaustion and an overdose of cocaine.

"A generation that had gone to school on a horse-drawn streetcar now stood under the open sky in a countryside in which nothing remained unchanged but the clouds, and beneath these clouds, in a field of forces of destructive torrents and explosions, was the tiny, fragile human life." This is how Walter Benjamin described the state of helplessness that I mean.

I asked my Albanian 'grandmother': what are the most important things in life? She replied: believe in yourself, and fight. I am amazed by both parts of this answer. The woman I call my Albanian grandmother was born 89 years ago in Istanbul. As a child she came to Saranda, a fishing village on the southern coast of Albania that at the time was part of the Ottoman Empire. Her father was a general or high-ranking member of the military, perhaps an admiral. In Saranda she met the love of her life, the man she would later marry. They moved to Tirana. They were both communists and lived in the woods as partisans. They fought physically for what they believed in: an independent Albania, a socialist Albania. When the socialists finally took power under Enver Hoxha, 'grandfather' became a spy for the new government. But this did not last and he soon fell out of favour, spending the next 10 years in prison. His wife visited him every week with their three children who were growing up without him. It was a long and difficult journey to the prison, and at the end of it she was never allowed to see him alone. By the time he was released, his children had grown up and left home, his wife was an old woman and he was an old man.

> "During the First World War, many writers lined up to romanticise the war. Some of them volunteered to go to the front."

## *Arming ourselves inwardly*

Grandfather died aged barely 70 from lung cancer, and grandmother has now lived alone for 19 years. Not a day goes by that she does not talk about her husband, the love of her life, whom she has in fact been missing all her life. Most of the older people that I know believe in God. But this woman is perhaps the sole exception. She amazes me. She still maintains her own socialism, despite the disappointments that socialism has brought her. She believes in herself. She fights.

It pains me to say it, but I don't believe that art and science can prevent violent conflicts. Culture – used in its widest sense – can help us to arm ourselves inwardly. It can communicate experiences that we don't have in real life. It can turn us into people who are prepared to withstand the kind of suffering and violence that we are not naturally prepared to withstand. It gives us the ability to bear the unbearable, not by simply accepting it but by thinking about it and living it. Because it makes us curious about what is outside ourselves. Curiosity does not reach for its gun but is the sister of affection. I cannot think of a better way to end than to quote Elias Canetti, who believed being a writer was an exercise in transformation: "in its compelling experience of people of all kinds, of everyone, but particularly those that are afforded the least attention".

**Andrea Grill,** a writer, lives in Vienna. She was awarded a PhD in 2003 with her thesis on Sardinian butterflies. In 2007 she took part in the Ingeborg-Bachmann competition in Klagenfurt. She was awarded fellowships by the Literarisches Colloquium Berlin and the Schloss Wiepersdorf. In November 2010 she received an award as part of the 2011 Bremen Literature Prize. Her recent publications include the novels "Tränenlachen", (2008) and "Das Schöne und das Notwendige" (2010) and "Happy Bastards", a collection of poems (2011), (all published by Müller, Salzburg and Vienna).

# The language of music Bach, Mozart, Haydn and Beethoven provide solace amongst the sorrows of everyday life. In the National Youth Orchestra of Iraq young Kurds, Shiites and Sunnis come together to play a classical Western repertoire, along with a few compositions by contemporary Iraqi composers. But can music also create understanding and reconciliation? An artistic director describes his experiences.

*By Vladimir Ivanoff*

In 2010, around 60 musicians from Germany, Yemen, Lebanon, Austria, Morocco, Palestine and Syria came together in Bayreuth, Germany to seek out traces of the Parsifal myth, its Jewish-Arab roots and its musical treatment from the Middle Ages right up to Richard Wagner.

One year earlier, 50 German, Iraqi, Lebanese, Palestinian and Syrian musicians were brought together by the music of Bach. They took a new look at its baroque spirit and reinterpreted it within the living traditions of Arab music and jazz. Bach's Passions were set against the present-day situation in Jesus' native land and with the conflict between the Arab world and the West. The baroque precision and complexity of Bach's work contrasted with the spontaneity of classical Arab music and jazz: two traditions that have much in common, including their complex and highly-structured improvisation techniques.

In both these years, the musicians were taking part in the Orient meets Occident summer workshop. Faced with the religious, economic, cultural and political differences between the West and the Islamic world that tend to dominate the world today, this workshop tries to show that music is not just decorative but that it commands respect on both sides as a medium that is open to the world.

The potential for peaceful relations between East and West and between different religions has become a platitude in today's international cultural industry. A multitude of projects are trying to convey the message that the countries on the northern and southern shores of the Mediterranean belong together and that communication between different religions is possible.

## *Communication without constraints*

The idea behind the Orient meets Occident workshop is different in one fundamental respect from the many other musical projects that have sprung up with intercultural and pedagogical aims. With his highly-respected West-Eastern Divan Orchestra, Daniel Barenboim has been advancing the Arab-Israeli dialogue by bringing together young Arab and Israeli musicians to play a solely Western classical repertoire. Middle Eastern artists have come together within an established European cultural repertoire, in the music of Beethoven and Mozart. In contrast, the conscious focus of Orient meets Occident is on stylistic diversity. The Western classical repertoire is confronted with styles based on improvisation, such as jazz (both European and Arab styles); European music from the Middle Ages, Renaissance and Baroque periods is contrasted with traditional Arab music in all its regional diversity. New music from the Arab world is placed on an equal footing with the European avant garde. A colourful mixture of diverse musical styles serves to make the workshop participants aware of the polarities of Orient and Occident, tradition and (post-)modern, native and foreign; and encourage them to look behind the stereotypes.

In musical terms, I understand the word 'intercultural' in a broad sense, as in fact the saying that music is a global language that everyone understands only has limited truth in the real world of music. Different musical traditions and styles have their own very specific structures of communication and organisation. So for example, a German musician who mainly works in the area of classical chamber music might find it very difficult to understand the musical communication within an orchestra. Jazz musicians and classical musicians tend to speak totally different musical languages, and even their verbal communication is a kind of 'Double Dutch' that to a large extent is incomprehensible outside their particular specialist areas.

But my experience tells me that musicians from the Arab world and Europe who share similar musical backgrounds (such as jazz) can communicate with each other relatively easily and with few constraints because they share a common musical language. In contrast, musicians from the same country with different artistic backgrounds often have major communication problems, as is the case when baroque specialists and members of normal classical Western orchestras try to play together or communicate verbally.

But these inhibitions can also harbour a great opportunity, as musicians generally define themselves first and foremost by their musical backgrounds. As a result, when sharing musical and verbal communication with people of a similar musical background, issues such as political and religious differences are of secondary importance. A real interest in making music together is generally a greater priority than the need for creating delineations. If differences are verbalised at a later stage, conflict is always mitigated by their shared interest in music, even if it is 'only' to ensure that they can still play together. And if musicians are interested in getting to know a new, totally alien style (such as when jazz musicians are introduced to traditional Arab music), it is always curiosity about the new musical language that comes to the fore and that serves to mitigate any potential areas of conflict.

"The orchestras and stars of European classical music have created an identity that is simultaneously pan-European and global: Cecilia Bartoli is an Italian who sings European classical music and is a global star."

European nations possess musical and cultural identities that have grown up over time: with their love of classical music, the Italians are proud of Vivaldi and Verdi, while the French take pride in Lully and Berlioz and the Germans in Mozart and Wagner. Although traditional music has taken something of a back seat in today's modern Europe, regional folk music is still alive in most European countries and has its fair share of enthusiasts. The orchestras and stars of European classical music have created an identity that is simultaneously pan-European and global: Cecilia Bartoli is an Italian who sings European classical music and is a global star.

Jazz, pop and rock are global music styles that all have their roots in Western culture. The Beatles are British musical icons, Xavier Naidoo is one of Germany's biggest pop stars (regardless of his 'migrant background'), Lady Gaga is an Italian-American superstar who has had a global impact. But who knows Oum Kalthoum, Asmahan, Farid al-Atrash and Fairouz? They are the last (and in the case of Fairouz, the only still living) exponents of a popularised but at heart still traditional pan-Arab musical culture that was at its height in the 1940s and early 1950s and that is equally well-known and loved by older Egyptians, Lebanese, Syrians and Iraqis.

Western colonialism spread across Arab nation states and robbed the Arab world of its cultural unity and with it a large amount of its trans-regional classical music culture. For decades, it has been almost exclusively Western-style classical music and globalised pop music that has dominated the Arab world. The curricula of music colleges have focused on Western classical music and, increasingly, jazz; while almost every Arab oil state now has its own Western-style symphony orchestra with corresponding concert halls and opera houses. In this way, cultural policymakers, artists and their audiences are – largely unconsciously – transferring putative values from the area of culture to the area of social planning and policy.

## *Solace amongst the sorrow*

As the presenter of a discussion programme on German radio, I once had the opportunity of talking to some of the musicians from the National Youth Orchestra of Iraq about what was important to them and their dreams for the future. The orchestra operated along the lines of Daniel Barenboim's West-Eastern Divan: young Iraqis, including Kurds, Shiites and Sunnis, came together to play a classical Western repertoire, along with a few compositions by contemporary Iraqi composers. Under the lodestar of Western classical music, this was intended to help in de-escalating conflicts between various sections of the Iraqi population. Our conversation revealed the high hopes that these young musicians projected onto Western classical music. In short, they believed that Bach, Mozart, Haydn and Beethoven provided solace amongst the sorrows of their everyday lives. For these young musicians, and indeed for a proportion of their audiences, this music possessed an outstanding value that they linked in their minds to social progress, political openness – also in the West – and a process of democratisation that was worth fighting for.

Most of the Western classically-trained participants in the Orient meets Occident workshop were harbouring similar hopes. Particularly since the Arab Spring, most young Arab musicians believe that pop and jazz music – in both its global and regional Arab forms – is a medium for freedom and progress, the 'music of the future' for the Arab world's new political and cultural order.

In contrast, musicians trained in the Western tradition and their jazz and pop colleagues almost without exception view traditional Arab music as something that it obsolete and outdated, representing a step backwards and even religious fundamentalism. They consider this unisonous tradition to be more 'primitive' than the polyphonic Western tradition. So, for instance, the Tunisian malouf is viewed as a medium that supports the state (because of its importance for tourism) and is hence categorised as being part of the old political order.

This lack of regard and appreciation for one's own musical (and in the broader sense, cultural) traditions is the main cause of conflict in the Orient meets Occident workshop and also within my own Ensemble Sarband, an intercultural chamber orchestra that I founded in 1986. Those musicians who have been trained in the Middle Eastern tradition lack self-confidence and under intense peer pressure often find themselves relegated to a musical back seat. At first they tend to be much more reserved in terms of getting their music across to the other musicians, and often they simply sit on the sidelines rather than joining in with discussions.

When representatives of regional musical forms (Syrians, Egyptians, Lebanese, etc.) come together to play traditional Arab classical music, this often leads to disputes. Each country claims its pronunciation of the Classical Arabic lyrics is the 'only correct one', and different musical details such as intonation and embellishments are only considered 'correct' in the Syrian, Lebanese, Egyptian, etc.) form. As a result, musicians from the various Arab countries are often at musical odds with each other. One participant in the 2010 workshop suggested the title Orient meets Occident should be changed to Oriental Accident.

I believe this issue should be a focus of this and other similar musical projects, because traditional Arab musicians very quickly discern appreciation for their music amongst their colleagues and audiences. European participants are generally interested in getting to know more about this initially strange, but ultimately fascinating, world of music. They discover that it is an ancient yet living, complex yet still changing tradition that is the equal of the Western classical tradition. Now at least, many of our Arab colleagues with a Western musical background (whether classical, jazz or pop) who have in the past hardly listened to the traditional music from their own region but have almost invariably considered it to be inferior have gained a certain degree of respect for it. In certain cases it emerged that some of the Arab musicians who had trained in the Western classical tradition also had experience of traditional music but initially were reluctant to broadcast the fact. Traditional Arab music is often very warmly received by Western audiences at concerts by Ensemble Sarband and performers at the Orient meets Occident workshops. It stands on its own two feet, and indeed audiences sometimes prefer it to Western repertoires because of its lively performance style.

In contrast, audiences at concerts in Arab countries are often initially somewhat suspicious of their own tradition. This is because it is usually those on the upper rungs of the social ladder who attend concerts, and these generally tend to prefer Western culture. But after the concerts I have been surprised, proud and relieved to discover that a truly Arab repertoire can hold its own against a Western repertoire. This positive reception from colleagues and audiences creates a sense of pride and self-confidence in traditional musicians.

A healthy degree of self-confidence and an awareness of the fact that Arab musical traditions and hence Arab culture in the broadest sense can be positively received and respected can produce far-reaching consequences. It can create a basic pan-Arab unity, despite the wide range of regional differences. It can allow the emergence of a confident Arab identity that goes beyond nations and religions and helps to mitigate the diverse tensions within the fabric of Arab states and bring about greater equanimity in when communicating with the West. Partners who are confident in their own identity can talk to each other as equals.

It also makes it easier for Western musicians, like Western audiences, to gain a more equitable appreciation of Arab culture that goes beyond the mass-produced Arabesk pop music that plays in the doner shops of Europe. From playing with equal partners from East and West, the musicians (and subsequently audiences, from listening to concerts and recordings) learn that diverse music styles and traditions are equally valuable, even if the musical languages are totally distinct. The go beyond the daily body counts broadcast in the media to get to know artists from 'crisis zones' as people with their own ways of expressing themselves and with the desire and the ability to communicate.

This is where I see opportunities for promoting European culture: a truly polyphonic orchestra made up of young musicians from Europe and the Middle East, where a dialogue of equals is possible without bowing to the dictates of dominant European or Arab cultural values. This artistic and pedagogical model could also be applied to other conflict-ridden regions such as the Balkans and Eastern Europe. With a relatively small outlay of time and money on the part of international cultural institutes, a living and far-reaching medium could be established that is capable of being heard by many ears and hearts that perhaps remain deaf to other voices.

"Musicians trained in the Western tradition and their jazz and pop colleagues almost without exception view traditional Arab music as something that it obsolete and outdated, representing a step backwards and even religious fundamentalism."

**Vladimir Ivanoff** has been artistic director of the 'Orient meets Occident' summer workshops since 2009. In 1986 he founded the Ensemble Sarband, an "intercultural chamber orchestra". Its programmes bring together musicians from very diverse cultures and act as a bridge between past and present, linking historically-informed European performance practice with the living traditions of the Mediterranean. Working closely with other artists, ensembles and orchestras (such as baroque soloists from the Berlin Philharmonic Orchestra, the Modern String Quartet, Sidi Larbi Cherkaoui, the King's Singers, Mystère des Voix Bulgares), it investigates the differences between cultures and religions and between historical and contemporary concepts of 'the other'.

# Art and conflict

Artists do not believe any more than footballers that they can create world peace, even if both culture and sport have a very integrating effect on society. How can art have a positive effect and what conditions are necessary to achieve this? A curator looks for answers in Afghanistan and Eritrea.

*By Christian Schoen*

"Is art an active force that can have a global political impact, mitigate conflicts and promote peaceful relations?" This was the opening line of an article in the *Neue Zürcher Zeitung* of 7th July 2012 that looked at the project being run in Afghanistan as part of Documenta 13. This art exhibition takes place in Kassel, Germany, every five years, and this time it also focused on the Afghan capital of Kabul by staging an exhibition, symposiums and workshops in the city. We feel inclined to answer the "NZZ" writer's question about the integrative and peacemaking potential of art with a "yes" because we want art to speak the language of freedom all over the world.

In Germany we know what an important role art has played in helping us to work through our own history. The debate stirred up by our avant-garde artists and post-war American art at international events such as the Biennale in Venice and the Documenta in Kassel was all part-and-parcel of dealing with our fascist past and transforming our society.

But the author of the newspaper article gives an ambivalent answer to his own rhetorical question. In general terms, he is reluctant to deny the positive power of art, but in the specific case of the Documenta initiative in Kabul he is not alone in thinking it has been a failure because the artistic projects in Afghanistan in themselves have not produced any lasting effects for the local people. He also feels that this attempt to build a bridge to Kabul is more about cultivating the event's image than about concrete results.

This critical view of the Afghanistan project throws up the following fundamental questions:

- How do we come up with a project that makes sense to everyone involved in conflict zones that welcome the collaboration of artists?
- How can we unite the differing expectations of our project partners and others?
- What do we need to consider in order to set clear objectives for everyone involved?

In any event, one thing is clear: before art can be afforded a possible role within socio-political conflict, it is necessary to consider how every political conflict has its own particular origins and takes its own specific course. The word 'conflict' itself can be interpreted in various ways. Of course it has a negative connotation, but it also points to a positive process of transformation within society.

There is potential for conflict everywhere, even in so-called 'free' countries. When talking about development programmes for other countries or regions, we should first of all think about whether we are ourselves walking the talk.

It is also necessary to clarify the word 'art', so that we can be sure we are all on the same page. Even if here we want to concentrate 'only' on the fine arts, it is still essential to know the historical, geographical and cultural background to a work.

"Instead of producing objects, many artists today focus on structures linked to processes, dialogues or performances that have no or only a partial physical manifestation."

Whether we are talking about the Buddha statues in Bamiyan, Afghanistan, a baroque wall hanging in a French chateau or a canvas by German artist Gerhard Richter, we still use the word 'art'. Although the world has become smaller – which has had nothing to do with art and everything to do with modern communications technology and physical mobility – cultural reference points play a vital role in the way art is produced, and of course received.

So something that might be called art in Europe might be totally incomprehensible as art to someone with a different cultural background. This is particularly true of strategies that have emerged from Western art history and developed into movements such as conceptual art, performance art or public art. Instead of producing objects, nowadays many artists focus on structures linked to processes, dialogues or performances that have no or only a partial physical manifestation. Even at home, these expanded ideas of art often have to be 'interpreted' so that the public can understand them. So it would be very naïve to hope that these kinds of artistic formats would be understood as part of development programmes in countries such as Eritrea in the Horn of Africa.

The challenges of terminology are even greater when we bring cross-disciplinary projects into the equation, where artists work alongside specialists from other disciplines. The complexity of artistic strategies and specific cultural comprehension must always be respected. It should go without saying that no one partner can claim to have a superior understanding. The challenge of finding terminology that everyone can agree on goes hand-in-hand with the definition of one's own expectations and the formulation of one's own goals.

A great deal of research is needed if we want to decide which forms of cultural exchange, cultural dialogue and financial or practical support actually make the most sense in another country. How do we define 'sense' in this context? Paradoxically, the tired and often misused word 'sustainability' cannot be used to describe art itself – in contrast to the art market. Sustainability is not a criterion for art. This would seem to be a paradox when we consider medieval and modern art history, as the classical works of art were created with a view to eternity. An exception here is architectural art installations and permanent public art that can have a lasting effect on the character of specific places both physically and intellectually.

## *Art is the daughter of freedom*

The ability of art to open up spaces for creative thought that cross subject matter, cultural or social boundaries without having a set of clear objectives – as is required in politics and business – is something worth defending. The oft-quoted saying of Friedrich Schiller that art is "the daughter of freedom" is happily bandied about to emphasise our moral standards.

Where art can be created free from existential and material necessity and from political, social and religious repression; where the mind can have free rein: these are the ideal breeding grounds for art and also the places where art in all its varied forms can be the symbol of a free and evolving society.

This may also have been the motivation of the Documenta organisers when they decided to include Afghanistan in their programme. The problem with this kind of project may have lain in the difficulty of bringing together differing inter-disciplinary and cultural expectations. How are the individual interests of the artists, curators and academics involved different from those of the overarching political interests? Of course the project also draws the attention of the German and Western public to the political (and military) engagement in the Hindu Kush, as positive reporting creates support at home and adds to our understanding.

So the question is less one of whether the Documenta has been focusing on its own PR, but rather whether it has allowed itself and Afghan artists to be manipulated? One of the curators of the Kabul exhibition, the Afghan artist Aman Mojaddedi comments: "Over the last three years there has been a huge rush of international interest in anything to do with supporting and financing activities in the area of art and culture as part of a propaganda campaign. The USA, UK, France and other countries have invested a great deal of money in these kinds of activities in order to give the impression that the situation in Afghanistan is improving. This is largely due to the fact that they have to find a way to justify the withdrawal of international troops".

## *A discrepancy in expectations*

This is where we see the clear discrepancy between the individual expectations of the artists and curators involved and those of their political mentors who also hand out the funding. However, the chief curator of Documenta, the Spaniard Chus Martinez, insists she was guided by purely artistic ideas.

And what are the expectations of the 'NZZ' critic? He assumes that art feels it has to try to save the world, that the "Documenta in Kabul is labouring under the sweet illusion that Western art can be a tool of nation-building; civil society's midwife in archaic, war-ravaged corners of the globe." This reveals a certain danger of overestimating the role of the artist. Artists do not believe any more than footballers that they can create world peace, even if both culture and sport have a very integrating effect on society. Even when Daniel Barenboim set up the West-Eastern Divan Orchestra, made up of Israeli and Palestinian musicians, it was not with the expectation of resolving the problems in the Middle East. But it is still a fantastic idea that gives individual musicians the opportunity to do something productive together, and the simple fact that they are playing together has a symbolic value that goes beyond borders.

> "Even when Daniel Barenboim set up the West-Eastern Divan Orchestra, it was not with the expectation of resolving the problems in the Middle East."

Afghanistan has been the focus of world attention for many years. There is a political will to bring peace to the country, alongside both selfish and unselfish interests on the part of the Western world that are obvious to greater or lesser extents. But the situation in other parts of the world is very different.

In Eritrea, for example, it is only too clear how difficult it is to engage with a country where bilateral political and economic relations are almost non-existent; with a country where political backing and the attendant logistical and financial support are totally lacking. In places that may have a German or other European embassy but no cultural institute such as the Goethe-Institut in Kabul, the work of humanitarian and cultural engagement is left to the NGOs.

Fuelled by the vision of providing a cultural underpinning for existing projects in the areas of healthcare or water supply, about a year ago various German associations and foundations came together to create an cross-disciplinary network for Eritrea. The My Eritrea project was launched by the Pilotraum01 initiative in cooperation with the WINTA-Era water foundation and the NGO HumanPlus. I feel very proud to be one of their curators, along with my colleague, Serafine Lindemann.

The commencement of this work with national and regional authorities in one of the poorest countries in the world is remarkable in that it makes culture an integral component of its activities. The aim is to strengthen the social infrastructure and cultural identity of this young country that gained its independence from Ethiopia in 1993 after 30 years of struggle.

In light of the country's need for basics such as water, food and medical care, the shocking lack of hygiene, the precarious political situation, and the simmering conflict on the Ethiopian border, a few eyebrows may be raised at the inclusion of art in the programme. What is the use of art when the country does not even have the basics for survival?

But people have long been aware that imported development aid only brings lasting results if it is sensitively adapted to the traditions, ethnic situations, social structures and cultures of the recipient. The initiative in Eritrea is based on a partnership of equals. It is not just the result that matters, but the journey.

Artistic processes play a role within didactic programmes, for example when families waiting for treatment at the Orotta hospital in the capital, Asmara, are taught about basic hygiene using playful and artistic methods. The main thing is that German artists understand the concept and right from the start provide the impetus for local artists to adapt the various projects to suit their indigenous concepts and styles. One of the project's long-term goals, apart from offering direct humanitarian aid, is to help the Eritreans to review and preserve their cultural heritage.

### *Consolidating the process of democratisation*

The country still defines itself through its hard-won independence, which threatens to send its diverse indigenous culture spiralling into oblivion. But we can look forward with a healthy dose of optimism to our long-term commitment resulting in a consolidation of the necessary process of democratisation, whether this is achieved through individual projects focusing on traditional music or the collation of folk stories and fairy tales, or through providing organisational assistance to the National Archive.

But one thing must be stressed: any meaningful cultural work across borders has to begin with a deep understanding of local cultural history. This is where art and aesthetics have a role to play in creating identity. The long history of cultural studies in Europe means that it is now our destiny to use our specialist and organisational knowledge to help build local institutions within the framework of joint projects.

### *Targeted partnerships*

The national and regional archives are particularly important in this respect as they have the job of preserving the cultural heritage. The best way forward would seem to be to promote more strongly than

"One of the project's long-term goals, apart from offering direct humanitarian aid, is to help the Eritreans to review and preserve their cultural heritage".

ever targeted partnerships between European universities, museums, foundations or associations and partners in the crisis regions who are involved in building or re-building. Meaningful and effective cultural work requires open and transparent handling of the expectations and objectives of all partners; it must be flexible and take into account cultural differences that may affect issues such as the longevity of projects and associated planning strategies.

Cultural engagement as part of development processes in conflict zones will always remain somewhat ambivalent. But it should be borne by the basic characteristics that make art meaningful for us as humans: our sense of opening ourselves up to the 'other', the vision to mobilise our minds and awaken curiosity. The curiosity that is based on the freedom of the mind provides the foundation for daring to do something different.

**Christian Schoen** is a freelance curator for international exhibitions. He wrote his doctoral thesis on Albrecht Dürer's "Adam and Eve". From 2005 – 2010 he was head of the CIA.IS Center for Icelandic Art in Reykjavík. As Commissioner, he was responsible for the Icelandic Pavilion at the Venice Biennale in 2007 and 2009. He is currently working with Pilotraum01, an initiative for cross-disciplinary projects and for development cooperation and activities to counter climate change.

# The role of EUNIC in crisis regions

**Democracy, multilateralism and decades of experience in peaceful co-existence – Europe has a great deal to offer and should be investing more heavily in cultural relations around the globe as a way of sharing these specific experiences with others and helping to mitigate crisis situations. No organisation is better placed in this respect than EUNIC, the network of European cultural relations institutes, with its 2,000 branches around the world.**

# A buffer for pacifying the people

Identity is not something abstract but is symbolised by objects, places, a church, a mosque, a bridge – places where everyone can relate to their own history. This history and these memories form the foundation for the future. This is why conflict intervention and cultural work both have to place great importance on protecting and reconstructing the cultural heritage.

*By Delphine Borione*

Since the middle of the 19th century, the nature of violent conflicts has changed. They are no longer played out by armies on the battlefield, but have become conflicts between countries, regions, or even communities that affect whole populations. Nowadays, conflicts no longer progress in a linear fashion but create a framework for the close intertwining of civil society and the military. This development can also be seen in the growing number of parties involved. This no longer includes just armies, but also NGOs, the civilian population and businesses. It has also become clear how nowadays crises have really become symbols.

Culture in its broadest sense – which includes education, shared heritage and language, as the latter generally represents an extremely strong badge of identity – can become a target and even a cause of tension during the course of a conflict. Therefore it is important to include the cultural dimension in both crisis prevention and conflict resolution. Cultural work as a factor in intercultural dialogue and understanding between peoples needs to be strengthened in this respect.

Cultural heritage, whether this is of a material or immaterial nature, is often targeted during conflicts because of its symbolic value. So a primary goal of those involved in conflicts is often the destruction of whatever it is that gives their opponents their identity. Their cultural heritage is therefore often attacked and as a result it becomes impossible for communities to restore themselves in a lasting way. This was the case in Sarajevo, where the warring parties attacked the library and even street signs, with the aim of removing all traces of a multi-ethnic community and shattering its very foundations. In the case of the destruction of the Buddha statues in Bamiyan, Afghanistan, the Taliban went ahead with the eradication of this symbol despite the intervention of Muslim clerics because they could not identify with the statues and simply could not accept their existence. The same mindset was behind the destruction of Islamic mausoleums in the north of Mali and its capital, Timbuktu.

Restoring and rebuilding cultural heritage that has been damaged during conflict helps to bolster resilience and heal the psychological scars amongst the civilian population. Everyone has the right to choose their own identity, but also the duty to respect that of others. This identity is not something abstract but is symbolised by objects, places, a church, a mosque, a bridge – places where everyone can relate to their own history. This history and these memories form the foundation for the future. This is why conflict intervention and cultural work both have to place great importance on protecting and reconstructing the cultural heritage.

In 1954 The Hague Convention laid down the principles for protecting cultural property during armed conflicts. But more still needs to be done. The UNESCO Convention of 1970 provided an agreement on the illicit trafficking of cultural property during peacetime. Since then, many institutions and organisations have been working together to fight the pillaging of cultural heritage. Interpol, Unidroit (International Institute for the Unification of Private Law), customs and police in many countries, museum staff and people involved in maintaining and restoring cultural property have all been working with ICCROM (the inter-governmental organisation dedicated to the conservation of cultural heritage) to restore and return damaged cultural property and scattered works of art to the peoples where they originated.

As part of protecting cultural heritage and strengthening the rule of law, the French foreign ministry has set out a strategy of practical collaboration in post-conflict situations. In order to increase the protection of cultural property and make a contribution to the fight against the illegal drugs trade, the ministry has organised regional conferences in the Middle East and South East Europe as a means of encouraging debate and sharing proven strategies. The aim is to set up joint actions and networks involving customs, the police and the judiciary in order to promote collaboration and carry out joint projects. These actions are also designed to closely involve local people in the protective measures and to press forward with the renovation of cultural property. Appropriation and inventory-taking of cultural property are the two flagships of this strategy for the protection of cultural heritage.

This protection can also be an important economic factor and contribute to local development if, for example, buildings undergo restoration. This has an effect on urbanisation, rural development, cultural activities and sustainable tourism. Positive effects can also be seen with regard to the country's image, symbols, well-being, sense of social cohesion and attractiveness. For example, in 2009 the French and Palestinian authorities set up a primary solidarity fund to maintain and improve the Palestinian cultural heritage in Bethlehem. Funding will also be provided for a new museum close to the Church of the Nativity in the heart of Bethlehem's old town. This will be the first museum to display the history of the town, its inhabitants and the urban area, and is also intended to act as an information centre for tourists and pilgrims.

NGOs have also been set up with the same idea of protecting cultural heritage in times of conflict. These include the International Committee of the Blue Shield and the French organisation Patrimoine sans Frontières (Heritage without Frontiers). With the assistance of the German and French governments, this latter organisation restored the Orthodox Church of the Saviour in the Kosovar town of Prizren that was damaged during the war. It is also worth mentioning the reconstruction of the bridge in Mostar, a symbol of the link between the two sides and also between the two ethnic and religious communities. The people of Mostar are proud of their historic bridge and feel it represents the bond that unites them.

The Bophana Audio Visual Resource Centre in Cambodia provides another example of the preservation of audio-visual cultural heritage. The Centre's stated objective is "to gather, image after image, snatches of life and a volley of voices. In order to try to understand, to try to give a name, a soul, a face and a voice to those who had been deprived of them. To return to the victims of a murderous history their destiny and their memory. To recover freedom of speech by integrating reflection about the past with the construction of the present (...). It is not only a question of recovering memory, but also of knitting up the elusive warp of a multiple and living identity, that of contemporary Cambodian society."

But despite all these initiatives, how many traces of the past are still being erased from our present-day world? How many cultural properties have been pillaged, stolen or destroyed in warring countries or in places where the rule of law has been trampled underfoot? How many films, audio recordings and photographs are being lost to the country's audio-visual heritage because of a lack of opportunity to archive and digitalise? These questions make it clear that there is still a great deal of work to be done.

## *Equipped to face the future*

Education can also be a significant factor in the link between culture and conflict. Education not only helps people to develop their intellectual capabilities, but in terms of economic, social and human development, the right education can also provide whole generations with the necessary tools to build a future that is not built on destroying others or on conflict with their neighbours. Once a violent crisis has come to an end there needs to be focus on ongoing education and its structures to create a kind of buffer for pacifying the people and as a means of accelerating the process of rebuilding.

It has been shown that the more quickly people can return to some semblance of normality after a crisis, the easier it is to diffuse tensions and create a future for all concerned. This is why it is so important for education to play a central role in any rebuilding process. Good examples here would be Haiti and Kosovo, where the authorities ensured that the school system was functioning again as quickly as possible once the crisis was over. This provides people with a sense of normality and can help them to gain self-confidence and regain trust in other people. They should then be able to look to the future in a more optimistic way.

And there can be no doubt that the main constituent element of our relationship with others is language. Language is a key component of our belonging to a community, a prerequisite for our existence and a basic assumption underlying our social ties. Any attack on language is therefore an attack on people themselves and their own sense of identity. A language dispute can quickly escalate to such an extent that it becomes the source of unrest or even war. In 1976, for example, the demonstration by school children and students against the government's decision to introduce Afrikaans as the official language in schools ended in tragedy. Nor should we forget the revolt by Albanian students in Kosovo who protested against being forced to speak Serbian. Respecting multilingualism or the language of a particular community can be a major contributory factor in assuring peace and stability.

In general terms, the more a crisis contributes to the destruction of the physical and material, as well as the psychological and moral existence of the people, the more important it is to try to strengthen ties forged through common identity or even to create a new cultural identity. This is where cultural work has an essential role to play.

By setting up the Institut Français cultural centre in Afghanistan, France has been able to encourage film production, the training of filmmakers and the development of a range of cultural activities. The name of the centre was changed to the Centre Séverin Blanchet in memory of the film and documentary maker of the same name who was killed in a bomb attack in 2010. Blanchet, a highly committed lecturer at the Ateliers Varan (workshops for documentary film makers), where the focus is on practical learning by doing, paid with his life for his belief in the value of cultural engagement in crisis resolution. He wanted to encourage young Afghans in Kabul to make films based on the views of others. The subject of the films was guided by the film makers'

"For me, there is a connection between a lack of reminiscence work and a lack of democracy, a lack of the rule of law and a lack of development."

Rithy Panh, documentary film-maker and founder of the Bophana Centre declared wish to show people both inside and outside of Afghanistan the difficulties, but also the riches, of their country.

Cultural activities help people to articulate themselves, to overcome the desire for revenge or the feeling of being a perpetual victim and to develop a less negative view of the world. Only then is it possible to find a way back to normal life. It is for this reason that France has stepped up its cultural work in Iraq with the help of its cultural centres. It wants to make a contribution to rebuilding the country, and projects carried out so far include financial support for the renovation of the Iraqi National Theatre and an upgrading of the National Museum.

The five French cultural centres in Jerusalem and the Palestinian territories are making a valuable contribution to the dialogue for peace between its peoples, a dialogue that demonstrates the possibilities for the future. The German-French cultural centre in Ramallah represents a symbolic but at the same time pragmatic example of cultural cooperation in a region where culture and tradition are decisive factors and where maintaining dialogue between the various communities is a constant challenge. The French cultural institute in Gaza, whose new building is due to be opened in 2013, is currently the only active foreign cultural institution there. The presence of a cultural institute that is imbued with the spirit of freedom and creativity can act as a kind of release valve for pent-up emotions in all these countries that have been rocked by crisis, tension and conflict and can help to create resilience.

## *Clowns without borders*

Clowns sans Frontières is a French artists' association that has been helping children in emergency situations around the world for eighteen years. The association includes volunteer artists, clowns, musicians, acrobats, dancers, puppeteers and actors who put on shows in refugee camps, slums, prisons or orphanages to help children and their parents to find their way back to some form of normal life after a war or catastrophe. Their work augments that done by NGOs in crisis interventions and is carried out in cooperation with local organisations. Since 1994, the organisation has planned and carried out projects to help refugees and displaced peoples in Kosovo, Albania, Bosnia, the Lebanon and the Palestinian territories. Clowns sans Frontières is currently involved in two similar projects in Burma and Thailand.

Cultural activity is also at the same time a form of preventive diplomacy, so it is a real tool for promoting understanding between different groups and for conflict prevention. The artists' own sensibilities can bring to light potential areas of tension, articulate them and thus serve to defuse them. The role of culture in encouraging the exchange of ideas and intellectual open-mindedness also promotes tolerance and understanding for the ideas of others. Cultural projects also provide an opportunity for quarrelling communities to work together on joint projects.

The German-French Elysée Fund for cultural programmes in non-EU countries also provides a good role model for strife-ridden communities. Two former enemies are now working hand-in-hand to support projects with a message of peace that also holds the promise of reconstruction and cultural development.

### *German-French fund for cultural programmes in non-EU countries to promote reconciliation (Elysée Fund)*

Germany and France contribute equally to this fund, which supports cultural projects in non-EU countries. It funded many projects in the Balkans after the end of the war as part of reconciliation efforts in the region, including:

- Lectures on reconciliation in Bosnia and Croatia;
- In Serbia, a congress on: "Promotion of a youth exchange programme in the countries of Southeast Europe with the aim of advancing reconciliation, cooperation and European integration";
- Establishment of a youth exchange programme in the countries of the former Yugoslavia.

"Culture can become a target and even a cause of tension during the course of a conflict."

Since 2003, an annual cultural project has also been supported in the Palestinian territories that has included the following initatives:

- Since 2010, the establishment of a mobile library (comprising a total of 1,500 French, German and Arabic works) travelling between the West Bank and Gaza;
- In 2011, the international circus festival in Ramallah, the first circus festival anywhere in Palestine;
- Since 2005, publication of a culture magazine in three languages.

In 2012, the Fund has been financing a project to train theatre professionals in Afghanistan with a view to supporting theatre as a whole, along with school drama projects.

Another example of how people from different ethnic backgrounds are being brought together is the West-Eastern Divan Orchestra, created by the Argentinian-Israeli director Daniel Barenboim and the American-Palestinian literary critic and author Edward W. Said. This orchestra brings together young musicians from Israel, Palestine and neighbouring Arab states with the aim of promoting intercultural dialogue and creating a common foundation for collaboration. With its many concerts in Europe, America and the Arab World, the West-Eastern Divan Orchestra has consistently proven how music can overcome political hurdles and encourage people to listen to each other.

Cultural work is aimed at the heart, mind and spirit and in this way it touches the people it wants to reach, unlike propaganda, which only has a superficial effect on its audience. A play can also send out a strong signal: a good example of this is the plays put on in the French cultural institute in Afghanistan by Afghan actors in collaboration with French theatre and film director Ariane Mnouchkine and her theatre company Théâtre du Soleil.

The "Shadows of War" photo exhibition has also had a major effect. This project was organised by the Italian foundation Fondazione Umberto Veronesi to encourage progress in the sciences. Held in 2011 in the Maison européenne de la Photographie in Paris, the work of top journalists and photographers demonstrated the fear and futility that permeates armed conflicts. Could there be any more convincing argument than these images for peace, dialogue and understanding between peoples?

These cultural projects encourage economic development, the labour market and income opportunities by supporting arts and crafts, cultural production and the creative industry. They help countries to develop and, importantly, to regain their sense of dignity.

What role can EUNIC play in this? All the members of the EUNIC network are convinced of the important contribution that cultural work can make to security and development by helping to mitigate conflicts and crisis factors. This is why their focus has been on the topic of "Culture and Conflict" and why they have supported the ifa project at its seminar of the same name held in December 2011, along with the publication of this annual review.

Indeed, the members are keen to work together even more closely because they understand the value of collaboration and the power of solidarity between countries that have historically been enemies. This is the job of EUNIC – to highlight the vital contribution made by culture to economic, social and human progress. In this way, the activities of the network's members and their joint projects help to reduce conflict in our society and safeguard peace between peoples.

This is why it is essential that European governments and international donors continue to provide financial support. Despite being persuaded of the connection between culture and conflict, this conviction is not always matched by appropriate levels of funding. Let's hope that the work done by EUNIC will now receive greater financial recognition.

**Delphine Borione** is Director of Cultural and Language Policies at the French Ministry of Foreign Affairs and President of EUNIC, the network of European cultural institutes.

# Far from the feasible

If we are to give Europe a 'face' and throw Europe's soft power into the pot in a world full of conflict, then public debate is essential. The world's conflicts need to be addressed by European policies on cultural and other issues. We are still a long way from creating the necessary consensus on this, let alone from being ready to take action. What is to be done? *By Gottfried Wagner*

The old and new debate about culture and conflict in external and internal cultural policy is rife with both complaints and expectations. It is customary to bemoan the failures of cultural and other policies during and after times of crisis, conflict and potentially violent altercations. The tragedy of the exploitation of culture is repeatedly stressed, such as was the case during the 'Balkan wars' at the end of the 20th century. But there is also the invocation of the holy cultural trinity of hope for everything culture can achieve in the avoidance of conflicts and their escalation, in promoting dialogue and, in certain cases, in reconciling conflicts (as happened in the South Tyrol).

As soon as political correctness is drawn into the equation, it makes sense to take a critical look at the relationship between abstract theory and verifiable empirical practice, between politics and real life.

In the business of democratic politics, the emphasis always falls on the feasible and that-which-must-not-fail, on worry over what has failed and the will not to (ever) again fail to invoke the benefits of culture. Any reference to culture as a potentially negative force for destruction during a conflict often serves as little more than an opening credit to the main feature, which then goes on to show how beneficial culture can be if only it is 'used in the right way'.

It is worth noting how culture is once again being exploited, this time in an optimistic scenario; but this is hardly surprising when we find ourselves in the sphere of external and internal cultural politik – where politics predominates – rather than in the temple of the liberal arts.

This position then seems particularly 'enlightened' when everything is done right; when the true freedom provided by culture, and particularly art, provides the best guarantee of its ability to promote peace and have a beneficial effect on conflict situations.

We know only too well how easily and unexpectedly such situations can escalate; we only have to look back at some of the bleaker chapters of European history and plays such as Hanns Johst's 'Schlageter' (1932/33) containing the line falsely attributed to Hermann Göring: "When I hear the word culture ... I reach for my gun" (Act 1, Scene 1). When faced with more recent conflicts around the globe and their 'cultural images' it requires a great deal of courage to use identity-based and hostile arguments to counter the 'production of the good'.

## *A tangled situation*

The list of philosophical writings and essays in this respect is both long and enlightening. What we are lacking in any discussion of a realignment of external cultural policy at a time when we are seeing the emergence of polycentric 'new orders', and also above all in terms of constructing new European approaches, is an open debate on the aporia of this question, on the contradictions and potential taboos in this context, so that we can avoid building our new constructions on sand. We can be motivated to do this by some of the factors listed below (in no particular order):

Conflicts can provide the essential ingredients for growth. A society's progress is based on protest and fierce struggles for positions and interests; one 'culture' follows on the heels of the next or new hybrid forms are created. The road to 'progress', like the road to hell, is paved with good intentions, but also often with conflicts that leave behind many victims. It is necessary to fight for democracy and strong economic systems, and cultural products – that will later form the core of the 'legacy' – bear living witness to the physical conflicts; indeed, even scientific progress is subject to victories and defeats, triumph and despair.

At present we are witnessing a battle between the 'tired' cultures that it is claimed are afraid of losing what they have and the hungry and dynamic new kids on the block: the starving, desperate people who are quite literally shifting the fight towards the prosperous north. Once again it is artists who are bringing us into the discussion with their words, images and sounds. And once again, the most exciting theatre is that which tackles the major issues of protest and conflict.

Shakespeare's hero courts the widow of his murder victim at the graveside; Lessing's tale of intrigue and love exposes nothing but reveals everything about privilege and the curse of social class on affairs of the heart. Today, the keenly committed teacher in the post-migrant German play *Verrücktes Blut* struggles to deal with young Turkish adolescents; their battle is never fully resolved, their anger is held up to the mirror of Sturm und Drang, but at first they refuse to recognise themselves in Schiller's 'robbers'. The appearance of a gun shakes up the conflict; the pistol becomes a tool that is used to enforce the 'game' and the understanding of the greater good that it represents. What calls itself the aesthetic education of humankind almost turns into a violent climax but – in a stroke of genius by the writer – in the end it triumphs in a most strange and remarkable way.

"Conflicts can provide the essential ingredients for growth. A society's progress is based on protest and fierce struggles for positions and interests."

This is not to say that everything has already been said, but the 'art' lies in wringing meaning out of simple happenings that we have still not or have never quite managed to grasp; creating meaning is creating freedom. "Set yourself free!" is also the secret agenda of aesthetic teaching that always avoids fear and shame by a mere hairsbreadth. The art lies in designing the 'serious game'. It is possible for new players to be won over by seriousness, for free spirits to learn how to change some of the more serious parts of life under the banner of freedom, but it is not exactly urgent.

So it takes at least a second glance to understand it all, if it can be understood at all. This also applies to the intention and outcome of the honourable desire to bring 'culture' into the equation (or perhaps we can say 'bring into play'?) as a defence against bloody conflicts, to act as a bearable way of dealing with terrible conflict situations and their consequences. In the furore over the "Seven Deadly Sins", delayed or renounced gratification, sublimation or repression cannot or can only to a lesser extent be initially balanced out by a friendly but strong ego and an empathetic super-ego – and only at a high price.

On the other hand, doing nothing or adopting an attitude of resignation cannot be considered as humane cultural alternatives. This means renouncing 'meaning for all' and giving up on the free creation of meaning in favour of a putative 'natural', revolutionary, zealously religious or ethnically racist 'law'. A relapse without prospect of paradise (before banishment); paradise can however also not promise the most ingenious system, unless it is the nightmare of totality. What remains – and here the high art of Freud and others are reduced, at least verbally, to a post-modern philosophy of life that is little more than an advisor's mantra – is learning how to handle conflicts in a cultural and cultivated way.

Culture then provides the space to deal with interests that are rife with potential for conflict, with antitheses, with 'other' ideas, with differences and similarities, with old and new; culture is conflict – and it is also the right (or wrong) way of dealing with conflict. Conflict relativises and gives dynamism to moribund relations and to this effect art is continually creating new conflicts. Art has never lost its dynamism; it can itself be uncultured in the midst of conflict; it can undermine the culture of peaceful problem-solving; indeed culture itself can mutate or be mutated into the uncultured.

What makes it so difficult is the fact that we as humans are quick to cast aside what we think of as the burden of responsibility when we are overwhelmed by circumstances. This means we then have to justify our violent impulses and invent and tell stories to turn these impulses into doctrine. Art has laid bare these stories a thousand times, but it will have to do so another thousand times. Any hope that this would come to an end has faded over the course of history; it seems hopeless to even have this hope.

In Europe, perhaps the bloodiest continent in recent history, the second half of the last century saw the creation of space for a political culture of negotiation, for the waiving of sovereignty in favour of the common wealth. This was a unique event in its history. The triad of democracy, the rule of law and the social market economy unleashed a massive energy. Productive conflicts can be experienced and limited in this way and bloody conflicts can be avoided between the Member States. Many people were brought into this 'culture', and more still were excluded. A great deal of what works internally has been gained through externalisation: the outsourcing of business models and conflicts.

Of late, the island of Europe has come under massive pressure. The tide is building in favour of internal consensus and external dominance; anxiety is spreading and sophisticated negotiation processes are increasingly turning into confrontational talks and populist policies; at the same time, the power to tie the main economic players into a set of basic rules that benefits everyone is waning. Faced with this situation, many people and their elected representatives are seeking out apparently safe harbours in a bid to find old ways of freezing conflicts and creating aggressive isolation: the 'nation states' that are no longer what they once were. Complexity creates fear. Reducing complexity will soon create even more fear.

Cultural policy that is orientated towards democracy and peace often contributes to a 'conflict culture', both internally and externally as a result of the disappearing demarcations between local and global, national and international. External cultural policy can no longer ignore its own contradictions and can no longer be local. The processes of global interaction and interdependence mean that it is now cosmopolitan and becoming more and more European.

Sound cultural policy – which must be both national and transnational – can also no longer simply be carried out under the naïve banner of the rhetoric of cultural conflict. But it can also not stop encouraging those who have the power to uncover the nature and problems of conflicts in a cultural and self-reflective way: the artists, intellectuals, cultural workers, the 'us' and 'them' and their joint projects.

## *The European players*

In practice, Europe is still experiencing difficulties in coming to terms with joint policies on culture and conflict, both internally and externally. Europe has tools at its disposal that are not available to everyone. In its latest round of reforms, the Council of Europe relegated culture and education further down the agenda of its core business of democracy and human rights. But on the other hand, it hands out more powers when the various conflicting cultures (the Member States) try to align conflict negotiations, as has already been the case. So the Cultural Policy Review programme has stalled over certain issues (the report on Turkey) and there were some remarkable incidents, as in the case of Russia. Interestingly, in this latter case the Council did not try to produce a national and an international report, but right from the beginning tried to produce one joint report. When the first conflict arose amongst the team of experts themselves and between the experts and cultural policy, this led to the removal of the critical member of the international group. So far there has been no public debate on this.

Other players include the EU's national cultural institutes and the EUNIC network. Of course we should not mention how, at the time when the UK's EU policy was doing an about-turn in the winter of 2011/12, the British Council had to step away from the main events being run as part of European external cultural policy within the "More Europe" programme;

(contrary to the British mantra of liberal debate, no event was held in London). We also should not mention how the German foreign ministry's 2011 paper on external cultural strategy came about without the input of the quangos whose involvement and autonomy had until then been held up as an example around the world. This resulted in several points being met with great controversy, including the assessment of the 'power' (and impotence) of culture during conflicts. We will just make a passing reference to the fact that EUNIC remains almost unknown amongst the European public, in stark contradiction to the notion of Europe as a 'civilian power'. If we want to give Europe a face (in all its variety) and throw Europe's soft power into the pot in the interest of all citizens (both European and global) in a world full of conflict, then public debate is essential. It is good that reality continues to arise of its own accord, at times painfully, as in the debate about the "Art of the Enlightenment" exhibition in Beijing in 2011, and in the way the hosts interfered in the composition of the expert delegation from the West. But this reality has some quite other conflicts in store that need to be addressed by European policies on culture and other areas. We are still a long way from creating the necessary consensus on this, let alone from being ready to take action.

Here the third European player would be needed, the EU and its institutions, and the European External Action Service (EEAS), an institution whose creation was held up by many as a prime example of low-level conflict avoidance. According to critics, the match between the Member States (the Council) and the EU, and between the EEAS and the Commission has ended up as a nil-all draw thanks to a state of 'institutionalised ambivalence', rather than the classic 'win-win' situation. And culture? This cannot be found in the EEAS set-up, despite the fact that the Council and the European Parliament have repeatedly emphasised the importance of culture in European external relations, and the Commission highlighted it as the third pillar in its programme for culture in an increasingly globalised world. This is also a striking example of conflict avoidance, with the effect that in the meantime the discussions (that we hope are enlightened) about conflict and culture can only take place in the heads of a few incorrigibles, as is the case with this publication from the Institut für Auslandsbeziehungen (German Institute for Foreign Cultural Relations, ifa). We are still a long way from hitting the right note when it comes to what is feasible.

**Gottfried Wagner** is an advisor to the Austrian Federal Ministry of Culture and Education. For many years, he was Director of the European Cultural Foundation, Europe's only independent, cross-border and pan-European cultural foundation. He was also Director of Kultur-Kontakt Austria, a European competence and research centre for education, culture and art, based in Vienna.

# Beware of vaulting ambitions

Although a painting can never stop a bullet, a painting can stop a bullet from being fired. Executing that painting and putting it in place, however, is a specialised and complex affair. The author wonders whether this is really EUNIC's business. *By Yudhishthir Raj Isar*

A striking feature of the culture sector today is the degree to which its institutional players – cultural operators, activists, advocates and organisations – readily invoke cultural expression and practice as expedients, in other words as instruments for the attainment of other ends. Does this always make sense? Recent years have seen a succession of causes external to 'culture' itself to which cultural actors have hitched their wagon, often opportunistically, sometimes idealistically, but not always with the intended effect.

These causes have included 'culture and development', 'culture and social cohesion', 'intercultural dialogue', the 'creative industries' and, most recently, 'cultural diversity'. Each of them has generated its own narratives and these narratives in turn have often been understood and deployed rhetorically in rather loose and undifferentiated ways. They have generated catch-all terms lumping together a range of different kinds of practices designed to meet different kinds of goals.

'Culture in conflict resolution' is one of these discourses and it has become a flourishing field of theory, practice and research. Its specialist practitioners generally define their goals in clear and precise terms. This is not always the case when such ideas are used discursively by non-specialist individuals or organisations, many of whom deploy them as vogue terms that are dictated by a certain 'political correctness'. This becomes problematic when conflict resolution as such is not central to the core mission or competencies of actors or organisations that identify with these buzzwords or claim to want to apply them. There are several organisations, even among those that define themselves as devoted to conflict resolution, such as those promoting interfaith dialogue, where a direct connection to any kind of on-the-ground conflict resolution is far from evident.

## *Cultural buzzwords*

The reader should not be surprised to learn, therefore, that while cognisant and highly appreciative of the potential of the arts as vectors and tools of conflict resolution, I am far from convinced that a body such as EUNIC should invest its energies in this area, other than being morally supportive of the opportunities it offers. Because of this, and because I am myself not directly conversant with actual practice in the field, I was initially reluctant to accept EUNIC's invitation to contribute to the present volume. Having been persuaded to do so, however, I have been afforded an opportunity to begin a mapping of the field that will be presented briefly below. The evidence provided by this preliminary survey reinforces my initial doubts as to whether involvement in projects relating to the use of the arts in conflict resolution would be the best use of either EUNIC or the bodies that compose it.

> "While cognisant and highly appreciative of the potential of the arts as vectors and tools of conflict resolution, I am far from convinced that a body such as EUNIC should invest its energies in this area, other than being morally supportive of the opportunities it offers."

Before I briefly make this dissident and perhaps provocative case, however, I need to make a brief detour to explain that, when I refer to 'culture', it is not in the broader sense of 'ways of life' with which the narrower understanding of culture as the arts and heritage is increasingly conflated. Indeed, a range of players, and nation-states in particular, now invoke the need to support, or 'protect' or 'promote' the arts and heritage, not for their own sake but because they embody or represent different 'ways of life' that need to be 'protected' or 'promoted', to use the language of the 2005 UNESCO Convention on the diversity of cultural expressions.

When the term is deployed in the 'ways of life' or group identity sense, the relationship between 'culture' and conflict is ambiguous from the outset. The baneful influence of the 'clash of cultures' paradigm has caused many to see cultural difference itself as a cause of conflict, without understanding that in all our contemporary societies politicised difference has become a pawn of contests over the control of power and resources, all of which can so easily be 'culturalised'. So here it is rather difficult to speak of a role for culture in conflict prevention and/or resolution.

It is of course possible to promote dialogic exchange around the values and ethos of different ways of life at the meta level, as it were, through conversations that take the form of 'dialogue between cultures' or 'inter-religious dialogue' in order to find common ground between different ways of seeing and being in the world.

But such practice, commonly referred to and practised as 'intercultural dialogue', is not 'the positive use of culture in conflict situations round the world' that EUNIC wishes to report on. And it simply cannot be, since the 'culture' that is being 'used' in this case is necessarily the arts, together with ideas of heritage and collective memory, while institutions such as museums serve as crucibles for such work. It is these expressive areas of human activity that provide powerful sources of energy and emotion, feeling and passion, imagery and imagination, and sheer human desire for building bridges or searching for common ground.

## *Multi-disciplinary conflict resolution*

So what is this expert field of conflict resolution, also referred to as peacebuilding, conflict transformation, conflict prevention, conflict management, conflict mitigation, conflict reduction, cross-sectoral conflict work and conflict sensitivity? As the American specialist Craig Zelizer has pointed out, the domain of conflict resolution is multi-disciplinary, drawing on theory and practice from disciplines as diverse as sociology, psychology, international relations, law and economics as well as from work on the ground by practitioners (naturally, many of these are artists when the techniques are arts-based). "The central goals of conflict resolution", he observes, "regardless of the particular disciplinary approach or frame used, are to develop a greater understanding of the sources and dynamics of conflict and to develop and implement more effective responses to preventing, managing, and reducing the effects of conflict."[1] Common to all approaches is the figure of the mediator or the process of mediation – between individuals or groups in conflict – that helps the parties to achieve some kind of mutually agreeable resolution of a conflict-ridden confrontation of some kind.

The bulk of these activities appear to be initiated, funded or led by US bodies, including well-known not-for-profit organisations such as Search for Common Ground (which now has offices in more than 15 countries), and governmental institutions such as the Conflict Management and Mitigation Unit of the US Agency for International Development, or intergovernmental entities such as the United Nations Development Program (UNDP).

European players are slowly becoming increasingly involved. One of these is Sweden's International Development Cooperation Agency (SIDA), which includes the topic in its culture and media development cooperation activities. Pan-European bodies understandably seek to rival American agencies, notably in fields where the latter have been pioneers. From a European perspective, this is no doubt a laudable objective. But is it the right one for every category of organisation, and more specifically EUNIC?

Today, a very diverse range of arts-based conflict resolution activities are being carried out by local and international organisations as well as many artists, mainly within the framework known as 'community arts', in which professional artists collaborate with people who don't normally engage in arts practice in a professional or full time way. These activities can be summarised as follows:

- Arts for peacebuilding – largely based on community arts, in which groups from different sides of a conflict are gathered together to conduct joint artistic products, sometimes focusing on the conflict.

- Social protest art – although this does not fit within a traditional model of peacebuilding, this type of art is often used during higher stages of conflict. Through artistic processes, individuals seek to resist and protest against violence through cultural means. Work that uses the arts to create awareness, understanding and trust with regard to issues of cultural freedom that may be threatened by oppression or discrimination can also be included in this category.

- Creative therapies – these processes largely focus on promoting the healing of individuals who have suffered because of conflict and/or trauma.

"The baneful influence of the 'clash of cultures' paradigm has caused many to see cultural difference itself as a cause of conflict"

Within this diverse range of arts-based activities, some projects may directly intervene in, or address the substance of, a particular conflict in a community. Art is often used to help people to explore specific conflicts from multiple perspectives and envision alternative possibilities, or bring together groups that are in conflict to address the relational aspects of conflict.

The specific arts-based process may not directly address the substance of a conflict, but it may facilitate increased understanding and interaction among the parties to it. Other efforts are more activist in nature and challenge unjust, regressive or repressive social, economic and political orders, while others aim to help individuals and communities deal with the potentially traumatic effects of conflict. Recent and still ongoing efforts of this type include initiatives in Palestine, the Great Lakes region of Central Africa, South Africa and the countries of the former Yugoslavia.

The theatre in particular has been a force for the exploration and transformation of perceptions, understandings and feelings. A typical example of the use of theatrical techniques for creative therapy is the support provided through SIDA for the development of the dramatic arts among children and young people in the West Bank/Gaza by the Swedish University College of Film, Radio, Television and Theatre. Although initially conceived following the signing of the Oslo Agreement for the development of a Palestinian cultural infrastructure, the project now focuses on relieving the deep trauma caused amongst children by the increasing violence and deprivation in their lives. Plays, drama training and video animation courses help these children to talk about and work through their experiences.

Although its positive impacts have, alas, been completely wiped out by subsequent events, another example of a performing arts-based peacebuilding initiative was the Centre for Performing Arts (CPA) founded in the Sri Lankan town of Jaffna in the 1960s. During the civil war it opened twenty centres across the country and many branches amongst exiled Sri Lankan communities internationally in order to involve young people in intercultural activities that promote peace and mutual understanding.[2]

These activities included the traditional dances of different communities. These were taken on tour to the various centres, thus allowing these art forms to be shared with communities that might have different languages and religions. They encouraged young people to create contemporary performances, often on the theme of the conflict, and to perform them to large audiences both within and beyond their own communities. They also comprised inter-community camps where young people from different communities worked together on performance and arts projects. The aim was to promote the interaction of cultural practices. Bringing young people together in cross-cultural programmes was a means of resisting the divisions in cultural forms by encouraging joint practices in which performances were created by drawing on the skills of all participants.

### *Alternative voices*

Initiatives on a broader canvas, also often based on the performing arts, include such emblematic projects as the West-Eastern Divan Orchestra (named after an anthology of poems by Goethe). This youth orchestra, which is based in Seville and is made up of musicians from Israel, the rest of the Middle East, Iran and Spain, was founded in 1999 by the Argentine-Israeli conductor Daniel Barenboim and the late Palestinian-American academic Edward Said . One of the young musicians in the orchestra sees the venture, which Barenboim himself calls a "project against ignorance", as "a human laboratory that can express to the whole

"The theatre in particular has been a force for the exploration and transformation of perceptions, understandings and feelings."

world how to cope with the other."[3]

The work of museums and sites of memory represents another type of conflict-oriented effort that uses cultural objects, documents and artefacts. The international network of 'peace museums', for example, stresses an educational role. Depending on their location and context, these 'peace museums' are "sites for historic narratives and survivor stories, centres for conflict resolution and transformative imagining or memorial and reconciliation sites." Their common value is considered to be their capacity to provide "an alternative voice or resistance to the dominant and dominating voices of violence."

## *Sites of Conscience*

Along the same lines, mention should be made of the international NGO 'Sites of Conscience', created in 1999 when the directors of nine historic sites – including the Gulag Museum in Russia, the Slave House in Senegal, Memoria Abierta in Argentina, and the Lower East Side Tenement Museum in the US – came together to explore a shared question: how can heritage sites promote human rights? These museums had little in common in terms of the history or themes they represented or the scope and scale of their properties, but they did share a commitment to placing heritage at the service of building lasting cultures of peace and democracy. They imagined a new type of space, which they called a 'Site of Conscience', defining this as a museum committed to three things: to interpreting history through a site; to engaging in programmes that stimulate dialogue on today's pressing social issues; and to sharing opportunities for public involvement in those issues. They decided to work as a coalition, operating at the intersection of historic preservation, human rights, citizen engagement, education, and the arts. Their work also fitted into broader initiatives aimed at transitional justice or democracy-building, such as Truth Commissions and other post-conflict programs. Tensions and creative innovations have emerged from these efforts in relation to three specific issues: memorialising practice; 'memory wars'; and the destruction and reconstruction of heritage, memory, and identity in post-conflict contexts. "Distancing itself from essentialist formulations of race, ethnicity, or national identity, Sites of Conscience seeks to shape heritage to construct a collective memory of moral acts and choices – of cruelty, compassion, and courage – and offer a space for the ongoing interrogation of the nature of those choices, the reasons for them, and what they suggest for the future."[4]

I have included these types of institutions and activities in this brief overview because their nature and the type of activities they undertake may be somewhat closer to the capacities of EUNIC than are the grassroots-based conflict resolution activities that I began with. But serious questions still remain.

*Where is EUNIC in all this?*

In the light of EUNIC's mission – "to improve and promote cultural diversity and understanding between European societies, and to strengthen international dialogue and co-operation with countries outside Europe" – what kind of added value could its members bring to such efforts, other than the channelling of moral and perhaps financial support mentioned above? In those countries that are represented by these cultural institutes, there must surely be specialised bodies whose members have the competencies and commitments that would enable them to do the job much more effectively. What place or what justification is there for the grouping to function as a conflict resolution organisation? What in fact would this mean? If it is supporting the work of organisations better qualified to carry it out, then there is no problem. But should they be adopting the role of a mediating organisation that seeks to carry out democratic communal problem-solving of the kind that is envisaged by conflict resolution?

This would require turning them into what the American political scientists Barbara Nelson, Linda Kaboolian and Kathryn Carver called 'concord organisations', based on their research into 100 cross-community organisations in Northern Ireland, South Africa, the United States, and Israeli and Palestinian groups working in the US. [5] The researchers defined concord organisations as those that bring together people with fundamentally opposing views or identities for the purpose of promoting civil society while recognising group differences, and they argued that even "liberal and (re)distributive regimes do not automatically convert conflict over domination into conflict over belonging."

They cited the work of Indian political scientist Asutosh Varshney, who found that it takes successful cross-community organisations, including the Hindu-Muslim alliance in the old-style Congress party, to activate the advantages offered by somewhat favourable structural relations. He noted that Indian cities with more cross-community organisations of all kinds had lower levels of communal violence. Importantly, he also found that in Indian cities cross-community contacts by themselves, such as going to the wedding of a friend from another community, are not predictive of lower levels of communal violence.

What is therefore needed to address these sorts of situations in divided societies is precisely the kind of concord organisations that can bring together people with fundamentally opposing views or interests in order to initiate dialogue, witness activities, provide education and training in conflict management and me-

"We Europeans need to be lucidly self-reflective about our self-assigned mission of spreading our positive messages, lest our efforts unwittingly mirror colonialist Europe's 'civilising mission' of yesteryear."

diation, foster community service, and so on. Are EUNIC's members equipped and/or mandated to do this, I wonder?

Aside from this last question, issues also arise with regard to the laudable European humanitarian impulse that underpins the desire to 'do good' elsewhere. The idea being, in this case, that European players can intervene effectively in areas of conflict that exist in other parts of the world. One would of course need to question the assumption that what I have called concord organisations are not something that we in Europe need, since ours is a 'zone of peace'. This is to forget the conflict situations that persist along the margins, or proximate 'outside' of Europe, such as in the Balkans. And, more importantly, this is also to ignore the ways in which ethnic difference has become a pawn to conflicts over power and resources in cities and suburbs right across Europe, something that cries out for effective resolution within our own house!

But this caveat may be a little academic, since it is clear that EUNIC's mission targets the rest of the world. EUNIC exists in order to forge a European whole that is more than the sum of its parts, in other words to forge a pan-European cultural image. Building on thoughts I shared with the 2011 European Cultural Forum with respect to the role of cultural operators in democracy-building elsewhere, I would like to reiterate in these pages that, when we as Europeans seek to 'support' therapeutic work of any kind in other settings, we need to be acutely sensitive to different understandings and priorities, as well as to potential clashes of perspectives.[7] No 'one size fits all' solution can even be remotely envisaged: peaceful conflict resolution, or democracy and human rights, have all become universal values to be sure, but there is no single global formula for their application on the ground. We Europeans need to be lucidly self-reflective about our self-assigned mission of spreading our positive messages, lest our efforts unwittingly mirror colonialist Europe's 'civilising mission' of yesteryear.

### *A marked assymetry of position*

While outsiders can make valuable contributions to conflict-resolution work, it is vital that local peacebuilders and civil society activists have a strong say in development activities. In most international development work, however, there is still a marked asymmetry of position whenever Western experts come in to help train, educate and work with locals. However, in recent years there has been a growing emphasis on collaborative partnerships based on local contexts and cultures. Peace studies expert Craig Zelizer highlights the increasing reliance on direct South-South interactions between conflict-ridden places, where individuals from one conflict region may share their experiences and expertise with those in other conflict regions. One example is the work of the organisation called Initiative for Inclusive Security, which has helped foster linkages and connections amongst women peacebuilders from the Sudan, Colombia, Iraq and elsewhere.

Projects such as these oblige us to recognise both the potential and the limits of the arts in conflict resolution, regardless of who carries out and who supports such work. As a community-arts practitioner reminds us, "although a painting can never stop a bullet, a painting can stop a bullet from being fired". Executing that painting and putting it in place, however, is a specialised and complex affair. Is this really EUNIC's business?

**Yudhishthir Raj Isar's** professional experience straddles different worlds of cultural practice and theory. He is currently Professor of Cultural Policy Studies at The American University of Paris, Eminent Research Visitor at the University of Western Sydney and founding co-editor of the Cultures and Globalization Series. He is a past president of the initiative Culture Action Europe.

1 http://wayback.archive-it.org/2077/20100906203351/http://www.communityarts.net/readingroom/archivefiles/2007/06/integrating_com.php. Accessed 23 September, 2012.

2 James Thompson, 'Performance, globalization and conflict promotion/resolution: experiences from Sri Lanka' in H.K. Anheier and Y.R. Isar (eds.) Conflicts and Tensions. The Cultures and Globalization Series, 1. London: SAGE Publications.

3 See the Wikipedia entry on the West-Eastern Divan Orchestra.

5 Sevcenko, L. (2011) 'Sites of Conscience: Heritage of and for Human Rights' in H.K. Anheier and Y.R. Isar (eds.) Heritage, Memory and Identity. The Cultures and Globalization Series, 4. London: SAGE Publications.

6 Nelson, B., Kaboolian, K. and Carver, Kathryn C. (2007 'Creating concord organizations: institutional design for bridging antagonistic cultures' in H.K. Anheier and Y.R. Isar (eds.) Conflicts and Tensions. The Cultures and Globalization Series, 1. London: SAGE Publications.

7 Y.R Isar, 'Civil society empowerment in third countries: are culture actors providing powerful voices in support of democratization processes?', discussion paper for the European Culture Forum, Brussels, 21 October, 2011 (http://culture-forum-2011.ec.europa.eu/index.jsp).

# Keeping doors open in difficult times

Let's be more precise about the word 'culture'. Let's be more confident and ambitious about what cultural relations can achieve for the EU as a component of its external relations. Let's allow the arts, education and intercultural dialogue to open doors and build trust between communities – and so help to prevent or resolve conflicts. *By Robin Davies*

Until recently, before I joined the British Council, I did not consider that culture had any special or significant role to play in international relations – least of all in the development of global prosperity and stability. I thought culture was museums, art galleries and theatre: something to look at. Only recently have I begun to understand the term 'culture', its importance to international politics and its centrality to the EU's external relations.

I now realise that for much of my life I have not only underestimated the power of culture as a transformational force, but I have also been confused about the term 'culture' itself. I find it clearer to distinguish between the anthropological and humanities concepts of culture. The former 'social-science' concept is about a collective meaning that encompasses people's shared memories, identity, values, norms, beliefs and purpose. The latter 'humanities' concept interprets culture as an agent for creativity: the literature, songs, poems, music, dances, plays, pictures, films, fashion and architecture produced by those who reinforce or challenge their own community's identity through the arts.

These two concepts are intricately linked. The arts foster identity, creativity, belonging and purpose within cultural communities, and play a key role in promoting understanding, sensitivity, and interaction across communities. The arts also promote cultural change, create flexible boundaries of inclusion and enable an overlapping of identities that prevents cultural difference from becoming a source of tension and violence. In this way, culture can generate stability and a sense of security by infusing individuals and communities with a sense of belonging. However, culture can also be manipulated into a negative force by seeking to establish division. By including only 'sameness' and excluding 'difference', culture can provoke tension and violence.

Much has been written about Europe's recent decline in the world's pecking order of growing economies and influence. However, in terms of population size, and commercial, economic and financial influence, the European Union still has a global impact. Even in these austere times, it still accounts for the greatest share of world trade and still generates one-quarter of global wealth. Despite the presence of larger and competing economies, the EU is still the biggest provider of financial assistance to poorer countries, and is increasingly involved in peacekeeping activities, conflict prevention and resolution, and post-conflict reconstruction. The EU has taken a leading role in dealing with the consequences of global warming, the emission of greenhouse gases and in carrying out research into cleaner energy.

### *Cooperation and integration*

The EU brings stability and prosperity to its citizens, is building close relationships with its neighbours and spreading the advantages of open markets, economic growth and democratic political systems. The EU does not seek to impose its political systems, economic principles or western values on others, but welcomes any democratic wider European country as a potential member, pooling resources in the common interest. As it expands, the EU's hallmarks are cooperation and integration.

The EU provides the largest share of all development assistance delivered by the major industrialised countries. Its objectives include eradicating poverty, promoting sustainable development, improving physical and social infrastructures and strengthening state institutions. The EU delivers its aid in many ways: through direct cooperation with governments, the implementation of individual projects (often through NGOs) humanitarian aid, assistance in crisis prevention and support to civil society.

Under its Common Foreign and Security Policy (CFSP), the EU defines the types of diplomatic and political activities it can undertake in conflict prevention and resolution. Influential in an increasingly interconnected planet, the EU seeks to support economic development and political stability in the wider world. The EU's interests go beyond trade and traditional development assistance. They cover support for economic reforms, health and education, infrastructure programmes, research and development and environmental policy, providing a framework for discussing democracy and human rights.

But the EU exports more than just the incentives, tools and skills for political development and economic integration. It also exports European culture – and I mean here both the 'anthropological' and the 'humanities' concepts of the term 'culture'. The EU exports a social and cultural framework within which stability, development and prosperity can flourish. It also exports culture as a creative agent that portrays and communicates this framework.

Our increasingly globalised world reduces the significance of political borders and cultural barriers and opens the way for cultural differences to be understood

"There is more to culture than meets the eye in a museum or art gallery."

and shared agendas to be established and engaged. At the centre of the social and cultural framework exported by the EU through its funded programmes and projects across the world are universally recognisable and accepted norms of behaviour and values, such as the rule of law, liberal democratic social order, the protection of human rights, and the acknowledgement of cultural diversity and respect for other cultures.

## *Going beyond narrow definitions*

The scope of cultural relations extends far beyond any narrow definition of culture as merely 'arts and heritage'. Such a narrow definition does not encompass all the tenets of what can be achieved through the vehicle of culture within international cultural relations. And, placed alongside the more traditional and familiar vehicles of international relations – diplomatic, political, trade and economic – cultural relations are often overlooked as a powerful contributor to stability and prosperity.

Collectively these values and norms represent European 'soft power' – the cultural influence that shapes the heart of European external relations and that should aspire to convey these values and norms to the outside world through a process of intercultural dialogue. Intercultural dialogue involves the promotion of the mutuality and trust that provide the foundation for successful international relations. While hard power is the ability to coerce (through military or economic means) and manipulate, soft power is the means to attract and work towards mutual understanding.

Traditionally, the success of the unification process of the European Union has relied principally on political and economic cooperation. The cultural dimension has been somewhat neglected. But since the end of the Cold War and with the increasing effects of globalisation, culture is moving to centre stage. Cultural relations, in terms of intercultural dialogue and the building of trust through a process of mutual understanding, are an essential component of both European integration and European foreign policy. They bond civil societies, not just government elites.

Because of this bonding power, cultural relations have a growing influence on conflict prevention and resolution. NATO, with its emphasis on preventing conflict rather than responding to it, has developed its 'Comprehensive Approach' to include the cultural angle to peacebuilding, because cultural difference often lies at the heart of conflict – language, religious belief and historical narrative all represent passionate reasons to fight for the survival of a cultural identity. However, culture can also represent the only way to bring people in conflict together.

Today education, sport, art, literature, music and dance are all cultural instruments used by mediators, cultural bodies and governments to reconcile warring factions and to build sustainable peaceful relations by identifying common interests and values. Culture divides, but it also heals. Culture is the soft power of attraction that builds bridges between communities.

Here are some recent examples that serve to illustrate the important role played by culture in many conflict zones:

'Book Cafes' in Zimbabwe have become places where people can meet for safe debate and discussion – and not just about books. That's the point.

A shocking photographic exhibition set up by young peace activists in Nairobi portrays and relives, very publicly, the recent Kenyan post-election violence. Today's Kenyan youth stands and stares and swears 'never again'.

From small beginnings, the Afghan Women's Network now has thousands of members, developing practical projects and activities in their local communities, and giving women a real voice in the country's embryonic governance. Before 2007 the national culture there prohibited decision-making by women.

In Palestine and Israel the sport programme 'Football for Peace' brings divided communities together, tackling cultural differences off the field as energetically as tackling each other on the field. Sport has become a vehicle for wider intercultural dialogue and mutuality.

In the immediate aftermath of the intercommunity conflict in the former Yugoslav Republic of Macedonia (FYROM), a transethnic Slav and Albanian network brought young people together to develop joint educational and cultural projects. By 2005 it had spread right across the country and was encouraging cross-community collaboration within a post-conflict situation.

In the aftermath of the Balkan wars, the Bosnia History Trail project was set up to engage young people from Serb, Bosniak and Croat communities in tracing their shared cultural heritage – a powerful way to value 'the other's' history and perspectives.

Throughout Europe, students are constantly being encouraged to take part in higher education exchange programmes, and international students receive grants to study at European universities. Education is culture too.

### *A sense of community*

These are the types of activities and programmes where the EU is increasingly focusing its investment. The essential rationale for including cultural components in the EU's external policies and relations lies in the power of culture, arts and education to foster a sense of community by means of education and intercultural dialogue. In foreign relations, this is a way of protecting the diversity of cultures, traditions, languages, cultures and different forms of artistic expression. The European Union itself is a collection of diverse cultures. Its gro-

"The European Union itself is a collection of diverse cultures. Its growing cultural footprint ensures that this model is applied at a time when elsewhere other cultural identities are wrestling with each other for dominance and survival."

wing cultural footprint ensures that this model is applied at a time when elsewhere other cultural identities are wrestling with each other for dominance and survival.

The European Union is an example of how fiercely antagonistic nations can gradually transform relations through increased interdependence and a sense of common destiny. Within the diversity of their cultures, they share ideas, norms and values that together constitute an 'abstract culture', in which Europeans see themselves as partners. This is a cultural practice worth exporting.

The development of cultural components for EU external relations and policies allows the Union to accentuate its role as a 'partner' for third countries and to support multilateral diplomacy rather than unilateral action. The strength of the European Union's soft power lies in its readiness to seek dialogue on matters of difference in order to reach mutual understanding, rather than resolving conflict by military or economic means. Culture is not a sector or sphere of society that is distinct from economy or politics but rather an integral part of them. Cultural experiences allow individuals to engage intellectually and emotionally and can provide personal connections that can outlive or override political disagreements. It is no coincidence that visits to cultural institutions are a permanent feature of diplomatic trips – this is where people-to-people relations are built, before the political discourse begins. Culture offers more than meets the eye in these cultural institutions. Culture keeps doors open in difficult times.

Over the last two decades, cultural relations have become progressively more influential as we have moved away from the predictabilities of the bi-polar Cold War to the vagaries of the multi-polar world of today. Cultural factors play a larger part in defining our sense of identity: our language, religion and historicity. People perceive and measure each other against a cultural yardstick. And as the effects of technology, wider access to news, ideas and knowledge and globalisation permeate every community, opportunities for contact and exchange grow. And because of this intercultural activity, cultures are meeting, mingling and morphing in an increasingly interconnected world.

We can no longer think of culture as being detached from mainstream politics and international relations. Understanding of, mutual respect for, and engagement with the other's culture are in fact at the very heart of political dialogue and foreign relationships. The EU is in a position to exploit the rich opportunities of cultural relations to enhance prosperity and stability worldwide.

**Robin Davies** joined the British Council in 2009 and is Head of the Council's Partnership and External Relations team in Brussels. Prior to that, his career included serving in the Royal Navy, where he planned operational routes for destroyers and frigates, working as a Naval/Defence Attaché in Moscow and the Hague and as a strategic planner at the British Ministry of Defence and at NATO Headquarters in Brussels.

# Little strokes fell big oaks Cultural Institutes may not resolve conflicts, but with courageous and thought-provoking programmes they can prepare the ground for breaking down stereotypes and prejudices so that societies can start to tackle sensitive issues.

*By Martin Eichtinger*

2011 was the year of democratic movements in the Arab world. These movements were supported by a new generation of Arab citizens who dared to challenge old regimes in order to make their dreams about an open society come true. 2012 will be the year that shows whether they have succeeded in their longing for more freedom and democracy. As the region's neighbour, the European Union has to ask itself just what it has contributed to these citizens' efforts.

As a representative of a country that was one of the founding fathers of the European Network of Institutes of Culture (EUNIC), I would like to take a closer look at a new role for cultural diplomacy that has developed over recent years in parallel to the institutes' primary goal of supporting young artists and creative and innovative talent.

Since the establishment of the EU's External Action Service, a series of very fruitful discussions have taken place, acknowledging the positive role of culture in the external relations of the European Union and the potential of cultural diplomacy in foreign relations. While some deplore the fact that cultural relations do not figure among the EEAS' tasks and that EU embassies do not include cultural officers amongst their staff, others still believe in the nation state's monopoly when it comes to cultural representation.

The world of culture is much too complex and diverse to fit into administrative organisational structures. Artists, cultural networks and civil society organisations in the field of culture now cooperate internationally thanks to the communication revolution. They do not behave like a big orchestra that can be conducted by anyone, but act more like molecules in the atmosphere, performing random movements, while at the same time constantly joining together to form new structures.

Cultural institutes have adapted to this new world of cultural cooperation. The focus has shifted from a culture of representation to a culture of participation in the global cultural dialogue. And in addition to serving as a springboard for the participation of artists and creative individuals or groups in international cultural exchanges, cultural institutes now consider it part of their remit to be involved in cultural diplomacy. These days the programmes of European cultural institutes increasingly reflect the political and social developments between countries and people.

Many cultural institutes have already become involved in intercultural and interreligious dialogue. I believe it is high time that the European cultural institutes, under the EUNIC umbrella, faced these challenges together: we need to change gear and transform our words into action. The decisions made at the recent EUNIC General Assembly in Brussels are a step in the right direction. However, we need to move more quickly and decisively and start implementing our first flagship project in this field, which we have been discussing since the summer of 2011.

"Diverse societies do not have to be divided societies; cultural and religious differences do not produce exclusion unless they are hardened by discrimination."

Jorge Sampaio, High Representative President Sampaio, United Nations Alliance of Civilizations at UNAOC's Annual Forum in Doha/Qatar 2011

In doing so, we have to ask ourselves some fundamental questions:

- Where do we want to go, i.e. what are our objectives?
- Where do we start and how do we divide up the work between EUNIC's member institutes, given their differences in size and budget?
- How do we achieve the desired results?

Thanks to their structural independence from political institutions, including those at European level, cultural institutes (i.e. EUNIC member institutes) can operate more freely and can successfully supplement the role of the EU, as well as national embassies or trade missions, as open meeting places for civil society and platforms for cooperation between people. Furthermore, their cultural activities in the host countries usually gain a higher profile than the work of other official representative bodies.

But intercultural and interreligious dialogue and cooperation is not an easy undertaking. We have all experienced the complexity of culture – there is a great deal of potential, but also a degree of risk. Culture as such is not a universal value and can even be a source of conflict. Intercultural relations force us to constantly deal with the Janus-faced nature of culture.

Confrontation between various cultures almost always results from a conflict of ideas, and yet it is precisely this conflict of ideas that can lead to creativity and, once again, to culture. We actually need creativity and culture to unite diversity. Diversity – be it ethnic, religious, cultural or linguistic – is a reality in our societies. It has in fact become the core element of our European identity and is reflected in our common motto "United in Diversity", something which should always be our top priority.

But of course it is still important to have the right expectations. We will not bring about democracy and human rights or actually resolve conflicts just by bringing creative people together. We cannot take the place of the fire brigade. Anything we do will seem like a drop in the ocean, but as we know, little strokes fell big oaks!

Cultural institutes may not resolve conflicts, but with courageous and thought-provoking programmes they can prepare the ground for breaking down stereotypes and prejudices so that societies can start to tackle sensitive issues.

Cultural institutes need to aim for tolerance and mutual respect while trying to be the driving force behind the promotion and safeguarding of diversity. At the same time, we must make sure that our activities are based on mutual respect for our global partners. We need to avoid anything which can be interpreted as neo-colonialism, expressions of superiority or lecturing.

We should strive to engage a wider audience, including citizens and civil society, and not just cater to elites that are often out of touch with sections of their own societies. For this reason, it will be increasingly important to create high-profile projects and to ensure that the successes of the cultural institutes receive regular coverage in the mass media.

## *Two immediate challenges*

As we are directly affected by developments in our neighbouring states, it makes sense that this is precisely where EUNIC is thinking of launching its first joint flagship project. The socio-economic differences between us and our neighbours to the south and east are certainly a potential source of conflict, especially if we fail to take advantage of the huge opportunities offered by the Arab Spring. We face two immediate challenges: firstly, we need to establish a sustainable dialogue with the new governments and secondly we need to offer the benefit of our experience in building peaceful societies through cooperation between governments and civil society. In doing this, we need to ensure that we take into account the differences between individual countries and societies. There is no one size that fits all when it comes to cooperation.

We can point to some lessons learned from recent history with respect to the dangers inherent in a lack of willingness to cooperate as equal partners, as illustrated by the fascinating brochure published

"We will not bring about democracy and human rights or actually resolve conflicts just by bringing creative people together."

by Poland on its road to democracy and EU membership.

As a starting point, we should prepare a clear roadmap of the joint steps that should be taken and ensure that we all have the necessary tools to proceed. More than anything, we need a high degree of intercultural competence and professional empathy (including trained mediators), along with the willingness of those involved to cross existing divides. In particular, we need to make sure that our partners really feel that we are all on an equal footing.

As EUNIC member institutes differ widely in terms of organisational structure, budget and personnel resources, we need to organise our joint endeavours in such as way as to allow for different forms of participation. It is more important to have maximum participation than to exclude members, just as long as there is a clear commitment to making a fair contribution, even if it is only in kind. We will be much stronger if we move forward together.

### *Sit down and listen*

In a conflict, it requires courage not just to stand up and speak, but also to sit down and listen, as Winston Churchill once put it. Sitting down and listening is the sine qua non for successful dialogue. And dialogue remains the only way of bringing us all safely to the end of our road together. I fully believe that, in terms of conflict resolution and prevention, the promotion of dialogue through all layers of society is a powerful instrument for raising awareness, fostering mutual understanding and combating negative stereotypes and hostility.

Let me emphasise in this context Austria´s commitment to the dialogue between cultures and religions. Austria, and in particular Vienna, has a long-standing tradition as a hub for dialogue and exchange at both national and international level. As early as the 1980s, we had already instigated various initiatives, such as a regular Christian-Islamic dialogue.

Cultural dialogue should be based on the universal application of human rights and fundamental freedoms, the respect of which is a precondition for a peaceful and diverse society. Therefore, it is of utmost importance to also recognise the importance of interreligious and intercultural dialogue in the context of the successful integration of minorities for the benefit of our societies as a whole. After all, integration is one of the most pressing issues facing our societies in a changing Europe, if not the most pressing.

Migration and integration will be one of the key leitmotivs of the 5th UNAOC Annual Forum, which is to take place in Vienna in the spring of 2013. Let me express my hope that EUNIC as an organisation will not only be able to participate in UNAOC's Fifth Annual Forum, but also to present the initial results of its activities in the area of promoting dialogue between cultures.

The feeling of arriving as a migrant in a foreign country, of experiencing linguistic and cultural barriers or simply being perceived as a minority in any society can all lead to insecurity and, in the worst case, to marginalisation and aggression. This is an experience that migrants have in common with all members of minorities, whatever their religious or cultural background.

Special attention should be paid to the development and support of women and youth during any dialogue. Among various national and international initiatives, we are currently organising a training seminar for Turkish women in Austria who will later act as dialogue guides and mentors in their communities. The main topics will be gender issues, education, migration and media. Our seminar's aim is to create bridge-builders within and between communities and to establish a sustainable network of women engaged in dialogue activities. This concept could also easily be transferred to the international arena.

So in my view, the way forward for cultural institutes is to embark on a constructive dialogue with our neighbours at all levels of society, both at international level and with the migrant communities within our own societies in Europe. While continuing the successful cooperation of our EUNIC clusters around the world on joint cultural activities, we also need to get involved in the new challenge for cultural diplomacy: its contribution to securing global peace, conflict prevention and post-conflict mediation through dialogue between different cultures and religions.

It is a noble task, but also a difficult one. It is a long-term project that often, unfortunately, offers very little in the way of immediate results. Its effects are generally not that easy to measure and are often only seen in the absence of conflict and war. However, this should not prevent anyone from being whole-heartedly involved in the project.

Based on EUNIC's principles, we need to continue to work on flagship projects aimed at furthering cultural exchange and cooperation between people and fostering tolerance and respect for each other or, in a nutshell, to promote the very ideal behind the idea of Europe: to foster unity in diversity and to support diversity in unity.

**Martin Eichtinger** is Director General for Cultural Policy at the Austrian Federal Ministry for European and International Affairs.

# A domain of peace

From the Age of Enlightenment to an Arab street, it has taken a long time to cross the Mediterranean. Finally, Europe can return the treasures of wisdom, philosophy and science to the Arab shores where they originated. *By Luciano Rispoli*

The wind of freedom that is blowing amongst the Arab peoples is first and foremost a wind of culture. Culture is essential for freedom, for the different approaches to democracy and for the very process of making demands. These different cultures worked together and characterised the moment of revolt among the Arab people. If the Arabs are to achieve their freedom and opportunities for expression – from a symbolic immolation in Tunis to a bloody conflict for liberty in Syria, and not forgetting the war in Libya – then they need to learn from European experiences of freedom and peace and from democratic, if sometimes contradictory, dialogues. From the Age of Enlightenment to an Arab street, it has taken a long time to cross the Mediterranean. Finally, Europe can return the treasures of wisdom, philosophy and science to the Arab shores where they originated.

Europe is now looking at the Arab world with new eyes. The time has finally come to understand what it is rejecting. And what perhaps is too dominant in our societies: absolute power, the dominance of money, the supremacy of one caste over another, the withdrawal of culture and its privatisation with the sole aim of making money.

It is not that trade in itself is harmful. It is also a creator of social standards. But it becomes dangerous as soon as it monopolises and colonises minds. In all cultures, uniformity is a killer.

In Europe today, one culture rules above all others: results. Yet, failure and futility are eminently fertile. Failure is a materialisation of the right to be different and art of the right to be unnecessary. Today, culture is only experienced and viewed as a vehicle, a means to an end. As a subject, it is disappearing from official discourse and programmes. Today it is also expected to bring development, along with projects, growth, harmonisation, not to mention harmony. And if it wants to attract funding, it has to bring results.

Culture, held hostage by collective security, should regroup and try to work together. Culture, held hostage by economics, should serve the interests of the creative industries. Culture, held hostage by war, should play its part in the prevention and resolution of conflicts via policy directives.

Let‘s assume that the era of art for art's sake is over, as is culture for culture's sake. Nevertheless, the fact that politics considers culture as an instrument proves the central importance of this social medium.

The wind of freedom is blowing through the Arab world while European economies are running out of steam, and social norms are being toppled and reinvented from reality. But despite this, culture is proving its essential significance through its creativity with no preconceived ideas and its lack of ultimate purpose other than to exist. Culture is a glue that holds society together, a collective project that allows the sharing of common standards. Culture is enriched by changes and constant evolution.

There is culture and cultures. They endlessly intersect and challenge each other. Cultures, "murderous identities" to borrow the title of a famous essay by the Lebanese-French writer Amin Maalouf, disappear behind culture, which prepares and creates the space of the word or of silence, permitting believers to change their minds and unbelievers to worship whatever they like.

Culture, a domain of peace, is made up of values or experiences that we Europeans would like to see shared worldwide. Culture as a reassuring factor that upholds individual and collective freedoms and the certainty that the 'other' has a right to be different. In this respect, culture goes beyond its cultural actions in terms of promoting events and experiences and is fundamentally universal.

EUNIC is an association that brings together all the national cultural institutes of the European Union's Member States. It has an ambitious objective: to use culture to raise awareness of the European experience. The experience of putting an end to centuries of war; the experience of promoting dialogue and pooling knowledge; the experience of plurality; the experience of individual rights and collective solidarity existing side-by-side. This sometimes includes the experience of failure, but above all it is the will to build something together while our destinies are inexorably interlinked.

## *Promoting the experience of plurality*

EUNIC has established five main priorities that are being disseminated and implemented by some eighty clusters worldwide:

1. To engage with civil society, with the help of clusters in the major countries of the Arab world, in order to encourage the exchange of ideas on a range of topics such as the media, cultural operators and their cross-training, networking of cultural spaces and the establishment of legal standards designed to protect cultural workers. EUNIC approaches the MENA region (Middle East & North Africa) with full awareness that our peoples already interact and live together. This peaceful coexistence is essential, although some extremists on both sides are doing their best to destroy it. Political and/or religious extremism is the enemy of culture.

2. To pursue a dialogue with China, a great cultural power and partner in all the areas relating to culture. This should include everything from creation to co-production, from marketing to distribu-

tion, from reciprocal influence to mutual discovery. In 2012, EUNIC and China are holding their fifth intercultural dialogue. The main topic of this dialogue is "cultural activities and urban development" and the subtopics are:

- The protection and exploration of local cultural resources and development of cultural brands for cities
- The role of culture for urban sustainable development
- Creative industries and (contemporary) art education
- Community culture and urban vitality

Alongside these dialogues between European and Chinese experts and artists, workshops are also contributing to a better understanding of our different and valuable experiences in Europe and China.

3. To make environmental culture a new social standard, in the process encouraging development and health.

4. To link the cultural actions to the idea of growth in the economic sense. Culture has to be understood as a sector of the economy that is given the full attention of governments and public authorities at national, European and global level. This part of the economy is subject to specific regulations and must be protected more than any other sector because it creates wealth, employment and improved living conditions.

5. Finally, to promote culture as a powerful tool for conflict prevention and, in some cases, in the processes of conflict resolution.

This fifth goal also places a considerable weight of expectation on the EU. The EUNIC network is calling for a better, more structured, and more sustainable collaboration with the Commission and the External Action Service. Our network holds firm to the idea of improving relations via dialogue with its partners, and this is given concrete form in the organisation of events, conferences, co-productions and cultural dissemination in order to create a greater understanding. The EU delegations also value the collaboration with EUNIC.

### *Cultural diplomacy really exists*

Today, EUNIC is feeling fairly optimistic. Europe's cultures are visible throughout the world and in EUNIC the EU has a strong tool for promoting this cultural visibility and showing that the EU is not just a tool for technical, political and economic administration, but also – even predominantly – a fantastic cultural experience. The joint projects of the National Institutes and the clusters ensure Europe is clearly visible and transcend Europe's technocratic and strictly economic image. Cultural diplomacy really exists, and is being carried forward by the cultural actions of the Member States.

It is also increasingly being borne by the way the EUNIC clusters are working together and "defending our shared inheritance". After all, with its 80 clusters all around the world running hundreds of activities that reach millions of citizens on all five continents, EUNIC is delivering a clear message: Europe is about the hope of being together, respecting our differences and turning them into strong, stable and sustainable power; a peaceful power. There have been no wars between EU members since the beginning of this adventure. A great deal has already been done, and we should be extremely grateful to the founders of the EU. But more still needs to be done, particularly in the area of culture. A visible economic programme needs to be launched in order to support the EU's external cultural activities abroad. As a powerful institution, the EU – which should not be confused with national cultures and domestic cultural policies – must promote peace, stability, development and health by supporting cultural actions.

We are told that culture is expensive, so we are always asked to prove its benefits. The EU has an important role to play in this respect by putting forward the idea that culture cannot be haggled over. Although Member States have no intention of delegating their domestic cultural policy to the EU, there is still a strong need for an EU cultural policy. This means having a clear view of the European experience so that we can promote it abroad, but also having enough culture professionals to do this, along with long-term funding. Failure to spread our successes via culture paves the way for possible wars, ethnic and social struggles and ultimately the risk of losing the advantages gained from 60 years of joint effort.

Can we seriously imagine, even for a second, what our world would be like without culture? No words, no music, no paintings, no sculptures, no theatre, no literature, no stories, no entertainment... in other words, nothing that we could have in common. Could we seriously envisage a Europe that does not promote culture through cultures? Culture protects against the worst enemy that lies within us. It provides us with money and deters us from the worst. It holds us, so we hold onto it. It makes us, constructs us, and in return, we shape it, day by day.

**Luciano Rispoli** worked for the France Télévisions Group for 12 years as director of the MENA region. He was then posted to Turkey for four years as media attaché for Turkey, Central Asia and the Caucasus region. He joined EUNIC in November 2011 and until early 2012 was Director of the Permanent Secretariat of EUNIC Global.

**Food for the soul** In South Sudan, poverty and hunger are widespread as a result of decades of civil war. Caring for refugees returning from neighbouring countries and other parts of the Sudan represents a major problem. Local fighting continues to flare up. Illiteracy remains at over 80%. What role can culture place in this kind of context? Interview with **Dr Jok Madut Jok**, Undersecretary in the Ministry of Culture, Republic of South Sudan.

**Ruth Ur:** It's almost one year since South Sudan declared independence on 9th July 2011. The world watched in amazement and excitement as the world's youngest country was born and a new sense of optimism emerged after almost 50 years of war. But this first year has not been an easy one, with conflict erupting both on the border and between tribes, and the break down in relations with the North resulting in drastic austerity measures issued by the government in Juba. As Undersecretary in the Ministry of Culture, how do you see the role of culture in contributing to nation-building in these challenging times?

**Jok Madut Jok:** My view is that if a new country must have infrastructure, deliver social services and be able to provide food for its citizens, it is just as important that it celebrates its cultures and promotes its arts, so that its soul is also nourished. Feeding the soul of the nation is even more important in circumstances such as now, when the economic situation is dire. If we assume that a sense of nationhood and citizens' pride in their new country emanates from the country's ability to deliver services to them, we should be able to assume that under austerity measures, when the country cannot provide any services, any programmes that attempt to imbue the citizen with a sense of pride and tie them more strongly to the polity, will be even more important now. It is as if to say that if we cannot give our people any services, let us at least offer them entertainment and preserve their cultural practices and values, and provide them with opportunities to refine their talents, all in the interest of building a collective national identity.

**Ruth Ur:** Putting to one side the idea of culture as entertainment, I wonder how you balance the need to build a collective national identity with the potential of culture to ask questions (rather than seek answers) and as a means of addressing the trauma of war and unresolved conflicts?

**Jok Madut Jok:** Indeed, culture performs myriad functions beyond the preservation and celebration of traditions. As a country that was united more strongly by the opposition to North Sudan and by the common goal of liberation rather than by any sense of historical oneness between all the people, South Sudan had always assumed that this unity of purpose would form the foundation of nationhood upon independence. However, when independence came, the country quickly found itself as little more than a mere geographical entity, having over 70 ethnic groups that see themselves as different from one another. There was need for a concerted effort to build its national unity and national identity, and the most obvious way to do this was through an equitable display, celebration and promotion of its cultures, building on cultural commonalities and pointing out that cultural diversity is an asset, not the liability that it has proven to be in many other African countries.

**Ruth Ur:** I'd like us to go back to this question of South Sudanese culture. Is there really a South Sudanese culture that differentiates itself from the separated North or indeed from neighbouring countries? And how do you see your work contributing to a positive identity for South Sudan that is not merely defined in opposition to the North?

**Jok Madut Jok:** Cultures cannot really be totally distinct from one another, regardless of the distance between people or the history of bitter conflicts. What one finds more often is that cultures engage in influence and counter-influence. So distance or closeness between cultures is not what matters. What defines South Sudanese practices as uniquely South Sudanese is the fact that these are practised within its territories, and so long as the country gives all of them equitable access on a national stage, they would all become just different components of South Sudanese culture. Whether a cultural practice is indigenous to South Sudan or was borrowed from somewhere else, so long as it is practised within South Sudan and its practitioners attach value to it and consider it an important component of their identity, no one would argue against it, but it would be promoted equally. Another thing that is undeniable is that there are more similarities between the different South Sudanese ethnic nationalities than between one ethnic group and neighbouring groups across the borders. The work of the Ministry of Culture is to create the national symbols that citizens can rally around as the core unifying practices, to promote the commonalities between ethnic groups, with a view to creating a national identity that every citizen can subscribe to whilst remaining loyal to his or her ethnic group.

**Ruth Ur:** As you say, South Sudan is the size of the Iberian Peninsula and has over 70 ethnic groups and languages. Does the concept of a nation state and a national identity therefore really make sense or is it simply a colonial paradigm imposed on a largely tribal society?

**Jok Madut Jok:** Though some communities in the territory that is now South Sudan were tribal kingdoms, there is no doubt that the concept of a nation state with a centralised authority was historically foreign to most ethnic communities in South Sudan. The notion of a nation state was introduced by the European empires, who, in the process of carving up the African continent, created 'the Sudan' out of an amalgam of ethnic nationalities. But the idea of a nation state is here to stay and having a sovereign state necessitates that its leadership forges its political unity, social cohesion, stability and prosperity. Since the state is now a reality and the people who live in it must coexist, it is crucial to find the symbols that bind them together to form a nation. The trick is that whatever the political leadership picks as the components of this country's identity must be symbols that every citizen sees themselves represented in, and that means inclusivity and equitable representation. We must be conscious of our own past. Some of the most significant factors in South Sudan's decision to secede from the Sudan were a feeling of exclusion from the symbols of the country's cultural identity and the favouring of Arab Islamic identity.

"The notion of a nation state was introduced by the European Empires, who, in the process of carving up the African continent, created "the Sudan" out of an amalgam of ethnic nationalities."

**Ruth Ur:** Despite significant oil reserves, as well as other natural resources, tragically South Sudan remains one of the least developed regions in the world. Looking at the economic potential of culture, what do you think might be a key growth area for South Sudan and how might this be exploited to generate wealth?

**Jok Madut Jok:** First of all, we are fully aware of the fact that oil is a finite resource and diversification of our economy is not only necessary, but essential for our survival. All potential sources of income are currently being explored, both by the state as well as by individuals and communities. Secondly, like in the rest of black Africa, the South Sudanese produce a variety of crafts and functional arts. A great many products, from pottery to basketry to agricultural implements to war objects and religious/spiritual objects, are not produced for the sake of 'art' but instead are artistically made for everyday use. So in addition to their convenience in daily life, they are also valuable trade items, with potential to supply tourist markets and exchanges between tribes. Unfortunately, many of these traditional crafts are under threat from the global market, particularly plastic and aluminium from Asia. It is the view of the ministry that if these crafts were to be maintained as part of the heritage of South Sudan, they will not only preserve the unique culture, but also generate income for their producers. We must be reminded that we might not accord them the value they represent for us until we no longer have them, and then it would be extremely difficult to revive that culture. To reduce the possibility of loss, we are now in the process of collecting samples of every one of these items from every tribe and arranging them into a mobile exhibition that will exhibit them to South Sudanese communities in ways that provoke debate on the nature of culture and nation. At the end of the travelling exhibition, we will then display them in museums in Juba, Wau and Malakal, grouping them not by tribe but by function. This will reveal the commonalities between all the tribal traditions, reduce discord, increase tolerance for difference, promote coexistence and could eventually demonstrate a degree of national unity.

**Ruth Ur:** One of the things that most struck me in Juba was the discrepancy between talent and creativity on the one hand and the lack of basic infrastructure for culture on the other. Even finding spaces for rehearsals or exhibitions is difficult because of inflated rental prices. Considering the years of war, the lack of infrastructure is hardly surprising, but I wonder, in such a challenging context, where does one start? Or perhaps one could look at it another way, let's say it's 2015 and we are looking back. What would you like to have achieved?

**Jok Madut Jok:** It breaks my heart every time a young talented artist comes to my office to tell me that she is unable to exhibit her paintings due to a lack of galleries or cultural centres. Or another is looking to rent a section of a restaurant to convert it into a theatrical stage, or a young musician cannot perform his art due to lack of venues. What used to be South Sudan's only cultural institution in Juba, Nyakorun Cultural Center, was leased off to a private business before the end of the war, and it is no longer available to artists for free. In this situation, South Sudan cannot reach its potential as a great nation if it does not offer its artists the opportunity to promote their talent and promote the arts in general as a medium of dialogue between generations and ethnic groups and as a way of dispelling the stereotypes between tribes that foment inter-tribal violence. To give arts and culture the opportunity to be the language of cohesion, it is important that South Sudan and its development partners invest in cultural infrastructure, beginning with establishing a national cultural centre, a performing arts centre in Juba that will facilitate a cultural dialogue between tribes and with neighbouring countries. It is our conviction in the national Ministry of Culture, Youth and Sports, that while nation-building projects may not be a panacea against ethnic violence, they are surely very important components of any effort to bring stability to the country. Another crucial investment that is in our plans, but unattainable due to lack or resources, are theatres in Juba, Malakal and Wau, followed by a theatre education programme, as this is a valuable vehicle for the promotion of coexistence, hygiene, and many other social values, especially if we start with school children so that they grow up with these ideas.

**Ruth Ur:** In a nation where 51% of the population lives below the poverty line and illiteracy remains at around 85%, what would you say are your priorities concerning cultural policy?

**Jok Madut Jok:** We are working together with the Ministry of Education on some of the basic requirements for a democratic educational system. The most crucial area is a curriculum and teacher training that emphasises instruction in native languages, at least in the lower grades. A curriculum and textbooks that build in the local culture and surroundings encourages children to stay in school. The next thing is a school arts programme, including a school theatre programme, which could be utilised as tool for conveying messages about peace, the importance of girls' education and to promote the values of coexistence and the shared history of the struggle for freedom.

"It breaks my heart every time a young talented artist comes to my office to tell me that she is unable to exhibit her paintings due to a lack of galleries or cultural centres."

**Ruth Ur:** Culture is the primary means by which different groups, societies and communities express their common values, beliefs and traditions. It can bind people, but can also lead to division and friction. Sometimes those of us working in the cultural field need reminding that culture is not always a force for good! Can you say something about how you see the relationship between culture and conflict?

**Jok Madut Jok:** Where culture is blamed for conflict, it is easy to see that it is really not culture that is causing it, but instead it is either a feeling of exclusion from the national stage or attempts at imposing one culture onto members of another culture. Otherwise, on the whole, culture is a very valuable vehicle for promoting coexistence. For example, in South Sudan there are some tribes that engage in wrestling as a sport. These are the groups that also happen to be competing for resources and fighting one another. In recent years, we have tried to promote wrestling as a national sport, trying to get the tribes to transfer their competition from shooting each other to wrestling each other. The more we can encourage these types of 'friendly' interactions and dialogue, the more we will be able to break down stereotypes and increase tolerance.

**Ruth Ur:** That's a fascinating idea. I'm interested in hearing more about your views on how cultural interventions can promote stability and social cohesion.

Do you have any other compelling examples, either from South Sudan or elsewhere?

**Jok Madut Jok:** Of all the cultural practices that I have observed between different groups, it seems to me that the most successful cultural item that mediates between people is language. The more people know of each others' languages, the less antagonistic they are to one another. If South Sudan were to invest in a language policy, whereby, say, the native language of any tribe is considered the national language, followed by English as the language of government and higher education and then a lingua franca such as Juba Arabic, the country would be more likely to emerge more united within a generation. I have also been impressed by the United States National Endowment for the Arts whose slogan is "great nations deserve great arts." The idea is that no matter how diverse a country may be, culture would be less of a problem if each is given equal space, and culture would be seen as contributing instead to the colourfulness of the country.

**Ruth Ur:** The EUNIC network has already established a presence in Juba and there is even a highly successful European Film Week, which takes place at the Institut Francais on the Juba University campus. Both the British Council and Institut Francais have offices in Juba, whilst others operate from centres in Nairobi or Khartoum. What role could you envisage for the European cultural organisations in promoting stability or do you think our contribution lies elsewhere? What I'm asking is, given the challenges, where do you think we could really make a difference?

**Jok Madut Jok:** Initially, we placed a lot of hope in European cultural organisations both in terms of financial assistance as well as expertise in cultural preservation, exchange, display and promotion, but we have become aware of the budgetary cuts that some of them have gone through. This makes it difficult for individual agencies to support big cultural projects in the developing world on their own. But there is still a great deal that Europe can accomplish in South Sudan, if programmes are coordinated and shared between agencies. This would prevent duplication and the possible thin spreading of capacity. Our priority areas would be school theatre and arts programmes, a cultural centre in Juba and tying arts and culture programmes to education. This would do preservation work, peacebuilding work and encourage and develop talents at a very young age, as well as providing young citizens with stories that tie them to their nation and promote tolerance towards difference.

**Ruth Ur:** Earlier this year, with help from the British Council, the South Sudan Theatre Company came to London to take part in the Globe to Globe festival

"Culture gets unquestioningly blamed for actions that are intrinsically more to do with gendered power relations than with cultural prescriptions."

with a production of Shakespeare's Cymbeline in Juba Arabic. One South Sudanese member of the audience wrote to us saying, "The euphoria generated by the performance among the diaspora is only second to the declaration of South Sudan as an independent nation on July 9th, 2011. It was nice to see, for once, that the negative image of South Sudan in the media, represented by a starving child, who is too weak to even chase our flies from their face, replaced by that of smiling casts of Cymbeline. The play has also made South Sudanese to start questioning the apologist phrases being churned out to cover our many failures. Phrases like: 'We' re a new nation starting from scratch' or its variant that 'Rome was not built in a day!' sounds increasingly hollow, when set against the accomplishment of South Sudan theatre, which four months ago, did not even exist!" How do you think you can build on experiences such as these to alter perceptions both within South Sudan and outside?

**Jok Madut Jok:** The first thing we did when the group returned from London was to have them perform here in Juba, one show for dignitaries and another for the public, with a view to developing a public appreciation for the arts. It is now common to hear people saying that they had no prior appreciation of theatre but are now interested in seeing more of such performances. We are trying to take advantage of this momentum to establish a South Sudan Theatre Company through parliamentary legislation, which would become a government-supported company, but independent of the government in terms of raising its own funds, in order to encourage play-writing and the performance of a variety of topics that have been raised throughout South Sudan in politics, economics, social order, security, hygiene and conflict. There is now a widespread conviction that theatre is not only a medium to reshape the image of the country internationally, but also to comment on our own society in ways that are corrective, to say nothing of its entertainment value. It is now our task as people who work in the field of culture to see into it that this momentum is not lost. One significant way of maintaining that momentum and increasing people's appreciation of theatre is the establishment of a national theatre in Juba and the renovation of existing theatres in Wau and Malakal. Furthermore, to produce the material for the theatre, it is important to build on the play-writing culture that already exists here and conduct annual prize competitions for writing plays, poetry and short stories. This is the material that would become the fodder for the theatre company.

**Ruth Ur:** Since you took up your post, you have worked tirelessly to build capacity within your Ministry of Culture and to develop an infrastructure for culture in your country. But your professional background is in maternal and reproductive health. I'm wondering – how do you see the connection between your academic work and your role in the Ministry of Culture?

**Jok Madut Jok:** What led me to studying women's health were a number of practices I had observed throughout Africa that negatively affect women, practices that are claimed to be cultural prescriptions. For example, women's health is affected every day by gendered violence, early marriage for girls, wife inheritance, labour expectations, and reproductive expectations. To understand women's health, it was important for me to study the social and cultural norms that relate to it. What I came to learn from this is that culture gets unquestioningly blamed for actions that are intrinsically more to do with gendered power relations than with cultural prescriptions. If cultures are meant to be adaptive, to enable their members to cope with change, then their negative impact on women seems to make them maladaptive. For example, bride price has always been favoured by most communities because of the role it plays in cementing social relations and marriages. But people are increasingly critical of this practice for its role in women's negative experiences in marital settings, whereby men may see their wives as property they have paid for and who can therefore be abused if they do not conform to certain expectations. Bride wealth may also be partly related to child marriage, with disastrous consequences for maternal mortality. Another example is the perception that women are only best as mothers and wives, and that they count for little else. This mindset is responsible for the lack of access to education for girls and to jobs outside the home for women, for the health consequences of frequent births, and for the physical abuse if they try to step out of these bounds. This is why engaging in culture could result in the promotion of positive practices and perhaps the shedding of practices that more and more members of society are beginning to criticise.

**Ruth Ur:** Finally, many people know little more about South Sudan than its tragic history of conflict. Can you think of one object or story that might give readers a different view of your country?

**Jok Madut Jok:** Yes, the image that the world has about South Sudan has often focused on war and its citizens as victims of Sudanese state violence, much of which is true. But even though we have been of the most war-torn countries in the world since WWII, the humanity and resilience of the people of South Sudan has always been unmistakable. Only people who lived or worked in South Sudan during the war would really understand when we talk about the basic values that helped our people to sustain their values of generosity and sharing. I remember the 1990s when famines were rampant, when foreign aid workers would arrive to deliver humanitarian aid and the people they came to rescue would struggle to find a goat or sheep or a bull to slaughter in honour of their guests. While there are many cultural items unique to South Sudan that I can mention to you, it is really norms, traditions and values that are the most ubiquitous symbols of South Sudan's culture. For example, South Sudan is home to something anthropologists refer to as the "cattle complex." This is a reference to a cultural region that includes the Nuer, Dinka, Murle and Mandari tribes that raise cattle as the mainstay of their livelihoods. But because the cattle are central to every aspect of life, from marriage to payment of poll tax to school fees for children to purchasing market commodities, the cattle themselves have become seen as the most prized cultural items. South Sudan has more cattle than people, and the cultural norms that surround the cattle resources are complex, funny and nuanced in a way that makes it a true cultural resource.

*Interview conducted by Ruth Ur*

**Jok Madut Jok** is Undersecretary of Culture at the Ministry of Culture, Youth and Sports in the Republic of South Sudan and Associate Professor of History at Loyola Marymount University in California. His book entitled "Sudan: Race, Religion and Violence" was published in 2007. Jok Madut Jok is a co-editor of the "The Sudan Handbook" (2010) and recently co-founded a South Sudanese research organisation, the Sudd Institute.
**Ruth Ur** is Director of "Programmes and Partnerships, Wider Europe" at the British Council. During her 15-year career at the Council she has been Head of Arts & Development and held posts in Israel and Turkey, as well as being involved in curatorial work. She has helped with the launch of a major study on "Artistic Practices and Social & Political Change in Libya, Egypt, Tunisia and Morocco", which is being carried out by the University of York and is due to be published at the end of 2012.

**Opening the doors for Europe: EUNIC** **In the past there has been a lack of a common, coordinated EU strategy for the role of culture in the continent's external relations. EUNIC, the network of European cultural relations institutes, has jumped in to fill this gap. With its 2,000 branches in over 150 countries around the world it ensures that the cultural sector has a strong, independent voice and that there is recognition of its value as a means of promoting greater understanding between people, societies and nations.**

EUNIC was formed in 2006 as a network of national cultural institutes and ministries based in the various EU member states. At present there are 27 members from 24 EU countries. EUNIC is one of the largest cultural multilateral networks in Europe. EUNIC members work in the arts, languages, education, science, intercultural dialogue, capacity-building and development sectors. They seek to facilitate cultural co-operation, to create lasting partnerships between professionals, to encourage greater understanding and awareness of the diverse European cultures and to encourage increased language learning.
EUNIC's members are present in over 150 countries with more than 2,000 branches. This worldwide presence and the similar aims and objectives of the various cultural institutes resulted in a large degree of cooperation even before the establishment of EUNIC as a legal entity at the headquarters level. National cultural institutes came together in different cities around the world to organise events and common activities, such as European film and music festivals, European Book Days, European Day of Languages, etc. EUNIC's members have an international reputation as Europe's leading cultural relations practitioners.

**The EUNIC network is:**

- An active network: encouraging members to implement shared projects
- A learning network: sharing ideas and practices between members
- A partnering network: working with partners including European institutions, civil society organisations and partners around the world,
- An advocacy network: raising awareness and increasing the effectiveness of cultural relations between people worldwide

As an international association with legal status, EUNIC was formed to work in a more strategic way towards common goals. It is now possible for EUNIC to act as a partner of the European Commission, European External Action Service and other European institutions in defining and implementing cultural policy for Europe and the EU's external relations. The objectives of the EUNIC network are to advocate a strong and independent voice for the cultural sector and for the value of culture in promoting better understanding between people, societies and nations.

EUNIC set up a permanent secretariat in Brussels in November 2011. The office, run by two full-time staff, provides support to the EUNIC Heads and EUNIC Board of Directors by ensuring prompt implementation of strategic decisions taken at the Heads level.
The secretariat also has a dual role that involves advising the Heads of institutes on EUNIC-related issues and being the first point of contact for clusters and EU institutions.
The EUNIC permanent secretariat deals with communications, research and advocacy to support the whole network. It acts also as a coordinator of common projects and ensures that all the partners share necessary information and have the same level of understanding in order to achieve meaningful results. The mission of the EUNIC secretariat is to bring visibility to the actions of EUNIC clusters around the world and provide them with information and help on how to access funding for projects.
Clusters – the networks of EUNIC members in a given city, region or country – constitute the most important part of the network. It is the clusters that are most active in developing and running various events and activities in different locations around the world.
By September 2012, the EUNIC network had 82 clusters, the majority of them outside the European Union. Clusters established within the last few months include Mexico, Georgia, Thailand, Turkey, Albania, Greece – Thessaloniki, Egypt, Palestine and Ghana. Another three new clusters are in the process of being established and are expected to be up-and-running in early 2013.
A cluster event or project requires the involvement of at least three members of the cluster in order to obtain the EUNIC label. It is the clusters that decide what type of events and projects they want to run. Very

often the programme depends on local circumstances, opportunities and the expectations of audiences in the country where the cluster operates. Some clusters develop very complex and diverse programmes, while others focus on a small number of activities.
One interesting example is the Generation '89 project initiated by the Prague cluster and supported by the European Commission's Citizenship Programme 2007-2013. It brought together 140 young people from Austria, Belgium, Bulgaria, the Czech Republic, Germany, Hungary, Poland, Romania and the UK to share their experiences and expectations for the future. They had one thing in common: they were all born in 1989. In 2010 they met in Warsaw, Bucharest, Brussels and Prague. They had the chance to speak about what has happened in their countries in the past and their expectations as European citizens. Together they drafted the Generation '89 declaration. The Generation 89 project has been selected for inclusion in a booklet of iconic projects from the EU's "Europe for Citizens" programme. (Generation '89 can be found on page 46, as part of the section entitled "Civil society in action". The brochure has been published online and will also be available in print.)

**Strengthening creative industries in South Africa**

The EUNIC Cluster in South Africa has developed an initiative with the main objectives of strengthening the relationship between the EU and South Africa in the field of creative industries and supporting the development of this sector of the economy in South Africa. This project is a result of a successful application for funding under the EuropeAid 'European Union - South Africa Trade Development Agreement Facility'. One of the elements of this programme is the promotion of dialogue to strengthen policy debate between the EU and South Africa. Target groups include South African government departments, parastatal organisations, constitutional bodies and civil society actors, along with EU institutions and EU strategic partner countries. The Arts and Culture sector was included as a dialogue area within the Dialogue Facility for the first time in 2012. The EUNIC cluster in South Africa has taken the opportunity to form a consortium with Arterial Network – a pan-African network of NGOs, creative industry companies, festivals and individual artists engaged in the creative sector – and Visual Arts Network, the industry body and development agency for the Visual Arts in South Africa.

The principal activities over the lifecycle of the project are: research into the trade, policy and legislative frameworks between the EU and South Africa; workshops based on the findings of the research; seminars for a wider group of practitioners and civil society; a conference for key stakeholders from the EU, South Africa and other African countries; and dissemination of the recommendations from this programme of events.

The total budget for the project is €188,000, with the EU contributing €150,000. The co-funded element is shared between the EUNIC cluster members: the British Council (lead applicant), Camoes Institute, Goethe-Institut, French Institute, Italian Institute, and associate members the Embassies of Austria and Spain.
One of EUNIC's main interests lies in multilingualism. On 26th September each year, many EUNIC clusters organise events celebrating the EUROPEAN DAY OF LANGUAGES to promote multilingualism. In 2012, the clusters were especially active and creative in the events they organised for the day. Here are just a few examples.

- EUNIC in Almaty, Kazakhstan organised an event called CAFÉ. EUROPE, which included an exhibition on European education, theatrical and musical performances, a prize-giving ceremony and a concert. About 1,000 people attended CAFÉ.EUROPE where they were able to watch a theatrical performance by the Bremen Musicians in five languages, take part in a song competition and play typical national games from various different European countries. A competition was organised for the best video on the subject of "Two Faces of Europe" to celebrate the European Day of Languages. The winner of the competition was awarded a trip to Europe by Czech Airlines.

- EUNIC in Turkey organised an event called "Languages Open Doors". On 29 September, the cultural institutes and consular missions in Istanbul, representing 12 different languages, celebrated the European Day of Languages in the Sismanoglio Megaro of the Consulate General of Greece by offering fun language games, a treasure hunt in the historic district of Pera, traditional and contemporary dances, short films, and surprises for children and grown-ups alike.

- EUNIC in Spain prepared a ground-breaking cultural and linguistic marathon, giving the people of Madrid the chance to take part in over 40 original and engaging activities. The aim of the event was to promote the study of languages, to raise awareness of lesser well-known cultures and to encourage everyone to think about potential travel destinations and to discover new artists and talents, as well as food from other cultures. During the evening of 27 September, foreign cultural institutes and European embassies in Madrid opened their doors and hosted film screenings, concerts and performance shows, dramatisations, poetry readings, storytelling sessions, book swaps, exhibitions, guided tours, food tasting sessions and, more importantly, language classes where participants could learn about grants to study foreign languages and have the chance to win prizes.

- TRANSPOESIE is an event created in 2011 by the EUNIC in Brussels cluster in collaboration with the STIB transport association and the Loterie Nationale. It is now in its second year and aims to give poetry pride of place on the Brussels metro. 24 European countries have joined forces to present 24 poems in their original language on the Brussels metro, with the poems also translated into French and Dutch. The 2012 edition of TRANSPOESIE began officially on 26 September, to mark European Languages Day.

In 2012, EUNIC in Russia launched another Curatorial Exchange Programme for young Russian curators, which offers internships in European museums and galleries. The project gives its participants a unique opportunity to advance their careers, to study the European art market and build new professional contacts in Austria, Germany, France, Romania, Sweden, the UK and other countries. Young Russian curators have been offered internships in leading European museums and contemporary art galleries for periods ranging from 3 weeks to 2 months in leading museums and contemporary art galleries in Europe. A generation of young Russian curators now work both as freelancers and for cultural institutions in Moscow and numerous other dynamic cultural centres in Russia's regions. They will be decisive in shaping the exhibitions and cultural life of the country in the future and in modernising and developing exhibition centres, biennales and institutions.

### Optimising regional and global cooperation

How can EUNIC further improve its work? In the period from July 2011 to December 2012, EUNIC organised five Regional Meetings for EUNIC clusters in different locations aimed at enhancing regional co-operation, exchanging expertise, ideas and best practices and planning future joint activities. Regional Meetings are usually organised in collaboration with the EUNIC clusters in the country, city or region in which the meeting is to take place.
In the second half of 2011 there were two EUNIC Regional Meetings, one for the whole Middle East North Africa (MENA) region and the other for clusters based in Europe. The MENA meeting took place in Rabat in Morocco from 20-21 September, while the European meeting was in Tallinn, Estonia from 5-6 October. Three meetings took place in 2012. The first meeting organised for clusters from North and South America was held in Lima, Peru from 22-24 February 2012. The second for the sub-Saharan region was in Lagos, Nigeria from 11-12 October 2012, while the third meeting held for the MENA cluster took place in Beirut, Lebanon from 14-16 November 2012.
Preparations for the European Regional Meetings 2013 in Warsaw and a meeting for clusters in Asia are currently under way.

EUNIC members and clusters come together in varied groupings to develop joint projects and new directions based on common goals and interests. At present EUNIC is running projects related to multilingualism, culture in external relations and culture in the context of development, conflict and sustainable development.
At the EUNIC General Assembly in July 2012 in Paris, EUNIC members decided to create a special fund to support inter-cluster activities that are directly related to topics that are of strategic importance to EUNIC, such as culture in external relations or multilingualism.
A selection of EUNIC global and inter-cluster projects is presented below.

In autumn 2012, Poliglotti4.eu, a EUNIC-led project co-funded by the European Commission and developed within the Civil Society Platform to promote multilingualism in Europe, entered its final stage. What has become clear is that the success of the new multilingualism strategy partly depends on the active involvement of civil society.

The Commission's Communication "Multilingualism: an asset for Europe and a shared priority", adopted in September 2008, foresees two platforms for a structured dialogue with stakeholders from the civil society and business sectors. The aim is to create a forum for the exchange of best practices for civil society stakeholders, gathering relevant information from the culture, non-formal and informal education and learning sectors, as well as from the media, in order to bring multilingualism closer to the citizen.
The poliglotti4.eu project brings together 9 member organisations from the Civil Society Platform. The project combines PR events, networking and research in three subject areas: early language learning, adult education and social services. The project covers more than 10 European countries.

**Ambassadors for multilingualism**

In addition to successfully setting up the comprehensive website www.poliglotti4.eu, EUNIC members around Europe as well as various project partners have also recruited Multilingualism Ambassadors to lend their voice and image to the cause of multilingualism and the promotion of language learning and language diversity in Europe. These Ambassadors work in the fields of education and language learning or have reached their current positions in the fields of entertainment, politics or economics on account of their knowledge of several languages.
Videos of 22 Ambassadors from 11 European countries can be viewed on the poliglotti4.eu website. On the website, where content is now available in 65 languages, there are also reports on project events and research that has taken place to date. The website will remain online for at least 5 years after the end of the project in order to guarantee the continuity of the project, ongoing networking activities and the exchange of best practices, ideas and experiences.
Poliglotti4.eu's closing conference "One continent, many tongues: a spotlight on Europe's linguistic wealth" took place in Parma in Italy from 15-16 November 2012. The conference brought together experts and multilingual talents from across Europe and highlighted Poliglotti4.eu's project achievements. The conference, which was part of the Parma Theatre Festival, has also given a voice to those Europeans who live and work in multilingual Europe and who represent a range of fields including science, arts and culture, education, economics and politics.

In May 2012, the Language Rich Europe networking project, set up to discuss and develop better policies and practices for multilingualism, released the initial draft of a research publication that analyses trends in language policies and practices in 24 countries and regions across Europe. The survey covers languages in education, the media, cities and business. Tilburg University's Babylon Centre for Studies of the Multicultural Society carried out the research in collaboration with partner institutions and experts in participating countries.
Over the coming months, the networks of language stakeholders in each country will come together in a series of workshops to discuss the findings and develop recommendations for European, national and regional levels. The outcomes will be presented to policy makers in Brussels in March 2013.
Some of the study's key findings include the following:

- There is a shortage of language teachers in some countries/regions, and special recruitment campaigns are required.
- While traditional modern foreign languages such as English, French, German and Spanish are commonly offered in primary and secondary education, very few countries offer students the opportunity to learn languages from outside Europe.
- Learning languages through subjects such as Geography and History is becoming more widespread, but is far from common practice.
- Of the companies surveyed, 83% use language skills as a factor in recruitment.
- Two-thirds of the cities surveyed report that they are able to offer a number of public services in three or more languages, while 37% make it a policy to include language skills in staff job descriptions and 29% provide language training to staff. According to the survey, the 5 cities (out of 63) with the most developed language policies are Barcelona, Krakow, London, Milan and Vienna.

The aim of the Language Rich Europe project is to promote greater cooperation between policy makers and practitioners in Europe and to ensure that languages and cultural exchange continue to be encouraged at schools, universities and in society. The project is co-funded by the European Commission and managed by the British Council. The main issues to be explored through the project include:

- How do we address the apparent shortage of language teachers?
- How can we motivate people to learn languages at all stages of their lives?
- How do we ensure a broad range of languages is offered in schools?
- How can we teach other languages through subjects such as Geography and History?
- How can cities ensure that they are meeting the language needs of their citizens and visitors?
- How can companies get more involved in language education?

**Dialogue with China: more creative processes**

The tradition of organising a 'Cultural Dialogue China-EUNIC' goes back to the year 2008, when the very first of the meetings took place in Beijing, China. Two other conferences followed in 2009 and 2010, in Copenhagen and Shanghai respectively. The 4th edition of the Dialogue was held in Luxembourg from 26-28 October 2011. Unlike the preceding three events, the 'Cultural Dialogue China-EUNIC 2011' moved away from the standard programme of key speeches and presentations and put greater emphasis on more creative processes, interaction between the participants and face-to-face discussions in small working groups during the conference.

What made the 'Cultural Dialogue China-EUNIC 2011' such an outstanding and extremely effective event? First of all, it was due to the general structure and methodology of the conference. Twenty artists and curators from China and Europe were invited to Luxembourg a week before the event in order to work in three different workshops – the Photographers Workshop, the Installation Art Creation Workshop and the Design Works Creation Workshop. The works that were created were displayed on the first day of the conference and all the artists actively participated in the programme activities, contributing their own insights and explaining the project work carried out in the course of the previous week. On the first evening of the dialogue meeting, there was a successful attempt at combining the worlds of arts and finance in the shape of a conference called 'Art and Finance', attended by more than 200 people. Days two and three were dedicated to 'Cultural Heritage Protection and Urban development', 'Functions of Cultural Centres in the Process of Urban Re-construction', 'The Role of Creative Industries in the Strategy of Sustainable Urban Development' and 'The Role of Arts in the 21st Century'.
The last slot on the agenda was reserved for a presentation on the 'Europe China Cultural Compass,' effectively an instruction manual for anyone who wants to immerse themselves in the sphere between East and West.

Preparations for the 5th session of the Cultural Dialogue China-EUNIC are in full swing. The main theme will be Cultural Activities and Urban Development. This time the event will take place in Xi'an. It will be organised by the Chinese National Academy of the Arts (Beijing), the Tang King Market (Xi'an), the General Office of Xi'an Municipal Government, the Shaanxi Provincial Culture Department, the Xi'an Academy of Fine Arts, EUNIC Heads and EUNIC clusters in Beijing.
But this was not the only initiative involving China. Do we mean the same thing, when we say the same thing? This was the key question posed at the beginning of the Europe-China Cultural Compass project initiated by EUNIC partners in China, the Goethe-Institut, the British Council, and the Danish Cultural Institute. After a year of research, including over a hundred interviews and discussions with cultural practitioners with experience in collaboration between Europe and China, the outcome was a publication that included not only a glossary of selected key intercultural vocabulary, but also a huge amount of information relevant to cooperation issues: background knowledge on Europe and China, information on how cultural sectors work differently, case stories from cultural practitioners, a project cycle analysis that crystallises challenges, learning and practices, and an extensive chapter on resources.
The Europe-China Cultural Compass project is part of an ongoing dialogue between Europe and China. It responds to the need to document this dialogue and reflect on it. The goal is to continuously improve the process. This EUNIC initiative aims to contribute to the understanding of cultural cooperation between Europe and China. The intention is to help prepare cultural practitioners for the

process of collaboration. To meet the different needs of those two target groups, two separate publications were produced: one in Chinese and one in English. The job of developing the concept and creating the Compass was given to an intercultural working team headed by Katja Hellkoetter as editor-in-chief. Experts in the team included Shen Qilan, Katelijn Verstraete, Emilie Wang, Judith Staines, Yi Wen, Roman Wilhelm, and many more external authors and contributors from China and Europe. The editorial board was headed up by Peter Anders (Director of the Goethe-Institut in Beijing), Eric Messerschmidt (Head of the Danish Cultural Institute in Beijing) and Joanna Burke (British Council, China Director, Cultural and Education Section of the British Embassy in Beijing).

**Launch of the EUNIC MENA project**

The Middle East and North Africa (MENA) region is of particular interest to EUNIC. The EUNIC MENA project addresses issues such as democratic empowerment, cultural policy and the creative economy and includes regional and national projects in the MENA region. EUNIC, the European External Action Service and the European Commission support the project.
The project was launched at the "Euromed Forum on Creative Industries & Society" that took place from 13 to 15 May 2012 in Jordan. The Forum brought together around 170 representatives of the creative industries from the MENA region (Algeria, Egypt, Jordan, Lebanon, Morocco, Palestine, Tunisia) and the European Union. EUNIC clusters in the MENA region and EUNIC members in Europe sent delegates to the event. All sectors of the creative industries were represented: advertising; architecture; crafts; cultural heritage; design; education & leisure; software; fashion; film, video and audio-visual production; literature, libraries and publishing; music; performing arts & entertainment; television, radio & internet broadcasting; and the visual arts.
The Forum was organised in a creative and highly participatory format using Open Space Technology (OST) to bring the various stakeholders together to seek and discuss a joint solution. The performance group 'Improbable' from London supported the process, with participants putting forward potential topics, discussing them in groups and identifying needs and expectations. In this way each participant was able to contribute to the design of the long-term EUNIC MENA Project. The final report lists all the issues raised and is available on request.
EUNIC will use these recommendations as a guide in designing the long-term MENA Project. It should be launched by the end of 2012 and will be implemented by EUNIC's Global Office in Brussels in cooperation with EUNIC clusters in the MENA region.
The aim of another EUNIC publication, a brochure entitled 'Culture and Development - Action and Impact', is to demonstrate the fundamental role culture has to play in the area of development. The brochure contains a description of projects that have used culture as a way of making a significant contribution to socio-economic development. The brochure is the result of a fruitful collaboration between the European Commission, the British Council, the Federation Wallonia-Brussels and EUNIC. The 36 projects represent a wide variety of cultural activities and initiatives in developing countries and are being implemented by various actors – including members of EUNIC, the European Commission, national development agencies and local partners. They illustrate good practice in terms of impact on the development of the communities concerned and the many shapes, forms and dimensions in which culture is embedded in the development process.

**Catalyst for change**

This new version of the brochure focuses on the Mediterranean region and so dovetails nicely with EUNIC's interest in engaging in dialogue with the civil society in the Middle East and North Africa region in support of a peaceful transition to democracy. Major pro-democracy events have recently taken place there and culture has proven to be a catalyst for change, for freedom of expression and for democracy. Supporting the creative sector and cultural diversity in the region also promotes stronger collaboration and professionalism for those actors in civil society who are actively involved in changes to create more widespread democracy.
The online version of the brochure was agreed on at the Culture and Development Network meeting organised by the British Council and UNESCO in October 2011. A clear message emerged from the meeting: the need for stronger collaboration and professionalism. It is also for that reason that the online version of the brochure was created – to enable information-sharing and to encourage future collaboration.

'Culture and Development – Action and Impact' was presented by the European Commission's EuropeAid - Development and Cooperation (DG DEVCO) and the British Council on behalf of the collaboration at the EUNIC Forum on Creative Industries and Society in Jordan in May 2012.

**Culture in external relations - preparatory action**

EUNIC Global is an associated partner in the consortium made up of four national cultural institutions and specialist organisations that won the bid for the EU preparatory action 'Culture in external relations'. The aim of the preparatory action is to collect data and information through mapping and consultation in a large number of states in order to analyse the resources, strategies and opinions relating to the role and impact of culture in external relations. The mapping will define concepts that relate to culture and diplomacy issues. Countries covered by the project include 27 EU member states, ENP countries, Croatia and 9 strategic partner countries.

EUNIC strongly supports the More Europe campaign, an external cultural relations initiative launched in December 2012 that aims to convince policy-makers to place cultural relations – one of the strongest assets that Europe has – at the heart of the EU's external affairs. Based on best practice evidence and research, More Europe calls on Member States, civil society and EU institutions to work together to combine their visions, pool resources, and coordinate their activities.

**Conflict resolution through cultural and civil society initiatives**

With the help of Germany's Institute for Foreign Cultural Relations (ifa), the EUNIC network now has growing expertise in the field of conflict and culture. On 7 December 2011, 80 experts from the fields of conflict transformation, cultural affairs, civil society and EU foreign and security affairs met in Brussels at the invitation of ifa and EUNIC for a roundtable discussion on 'Conflict resolution through cultural and civil society initiatives?' The roundtable discussion focused on the role of cultural institutes in promoting peace in conflict and post- conflict regions, in establishing cultural dialogue and in working to rebuild civil infrastructure through creative and educational programmes.
The meeting was divided into two parts. In the first part of the discussion, cultural activists and experts in conflict resolution and peacebuilding shared their experiences, presenting best-practice projects and expressing their views and demands. In the second half, experts from the fields of cultural relations, EU foreign and security policy as well as from research organisations focused on the role of cultural institutes in European foreign policy.

Basically, the conference examined the long-term impact of cultural and civil society initiatives and the effectiveness of cultural and educational tools for conflict resolution.

During the conference the participants tried to answer a number of important questions such as: in what ways can EUNIC best use its cultural relations expertise and extensive networks for conflict resolution? How might these networks better cooperate and work together with civil society initiatives? How might they communicate their knowledge to decision makers in order to develop a more effective, integrated approach to EU peacebuilding efforts?

In order to better coordinate different ideas and approaches covered during the roundtable discussion, a EUNIC working group on culture and conflict was set up as part of the ifa-funded programme Civil Conflict Resolution (zivik) with the aim of drafting a policy paper for EUNIC to help effectively communicate this field of expertise to political decision-makers on a European and national level. The group is trying to create a deeper understanding of work in and on conflict through cultural projects. It is gathering together examples of projects in order to generate general good practice criteria for working in/on conflicts through cultural activities.

**Culture and Sustainable Development – Culture|Futures**

Culture|Futures, the project linking culture and ecology, has organised a number of exciting events in the last few months. Project leaders were able to involve cultural institutions, municipalities, individual actors, young people and other stakeholders in activities taking place in different locations around the world. The Culture|Futures project was launched in 2009 by the Danish Cultural Institute in cooperation with EUNIC, the British Council,

the Goethe-Institut, the Italian Cultural Institute and other organisations active in the field of culture and sustainable development.
In December 2011, Culture|Futures organised a conference called: "Eco-Leadership though Culture" in Durban during the UN Climate Summit COP17 in South Africa. The conference was co-organised with the Municipality of Durban, the Ecological Sequestration Trust and the Danish Cultural Institute in co-operation with many other partners. The programme featured keynote speeches and panel contributions from some of the world's best known specialists and activists which underlined the solutions needed to resolve the challenges faced by the African continent in relation to urban and regional development.
The conference delegates discussed the vision of an "ecological age" and the role of culture in making it a reality. The speakers and participants were also looking for ways to inspire institutions working in the field of culture and cities in Africa to become leaders in socio-ecological activities. The conference was a first step in creating an international Culture|Futures network for cultural institutions, individual actors, cities, regions and other stakeholders active in the field of eco-leadership.
In 2012 Culture|Futures organised events aimed at the younger public. In June, the project ran a Backstage Sustainability Workshop at the Roskilde Festival and in September it launched a student competition 'Co-creating Sustainable Solutions for the Future'.

**European Literature Nights**

The European Literature Nights initiative is being coordinated by the Czech Centres in cooperation with EUNIC. The aim of Literature Nights is to offer a platform for European countries to present their contemporary writing in translation and to present new European literary voices in a creative way. The European Literature Night concept is based on the assumption that literature is a unique and creative tool that reflects the elementary dialogue between individual voices and cultures through a shared reading experience. Literature is a tool for mutual understanding that helps to break down communication barriers.
In 2012, literature was presented in its various forms in a number of European cities including Amsterdam, Banska Bystrica, Berlin, Bratislava, Budapest, Bucharest, Dublin, Dusseldorf, Edinburgh, Yerevan, Kutna Hora, Kiev, London, Lvov, Madrid, Milan, Munich, Prague, Riga, Sofia, Stockholm, Warsaw, Vienna and Zilina.
A few examples of Literature Night events are given below, perfectly illustrating the creativity and energy that was unleashed among the organisers.

In Dublin, Ireland, the Literature Night took place on 16 May and its aim was to promote European cultural heritage by presenting different writers, including the well-known and those just starting their careers. Each participating country was represented by a translated piece of a novel, poem or short story, read by well-known Irish people at various unusual places, such as churches, museums, pubs or cafes. All the venues were within walking distance of each other and the public was provided with a map of the readings and venues so that they could move easily from one place to another.

The Munich Literature Night dealt with a very unconventional topic, that of Roma literature, which existed in oral form only until the 20th century. Stories, fairytales, traditions and language were passed from mouth to mouth and from generation to generation. However, there have been significant developments in written Roma literature over recent decades with novels, poetry, theatre plays and memoirs being published in the Roma language or in translation. Roma literature has emerged as a strong part of European literature as a result. The works presented at the event were translated especially for the occasion in cooperation with students of Slavonic studies in Munich.

The Literature Night in London brought together European writers who were shortlisted by members of the public and appropriate institutions. The authors read extracts from their works and discussed their books, inspirations, and the wider literary context of the countries they come from.

In Yerevan, the British Council in Armenia organised the Literature Night in cooperation with European colleagues, as part of the Yerevan World Book Capital 2012 celebration programme. Actors read extracts from Czech, Romanian and UK literature translated into the Armenian language.

### Fashion Road: Dialogue across Borders

Fashion Road: Dialogue across Borders is a two-year collaborative project in which fashion designers from different European countries and Armenia look to the past for ideas and inspiration. They are studying traditional costumes from Armenia, the UK, Germany, Romania, Denmark and the Czech Republic, exploring the role of those costumes in contemporary society, and discussing the ways in which people associate those costumes with their national identity and heritage. Key to this project was meeting other designers and having the opportunity to view clothing in a cultural context and to use modern technologies and approaches to present their interpretation of each country's culture and identity.
The project was officially launched on 4 and 5 May 2011 with an international seminar followed by the residency programmes in Armenia for the European designers and in Europe for Armenian designers. The designers were paired to work together to prepare their collections, which would contextualise the cultural heritage, values and traditions of the participating countries explored during their time abroad. The collection was put into an exhibition in Armenia and in the participating European countries.

The collection prepared by the designers raised understanding and appreciation of European cultural values and identity among the Armenian public, as well as of Armenian cultural history and heritage among Europeans. It also served as a forum for discussions about the importance of cross-cultural cooperation and exchange as well as the fusion of cultural traditions and heritage with modern trends and technological developments for more creative and innovative approaches to fashion.

### Members of EUNIC

Austrian Federal Ministry of European and International Affairs
Balassi Institute
British Council
Bulgarian Ministry of Culture
Centre Culturel de Recontre Abbaye de Neumünster, Luxembourg
Culture Ireland
Cyprus Ministry of Education and Culture
Czech Centres
Danish Cultural Institute
Estonian Institute
Finish Cultural and Academic Institutes
Flemish-Dutch House deBuren
Foundation Alliance Française
French Ministry of Foreign Affairs
Goethe-Institute
ifa – German Institute for Foreign Cultural Relations
Institut Français
Instituo Camões
Instituto Cervantes
International Cultural Program Centre Lithuania
Polish Ministry of Foreign Affairs
Romanian Cultural Institute
SICA – Dutch Centre for International Cultural Activities
Slovakian Ministry of Foreign Affairs
Slovenian Ministry of Culture
Società Dante Alighieri
Swedish Institute
Wallonie-Bruxelles International

### Presidents of EUNIC

| | |
|---|---|
| 2006 | Sir David Green – British Council |
| 2007 | Emil Brix – Austrian Federal Ministry for European and International Affairs |
| 2008 | Hans-Georg Knopp – Goethe-Institut |
| 2009 | Finn Andersen – Danish Cultural Institute |
| 2010 | Horia-Roman Patapievici – Romanian Cultural Institute |
| 2011 | Professor Ana Paula Laborinho – Instituo Camões |
| 2012 | Delphine Borione – French Ministry of Foreign Affairs |

## EUNIC clusters' activities between July 2011 and December 2012

### Multilingualism

September 2011, EUNIC in Warsaw, International Translators Day "Born in Translation"
September 2011, EUNIC in Kazakhstan, European Day of Languages
September 2011, EUNIC in Senegal, European Day of Languages
September 2011, EUNIC in Norway, European Day of Languages
September 2011, EUNIC in Warsaw, European Day of Languages in Warsaw
September 2011, EUNIC in Lebanon, European Day of Languages in Lebanon
September 2011, EUNIC in Morocco, European Day of Languages
September 2011, EUNIC in Bosnia and Herzegovina, European Languages Day in Zenica
September 2011, EUNIC in Canada, European Day of Languages in Toronto
September 2011, EUNIC in the Czech Republic, European Day of Languages in Prague
September 2011, EUNIC in Estonia, European Day of Languages in Tallinn
September 2011, EUNIC in Athens, European Day of Languages
September 2011, EUNIC in Hungary, European Languages Cocktail Bar
October 2011, EUNIC in Rome, One Europe - Many languages - New opportunities
October 2011, EUNIC in Uzbekistan, Teachers' Day in Tashkent
October 2011, EUNIC in Vietnam, European Languages Days – Conference in Hanoi
November 2011, EUNIC in Bordeaux, 10th Day of Languages - language and culture
December 2011, EUNIC in Warsaw, Read in Translation
February 2012, EUNIC in Washington, European Conversation Club
February 2012, EUNIC in Senegal, Writing in European Languages contest
March 2012, EUNIC in Estonia, conference - Languages of Smaller Populations: Risks and Possibilities
March 2012, EUNIC in Rome, Europe - Italy: the challenge of multilingualism
May 2012, EUNIC in Venezuela, Interactive White Board,
May 2012, EUNIC in Melbourne, European Language Festival in Anakie
June 2012, EUNIC in Warsaw, Fan's Dictionary for volunteers' communication during Euro 2012
June 2012, EUNIC in Athens, Launch of the Language Rich Europe Framework for Language Policies and Practices in Athens
September 2012, EUNIC in Bosnia and Herzegovina, European Languages Day in Mostar and Sarajevo
September 2012, EUNIC in Canada, European Day of Languages in Toronto
September 2012, EUNIC in Colombia, European Day of Languages in Bogota
September 2012, EUNIC in the Czech Republic, European Day of Languages in Prague
September 2012, EUNIC in Estonia, European Day of Languages
September 2012, EUNIC in Hungary, European Languages Cocktail Bar
September 2012, EUNIC in Jordan, European Day of Languages in Amman
September 2012, EUNIC in Senegal, European Day of Languages in Dakar
September 2012, EUNIC in Spain, Open Doors at the European Cultural Institutes - European Day of Languages
September 2012, EUNIC in Turkey, European Day of Languages - 12 Languages in One Day
September 2012, EUNIC in Chicago, European Professional Development Day
September 2012, EUNIC in Morocco, European Day of Languages in Casablanca
September 2012, EUNIC in Warsaw, European Day of Languages in Warsaw
September 2012, EUNIC in Romania, European Day of Languages
September 2012, EUNIC in Serbia, European Day of Languages
September 2012, EUNIC in Berlin, The art of speaking a language: Multilingualism and its opportunities
September 2012, EUNIC in the Netherlands, European Day of Languages by EUNIC in the Netherlands
October 2012, EUNIC in Lebanon, European Day of Languages in Beirut
October 2012, EUNIC in Warsaw, International Translators' Day in Krakow and Warsaw
October 2012, EUNIC in Krakow, International Translation Day
October 2012, EUNIC in Vietnam, European Language Days

### European Literature

January – December 2011, EUNIC in Canada, LISEZ L'EUROPE - Contemporary European Literature in Montreal
July 2011, EUNIC in Warsaw, Spoke'N'Word Festival - Slam Poetry from different countries
August 2011, EUNIC in Cordoba, FLiCba… + de 140: code name for new literature festival in Cordoba
September 2011, EUNIC in Sweden, joint EUNIC stand at the Bok&Bibliotek Book Fair, Gothenburg
September 2011, EUNIC in Canada, International Literature Festival in Montreal
September – October 2011 EUNIC in Brussels, Project TRANSPOESIE 2011
October 2011, EUNIC in Warsaw, Reading somewhere else, 2nd edition in Warsaw
October 2011, EUNIC in Serbia, Book Fair 2011 in Belgrade
October 2011, EUNIC in Finland, Helsinki Book Fair 2011
October 2011, EUNIC in Morocco, Open Days at Libraries in Rabat
November 2011, EUNIC in New York, Crime Scene: Europe - New Literature from Europe 2011
November 2011, EUNIC in Romania, European Comics Festival
November – December 2011, EUNIC in Tanzania, Dar Slam Poetry Championship Festival
February 2012, EUNIC in Morocco, International Fair for Publishing and Books SIEL (17th edition) in Casablanca
March 2012, EUNIC in Vienna, European Festival of Poetry in Vienna
March 2012, EUNIC in Athens, Six Voices, Six Women – short stories for the International Women's Day in Athens
April, 2012, EUNIC in Spain, European aid for book publishing - round table in Barcelona
April, 2012, EUNIC in Warsaw, Reading somewhere else, 3rd edition
April, 2012, EUNIC in the Netherlands, City2Cities: International Literature Days Utrecht
May 2012, EUNIC in Romania, European Literature Night in Bucharest
May 2012, EUNIC in the Czech Republic, Literature Night in Prague
May 2012, EUNIC in Vietnam, European Literature Days
May 2012, EUNIC in London, European Literature Night IV in London
June 2012, EUNIC in Croatia, regional multimedia literature festival "KROKODIL" in Zagreb
June 2012, EUNIC in Hungary, European Literature Night
June 2012, EUNIC in Denmark, Festival of European Contemporary Playwrights
August 2012, EUNIC in China, Beijing Book Fair
August 2012, EUNIC in Cordoba, 2nd Córdoba International Literature Festival
September 2012, EUNIC in Algeria, XIII International Book Fair in Algeria (SILA)
September - November 2012, EUNIC in Brussels, Project TRANSPOESIE 2012
September 2012, EUNIC in Berlin, The Superreal World – Graphic Novels of Europe: Vernissage and Graphic Novel Day
September 2012, EUNIC in Berlin, Europa literarisch: Norman Manea from Romania by EUNIC in Berlin
October 2012, EUNIC in Vienna, Literature Night in Cafes in Vienna, EUNIC Week
October 2012, EUNIC in Canada, EUROPE@

IFOA Toronto

October 2012, EUNIC in Canada, International Festival of Authors in Toronto
Oct ober 2012, EUNIC in Morocco, Open Day at the Libraries in Rabat
October 2012, EUNIC in Warsaw, VIII Spoke'n'Word Festival
October 2012, EUNIC in Serbia, Book Fair in Belgrade
October 2012, EUNIC in Berlin, Europa literarisch: Håkan Nesser from Sweden by EUNIC Berlin
October – November 2012, EUNIC in Melbourne, 'Myth, Magic and Mystery' public reading in Melbourne
October – November 2012, EUNIC in Lebanon, Fair for Books in the French Language in Beirut
November 2012, EUNIC in Rome, „Cinderella as a cultural text" - international conference in Rome
November 2012, EUNIC in Warsaw, Reading somewhere else, 4th edition
November 2012, EUNIC in New York, Artistic Fictions/Fictional Artists: New Literature from Europe 2012

## Arts

### Visual Arts

May – September 2011, EUNIC in Estonia, International Media Art Exhibition in Tallinn: 'Gateways. Art and Networked Culture' in Tallinn
July - September 2011, EUNIC in London, Active Witness/Photo Summer Exhibition
August 2011, EUNIC in Norway, the Norwegian International Film Festival in Haugesund
September 2011, EUNIC in Norway, Oslo culture night
October 2011, EUNIC in Estonia, art exhibition 'Tadeusz Kantor. Polish Avant- Gardist and Theatre Reformer' in Tallinn
October 2011, EUNIC in Croatia, 'The Great Five' film programme at the Zagreb Film Festival 2011
October – December 2011, EUNIC in Warsaw, Taboo in Children's Art in Gdansk, Poznan and Warsaw
November 2011, EUNIC in Romania, Prague through the lens of the secret police
November 2011, EUNIC in Bosnia and Herzegovina, Mini-INPUT Seoul - International Public Television Screening Conference in Sarajevo
November 2011, EUNIC in Bosnia and Herzegovina, Mini-INPUT Sydney - International Public Television Screening Conference in Sarajevo
November 2011, EUNIC in Hungary, 'Behind the Celluloid Curtain' film screenings
November - December 2011, EUNIC in Sudan, European Film Festival 2011 in Khartoum and Juba
November 2011, EUNIC in Rome, travelling exhibition 'Childhood - Tracks and treasures' in Rome
December 2011, EUNIC in London, Robotville EU
December 2011, EUNIC in Lithuania, The Celluloid Curtain – Europe's Cold War in Film
January 2012, EUNIC in Norway, Tromsø International Film Festival
February 2012, EUNIC in London, Ready Steady Doc/Documentary Film Festival
March 2012, EUNIC in Norway, Eurodok - The European Documentary Film Festival in Oslo
March 2012 – March 2013, EUNIC in Slovakia, EuroFilmClub in Bratislava
April 2012, EUNIC in China, Caochangdi Photo Spring
April 2012, EUNIC in China, Symposium on Public Cultural Policies: European and Chinese Perspectives on Supporting the Visual Arts
April 2012, EUNIC in New York, Disappearing Act IV – European Cinema
April 2012, EUNIC in South Africa, City of Gold Urban Arts Festival in Johannesburg
May 2012, EUNIC in Venezuela, Virtual Library/EUNIC Membership Identification
May 2012, EUNIC in Kazakhstan, EUNIC Almaty Film Festival
May – June 2012, EUNIC in Ireland, Climate|Culture|Change - screenings and discussions in Dublin
May 2012, EUNIC in the occupied Palestinian territory (oPt), European arts and culture Week in Palestine
May 2012, EUNIC in Bosnia and Herzegovina, European Film Week in Sarajevo,
May - July 2012, EUNIC in Warsaw, Young Film Critics Forum in Gdynia and Wroclaw
June 2012, EUNIC in Vietnam, 4th European Documentary Film Week
June 2012, EUNIC in Senegal, Image and Life Festival
June 2012, EUNIC in Ukraine, European Short film festival in Kiev
July 2012, EUNIC in South Africa, Durban International Film Festival
August 2012, EUNIC in Namibia, EUNIC Film Festival ‚Somewhere Else - Searching for a Home'
August 2012, EUNIC in China, EU – China Roundtable on Digital Publishing in Beijing
August 2012 – January 2013, EUNIC in Berlin, Exhibition and Accompanying Programme: Olympia: Myth – Cult – Games
September 2012, EUNIC in Norway, Oslo Culture Night
September 2012, EUNIC in Rome, audiovisual translation event in Rome
September 2012, EUNIC in South Africa, Moshito Music Conference in Johannesburg
September – October 2012, EUNIC in China, EUNIC Beijing Design Week
September – October 2012, EUNIC in the Philippines, 15th edition of Cine Europa Film Festival
September – October 2012, EUNIC in Croatia, Media-Scape Biennale Zagreb
October 2012, EUNIC Berlin, Mythos Olympia – The Documentary!
October 2012, EUNIC in Berlin, Europe's Golden Bears
October – November 2012, EUNIC in Melbourne, photographic exhibition 'Memories of a Pilgrimage' in Melbourne
November 2012, EUNIC in Vietnam, Hanoi International Film Festival
November 2012, EUNIC in Ethiopia, European Film Festival in Addis Ababa
November – December 2012, EUNIC in Ethiopia, workshop for moviemakers
November – December 2012, EUNIC in Sudan, European Film Festival 2012 in Khartoum

### Performing Arts

September 2011, EUNIC in Croatia, DUGAVE Street Art Festival in Zagreb
September 2011, EUNIC in New York, Moving Sounds - Annual Music Festival
September 2011, EUNIC in Brazil, AMEO – Andromeda Mega Express Orchestra: Music from another planet
September 2011, EUNIC in Venezuela, European DJs in Caracas
November 2011, EUNIC in Washington, concert by European Jazz Motion
December 2011, EUNIC in Zimbabwe, The Flame: Celebrating World Aids Day
February 2012, EUNIC in Zimbabwe, Live Vibe: The Smoke That Thunders
March 2012, EUNIC in India, Culinary Festival
April 2012, EUNIC in Croatia, EUNIC Cultural Fellowships awarded to emerging cultural leaders from Croatia in Zagreb
April 2012, EUNIC in Washington, outreach activities for the European Union Youth Orchestra
April 2012, EUNIC in Vietnam, Hanoi Sound Stuff
April 2012, EUNIC in Japan, European Baroque Music Festival
May 2012, EUNIC in Senegal,Festival Interférences
May 2012, EUNIC in Estonia, Tallinn Treff Festival in Tallinn
May 2012, EUNIC in Hungary, Europe Day Festival

May 2012, EUNIC in Senegal, Salam Music Expo
May 2012, EUNIC in Washington, Eurovision Song Contest Party
May 2012, EUNIC in Brazil, 8th European Week
May 2012, EUNIC in Slovakia, Concert for Europe in Bratislava
May – June 2012, EUNIC in the Philippines, Focus on European Contemporary Dance: International Dance Festival Manila
June 2012, EUNIC in Hungary, Scandinavian and Baltic Midsummer's Day
June 2012, EUNIC in Brussels, BreXpat - Manneken Speak - Fête de la Musique in Ganshoren
June 2012, EUNIC in Lebanon, music festival in Beirut
June 2012, EUNIC in Senegal, Festa2H
June 2012, EUNIC in Turkey, Night of European Culture in Istanbul
August 2012, EUNIC in Hungary, Park in Progress
August – December 2012, EUNIC in Denmark, Copenhagen Art Festival
September 2012, EUNIC in Vietnam, Festival of Contemporary Dance
September 2012, EUNIC in China, Beijing Fringe Festival
September 2012, EUNIC in China, Music and Design aka M.A.D.
September 2012, EUNIC in Warsaw, Summer Opera
September 2012, EUNIC in New York, Moving Sounds - Annual Music Festival
October 2012, EUNIC in Berlin, XXIII Berlin Early Music Days
October 2012, EUNIC in Norway, European Jazz Nights
October 2012, EUNIC in Turkey, Art in Movement
November 2012, EUNIC in London, EUNIC celebratory concert: „Inspired by Debussy" in London

### Culture in External Relations

EUNIC in New York, Visa Advocacy Initiative (ongoing project)
June – July 2011, EUNIC in London, Cultural Diplomacy Seminar
March 2012 – November 2013, EUNIC in South Africa, Dialogue Facility in Arts and Culture project

April 2012, EUNIC in the Czech Republic, EUNIC conference Culture + Culture and Diplomacy

May 2012, EUNIC in Serbia, Diplomatic Academy – presentations on cultural policy

June 2012, EUNIC in London, Cultural Diplomacy Conference in London

October 2012, EUNIC in Vienna, 'Pointing the Way' – international workshop on the dialogue between cultures in Vienna
November 2012, EUNIC in Hungary, Conference Dialogue between China and Europe
November 2012, EUNIC in Warsaw, More Europe Conference in Warsaw

### Culture and Development

May and September 2011, EUNIC in Brussels, Learning and Development workshop in Brussels
September 2011, EUNIC in Morocco, conference - Debate on Culture and Development in Morocco
October 2011, EUNIC in Brussels, Culture and Development Network meeting
July 2012, EUNIC in Tunisia, Three times fifteen? Debate on the role of cultural centres in local development

### Creative Industries

October 2011, EUNIC in Slovenia, Slovenia in fashion - the first Slovenia fashion week
January 2012, EUNIC in Algeria, A Bridge between the two Shores: meetings between young creators from Europe and Algeria
June 2012 – October 2012, EUNIC in Romania, Dialogue across Borders – a series of events in Romania, Germany, Denmark and the Czech Republic
From October 2012, EUNIC in Jordan, EUNIC MENA Creative Industries
November 2012, EUNIC in Jordan, Creative Jordan – Platform for Visionary Ideas
November 2012, EUNIC in the Czech Republic, Culture + Creative industries in Prague
November 2012, EUNIC in Senegal, participation at the International Conference on Creative Industries in Africa
From October 2013, EUNIC in the occupied Palestinian territories (oPt), cultural discussions in Ramallah
Discussion forums, lectures, workshops, conferences and projects
2011 – 2013, UNIC in India, EUNIC Lecture Series
July 2011, EUNIC in Japan, Embracing Solidarity and Diversity in Community Projects
July – August 2011, EUNIC in South Africa, Crossings – 2nd edition of Crossings, an international workshop for young artists in Johannesburg
September 2011 – autumn 2012, EUNIC in Brussels, series of events relating to 'Getting Smaller' About the Advantages of Shrinking in Europe
- Is Europe getting smaller? About nationalism in the EU
- Centre and Periphery - historical developments and current perspectives
- Multiculturalism in times of crises - is multicultural society a failed political notion in Europe?
- Collective memory, changing identities and cultural transformation in shrinking states
- What about the European dream?
October 2011, EUNIC in Melbourne, Series of lectures on European issues
- The Euro Crisis, Causes and Possible Solutions
- 'Maonomics' and the Chinese Economic Miracle
- The Victory of Communism with a Profit Motive
- The Implications of Transnational Crime and Money Laundering
November 2011, EUNIC in South Africa, Architecture Studio – 4th edition of a workshop and public events with architects and architecture students
November 2011, EUNIC in Vietnam, Open Academy Europe – workshops and lectures
January – December 2012, EUNIC in Russia, Curatorial Exchange Programme for young Russian curators 2012
February – April 2012, EUNIC in Ireland, How Migration Challenges Notions of Society – series of lectures in Dublin
March – June 2012, EUNIC in Serbia, series of debates on cultural policy and cultural centres in Belgrade
April 2012, EUNIC in Warsaw, conference on textbook design
April 2012, EUNIC in the Netherlands, The European Responsibility for Culture conference
May 2012, EUNIC in Brussels, EUNIC Inter-Cluster Meeting in Leuven, Belgium
May 2012, EUNIC in Senegal, Launch of EUNIC in Senegal Breakfast Meetings
May 2012, EUNIC in Stuttgart, Crisis as an opportunity? What values does Europe follow? International panel discussion in Stuttgart
June 2012, EUNIC in Egypt, focus group discussion on creative industries in Egypt
June 2012, EUNIC in Romania, Night of the Cultural Institutes open night
October 2012, EUNIC in Mexico, Cultural activities in prisons – why, symposium and workshop
November 2012, EUNIC in the Philippines, European Higher Education Fair 2012: Brighter Prospects

## Editorial information

Published by: EUNIC, Institut für Auslandsbeziehungen
(ifa, Institute for Foreign Cultural Relations) and
the Robert Bosch Foundation, in cooperation with the British Council,
the French Ministry for Foreign and European Affairs and the Calouste
Gulbenkian Foundation

Project Editors: William Billows, Sebastian Körber
Editor, English Edition: Gill McKay
Editorial Assistance: Katrin Mader, Kamila Gawronska, Helena Kovarikova
Graphic Design: Eberhard Wolf
Address ifa: Charlottenplatz 17, 70173 Stuttgart
Printers: ConBrio Verlag Regensburg
English translation: Neil McKay, Gill McKay

The views expressed in the articles within are those of the respective authors.

Photo credits, photo spreads: Frankie Quinn, Belfast
(www.frankiequinn.com)
Photos of authors: p.77 Jens Schulze

ISBN: 978-3-921970-84-3

EUNIC ifa CALOUSTE GULBENKIAN FOUNDATION Robert Bosch Stiftung BRITISH COUNCIL Liberté • Égalité • Fraternité RÉPUBLIQUE FRANÇAISE MINISTÈRE DES AFFAIRES ÉTRANGÈRES